Clinician's Handbook
Obsessive-Compulsive Disorder

Praise for *Clinician's Handbook for Obsessive-Compulsive Disorder*

The authors outline a fresh and creative perspective on cognitive therapy for OCD, derived from the development and testing of their Inference-Based Approach (IBA). This makes an important contribution by addressing components neglected or omitted in earlier approaches – a must read for anybody involved in the treatment of OCD.
Jan van Niekerk, Clinical Psychologist, Fulbourn Hospital, Cambridge, UK

The Inference-Based Approach (IBA) has transformed the treatment of OCD in my private practice. This finely detailed treatment manual will now give clinicians – and their clients–access to the most innovative horizons of OCD clinical research and practice.
Bob Safion, LMHC Private Practitioner, Anxiety Treatments, Massachusetts, USA

Building on a solid empirical and philosophical foundation, O'Connor and Aardema have written the definitive, practical guide to inference-based therapy for OCD for the practicing clinician that the field has been waiting for.
Gary Brown, Research Director and Doctor in Clinical Psychology, Royal Holloway University of London, UK

Clinician's Handbook for Obsessive-Compulsive Disorder

Inference-Based Therapy

Kieron O'Connor
Frederick Aardema

A John Wiley & Sons, Ltd., Publication

This edition first published 2012
© 2012 John Wiley & Sons Ltd

Wiley-Blackwell is an imprint of John Wiley & Sons, formed by the merger of Wiley's global Scientific, Technical and Medical business with Blackwell Publishing.

Registered Office
John Wiley & Sons Ltd, The Atrium, Southern Gate, Chichester, West Sussex, PO19 8SQ, UK

Editorial Offices
350 Main Street, Malden, MA 02148-5020, USA
9600 Garsington Road, Oxford, OX4 2DQ, UK
The Atrium, Southern Gate, Chichester, West Sussex, PO19 8SQ, UK

For details of our global editorial offices, for customer services, and for information about how to apply for permission to reuse the copyright material in this book please see our website at www.wiley.com/wiley-blackwell.

The right of Kieron O'Connor and Frederick Aardema to be identified as the authors of this work has been asserted in accordance with the UK Copyright, Designs and Patents Act 1988.

Library of Congress Cataloging-in-Publication Data

O'Connor, Kieron Philip.
  Clinician's handbook for obsessive compulsive disorder : inference-based therapy / Kieron O'Connor and Frederick Aardema.
      p. ; cm.
  Includes bibliographical references and index.
  ISBN 978-0-470-68409-2 (cloth) – ISBN 978-0-470-68410-8 (pbk.)
  1. Obsessive-compulsive disorder–Treatment. 2. Cognitive therapy. I. Aardema, Frederick. II. Title.
  [DNLM: 1. Obsessive-Compulsive Disorder–therapy. 2. Cognitive Therapy–methods. WM 176]
  RC533.O35 2012
  616.85'227–dc23

2011024329

A catalogue record for this book is available from the British Library.

This book is published in the following electronic formats: ePDFs 9781119960027; Wiley Online Library 9781119960027; ePub 9781119954996; eMobi 9781119955009

Set in 10.5/13pt Minion by Thomson Digital, Noida, India

1   2012

Table of Contents

List of Cartoons   vii
About the Authors   ix
Acknowledgements   xi
Introduction   xiii
Chapter One: Overview of the IBT Programme   1
Chapter Two: IBT: Evaluation Tools   9

Part I: Education and Foundation   **21**

Chapter Three: When OCD Begins   23
Chapter Four: The 'Logic' behind OCD   43
Chapter Five: The Obsessional Story   57
Chapter Six: The Vulnerable Self-Theme   73

Part II: Intervention   **89**

Chapter Seven: OCD Doubt is 100% Imaginary   91
Chapter Eight: OCD Doubt is 100% Irrelevant   115
Chapter Nine: The OCD Bubble   129
Chapter Ten: Reality Sensing   143

Part III: Consolidation   **157**

Chapter Eleven: A Different Story   159
Chapter Twelve: Tricks and Cheats of the OCD Con Artist   175
Chapter Thirteen: The Real Self   189
Chapter Fourteen: Knowing and Doing: Moving On and
    Preventing Relapse   205
Chapter Fifteen: Trouble-Shooting   221

Case Illustrations	231
Case Illustrations: Clinical Data	257
Answers to Common Queries from Clients	277
Therapist Queries	283
Quiz Answers Sheet	289
Appendix 1: Inferential Confusion Questionnaire (ICQ-EV)	291
Appendix 2: IBT Clinical Scales	293
Appendix 3: Therapy Evaluation Form and Scale	299
Appendix 4: Avoidance and Situational Profile Scale	307
Appendix 5: Diary	311
Bibliography: Key IBA Publications and Other References	321
Index	325

List of Cartoons

Cartoon 1.   The doubting dance.
Cartoon 2.   Just checking to be safe.
Cartoon 3.   The door prize.
Cartoon 4.   A clean break.
Cartoon 5.   Just to be sure.
Cartoon 6.   The hot spot.
Cartoon 7.   An offer to refuse.
Cartoon 8.   The crossing.
Cartoon 9.   Going beyond reality.
Cartoon 10.   The O'Seedys doubt depot.
Cartoon 11.   Safety first.
Cartoon 12.   Where's the sense?
Cartoon 13.   The useful hoard.
Cartoon 14.   Bad luck.
Cartoon 15.   Seeing yourself in O'Seedy's mirror.
Cartoon 16.   Uptight out-a-sight.
Cartoon 17.   In control.
Cartoon 18.   The untouchable.

About the Authors

Dr Kieron O'Connor received his doctoral degree and clinical training at the Institute of Psychiatry, Maudsley Hospital in London. He is currently the Director of the Centre for Research on Tic and Obsessional Disorders at the Fernand-Seguin Research Centre, Hôpital Louis-H. Lafontaine, and full professor in the Department of Psychiatry at University of Montreal. He is also associated professor at the University of Quebec in Outaouais. His research focuses on improving understanding and treatment of people suffering from obsessive-compulsive spectrum and related disorders. The inference-based therapy (IBT) programme described in this handbook is a product of this research. He has created three multidisciplinary research teams working, respectively, on the treatment of three tic disorders: Gilles de la Tourette syndrome, delusional disorders and obsessional disorders. His approach combines clinical and psychophysiological methods. His recent research extends treatment programmes into eating disorders and body dysmorphic disorder and to children and adolescents. He is also involved with community education and workshops and has authored four treatment manuals. He has developed innovative treatment approaches to obsessions, tics and habit disorders including the inference-based approach. Dr O'Connor's publications include *Behavioural Management of Tic Disorders* (Wiley, 2005), and *Beyond Reasonable Doubt: Reasoning Process in Obsessive Compulsive Disorder* (with F. Aardema & M. C. Pélissier; Wiley, 2005).

Dr Frederick Aardema studied clinical psychology at the University of Groningen and the University of Amsterdam in the Netherlands. Presently, he is a clinical researcher at the Fernand-Seguin Research Centre, Hôpital Louis-H. Lafontaine, affiliated with the University of Montreal. He is also Co-director of the Centre for Research on Tic and Obsessional Disorders. Frederick Aardema has played a vital role in the development of an inference-based approach to the treatment of OCD, including the development of a new questionnaire that reliably measures a characteristic reasoning style in those with obsessive-compulsive and delusional disorder, the Inferential Confusion Questionnaire. In addition, his work in reasoning has led to the development of an innovative theoretical approach to pure obsessional ruminations. Dr Aardema has published widely in international journals in the field of obsessive-compulsive and related disorders, and is a frequent presenter at scientific conferences. In particular, his research interests include psychometric and experimental methods in the measurement of reasoning processes in OCD, as well as the application of inference- and narrative-based models to obsessions without overt compulsions. Other aspects of his research include dissociation, virtual reality, introspective ability, self-constructs and psychological assessment. Dr. Aardema's books include *Beyond Reasonable Doubt: Reasoning Process in Obsessive Compulsive Disorder* (with K. P. O'Connor & M. C. Pélissier, Wiley, 2005).

Acknowledgements

Our thanks to Annette Maillet, Karine Bergeron, Jan Woodley, for active contributions to the manual, to Annie Taillon, Marc Lavoie, Ariane Fontaine, Marie-Claude Pelissier, Stella Paradis, Marie-Eve Delorme and Sarah Roberts for research contributions. To the Canadian Institute of Health Research, Fonds de la Recherche en Santé du Québec, Hôpital Louis-H. Lafontaine, Centre de Recherche Fernand Seguin for research support and funding and to all the personnel, clinicians, assistants, students and especially clients of the OCD spectrum study centre (CETOCT), at the Fernand-Seguin Research Centre, University of Montreal and University of Quebec in Outaouais. We would also thank Prakash Naorem and Karen Shields of Wiley-Blackwell for their editorial efforts.

We thank:Bob Safion, Natalia Koszegi and Genevieve Goulet for supplying case illustrations. Finally a huge thank you to Jacquelene Chegrinec for bringing clinical issues to life with her cleverly crafted cartoons.

Introduction

This clinician handbook provides the most comprehensive clinician guide so far for the application of inference-based therapy (IBT) to obsessive-compulsive disorder (OCD). It complements our previous book *Beyond Reasonable Doubt* which remains the base source text for the philosophical and reasoning theory underpinning of the inference-based approach (IBA) and the therapy programme (IBT) that derives from it. In the 5 intervening years since its publication, IBT has considerably expanded its reach in therapeutic work. This expansion largely stems from empirical research and replication of IBA principles in the literature, the clinical adaptation of IBT to diverse OCD and related populations and also from our own evolving conceptualization of OCD primarily as a reasoning disorder.

We do allude to this philosophical and research base in the text and provide support references for the curious and scientific minded. However, the target audience of this current handbook is the therapist–client dyad collaboratively engaged in IBT in clinical and non-clinical settings. It is hence a hands-on clinical how-to-do-it book. We have slow-motioned the course of therapy to hopefully permit an errorless and timely passage through all the steps of the programme. The text enables the therapist to identify key transition points in client thinking and behaviour, clear criteria for mapping client progress and sign posts for precisely locating the 'Where am I now?', 'How did I get here?' and 'What happens next?' for most eventualities arising in the therapeutic process.

IBT[*]

Since IBT is a distinct cognitive approach, we consider it worthwhile in this introduction to pinpoint some of its key original components as a way of priming

---

[*]In order not to encumber the text, we have not followed the standard textbook procedure of citing references in the text. However, the bibliography, entitled 'Key IBA and other publications', lists supporting literature.

Clinician's Handbook for Obsessive-Compulsive Disorder: Inference-Based Therapy, First Edition.
K. O'Connor and F. Aardema.
© 2012 John Wiley & Sons, Ltd. Published 2012 by John Wiley & Sons, Ltd.

the reader for what is to come. In our inference-based approach to understanding and treating OCD, an, the obsessional sequence begins with the initial inference of doubt. An inference is a conclusion about a state of affairs arrived at through prior reasoning. This doubt precedes the images of consequences, the appraisals and other downstream elements of the obsessional thought sequence. We acknowledge that these latter processes may be clinically relevant and may, therefore, also need to be addressed in therapy. However the target of IBT is the initial obsessional doubt and the reasoning processes which underpin this doubt.

1. Intrusion or Inference?

It is important to note that the primary obsessional doubt is an inference, not an intrusion. The word 'intrusion' is frequently used by therapist and client alike to denote the obsessional thought. But obsessional doubts do not intrude, or simply jump spontaneously into the head. Of course the thoughts are often unwanted, are alien to the client and can feel invasive but they do not in fact intrude into thinking. The obsessional doubts are rather created and maintained by the client's way of reasoning. The obsessional thoughts may be noisy residents but they are not intruders. We think it misleading also to consider that obsessions can develop from reactions to otherwise normal 'pop up' thoughts, that is, random thoughts triggered by spurious observation in the course of the day. Examples include 'Oh, there's a green hat with a propeller. How funny', 'Wow, those women's shoes are huge. They could trip up' and 'Who's *that* guy shouting at? Not me, I hope'. In other words, for IBA the reactions to so-called 'intrusions' do not create obsession, rather the client inferring doubt unnecessarily leads on to the chain of obsessional thinking and behaviour. Eliminate the doubt and logically all other components of the OCD sequence are eliminated. Appraisals certainly induce distress. But cognitive models emphasizing the exclusive role of appraisals *may* offer a satisfactory account of how thoughts hang around in people without OCD since, here, the doubting inference is not in the way.

2. Inferential Confusion

In the inferential approach to therapy there is only one principal process responsible for obsessional doubt : inferential confusion. Admittedly, inferential confusion has complex inputs and effects, but our clinical research shows that this singular process accounts well for most aspects of obsessional thinking and behaviour: the ego-dystonicity, the repetitive behaviour, the dissociation and the lack of confidence. Inferential confusion is a robust and identifiable construct and consists of two processes: (1) distrust of the senses or of self and of common sense, and (2) over-investment in remote possibilities. These two processes are part and parcel of the same construct. We've tried all sorts of statistical and clinical ways to separate them, but the two processes work in tandem and go hand in hand. Our research indicates that distrust of the senses or self fuels a reliance on subjective narrative, and the obsessional narrative justifies the distrust in the senses. The important clinical implication is that both must be addressed *together* since addressing one without the other goes only halfway. This caveat may seem like a catch 22: you can't do this before that, or that before this. But the metaphor to use here is of two revolving pistons where one piston represents trust in self and senses, and the other piston is investment in remote possibilities. As one piston goes up, the other goes down in tandem. So working on both at the same time moves us along faster.

Our research indicates that where there is successful resolution of inferential confusion, the obsessional thinking and behaviour reduces to zero, together with all associated obsessional emotions.

3. Thinking Before Acting

The focus in IBT is on cognitive change as a first priority with behavioural change following seamlessly behind. Behavioural experiments, exposure, or reality testing may not be necessary to eliminate compulsive behaviour. In IBT the aim is to reorient the client to reality through cognitive education and insight, so that the client relates to reality as reality by performing what we term 'reality sensing' which entails relating to reality in a normal non-effortful way. This cognition-behaviour sequence does not detract from the proven efficacy of behaviour therapy nor its power to impact on thoughts. IBT can be combined with exposure-based treatments. There is still debate over the exact processes operating in exposure, and there is evidence (though not causal) that where traditional behaviour therapy is successful, inferential confusion also changes, so reduction in inferential confusion is related to successful exposure.

The location of the source problem of OCD lies for IBT within a reasoning about possibilities. It is not located within an anxiety disorder or a phobic reaction to a real sitmulus event. The goal of IBT in the *first instance* is not to change a client's behaviour but to modify obsessions. IBT does not expose the client to do what they don't wish to do in the guise of eliciting anxiety to better tolerate it. Rather IBT addresses a confused way of reasoning about possibility. For example, a woman may believe she has contaminated her hand through touching a handrail, or a man may be convinced he has inadvertently left his oven turned on. According to IBT, these clients do not initially require exposure to handrails or ovens but rather insight into the inferentially confused nature of their obsessional doubts ... confusing real probability with an imagined possibility which convinces them they may have done acts they did not. A major principle of IBT is that clients already possess within otheir repertoire the ability to vercome obsessions. They require a shift from OCD reasoning to non-OCD reasoning and reality sensing as already performed in non-OCD situations.

4. A Constructionist Approach

IBT implicitly adopts the constructionist principle of information processing that views perceived personal reality as a construction. The pragmatic therapist need not be too worried here since, firstly, the constructionist model is implicit in IBT and not laboriously elaborated; and, secondly, the constructionist approach offers a more obvious and direct fit with the creative way we all interact with the world. There is no need for explanations involving hypothetical black boxes mediated by arrows to-ing and fro-ing in between. Reality feels no less 'real' by being constructed, and we appeal frequently in the programme for a return to an authentic personal reality and real self.

The constructionist view of the world is that attitudes, beliefs and reality are continually reconstructed depending on our doings. The office cabinet metaphor of mind which reifies beliefs as memos filed away in the brain is replaced by a creative process which generates feelings, stories and experiences in the 'here and now' through individual interactions with environments in the 'here and now' launched by my intentions in the 'here and now'. The past is constructed in the present according to planned doings in the future, and it's always 'now' somehow. This focus on the person's 'now' and all he or she is doing 'now' as the key to understanding suffering 'now' is in one sense a modern development of basic behaviourism, where behaviour is viewed as entirely maintained by current contingencies. However, cognitive constructionism adds the 'creating' to the 'maintaining'.

Constructionist approaches emphasize narrative construction and active immersion as a way to access beliefs. Beliefs are stories we tell ourselves and keep on telling ourselves, not some deep down, hard-to-get-at 'node' necessarily requiring heavy-duty psychological drilling and excavation! The stories we construct give our lives meaning. This is why we place a lot of emphasis in IBT on narrative immersion and the role of language in implanting and transporting ideas effectively. A bonus by-product of using IBT is that the therapist as well as the client learn the art of effective self-story telling.

5. Doubt Creation

Doubt in OCD is 'created' by the client and then actively rehearsed and maintained by the client's neutralizing thinking and behaviour. Of course, to the inferentially confused client, it seems the uncertainty is out there, a fact of life difficult to tolerate. 'How can I or you know for sure it's really safe?' the client asks. 'I really just don't know how to clean my teeth', another client pleads. 'Please tell me how can I know when they're clean?' Such pleas imply that a genuine uncertainty or incompleteness in knowledge exists when in reality such interrogations are themselves usually the sequel to an inferentially confused obsessional doubt. The client knows when other people's teeth are clean, and he knows the teeth he sees in his mirror are clean. So certainty is not at issue; the dilemma is rather a distrust of sense information and doubt of given perceptual knowledge.

Finally, the IBT programme in this is designed to be interactive and user friendly with quizzes, exercises worksheets and training cards. We have also introduced humour through cartoons and illustrations, partly in recognition of the constructive impact of humour on the creation of a successful therapeutic alliance, but also because in clients with OCD and in therapy generally vivid visualization can be as captivating as words. One last point . . . our view is that all therapy programmes are works in progress and we welcome feedback from users, both therapists and clients.

Kieron O'Connor and Frederick Aardema
Montreal

Chapter One

Overview of the IBT Programme

Overview of the IBT Evaluation and Treatment

The present inference-based therapy (IBT) has been developed over the course of the last 15 years utilizing information building upon clinical case studies as well as numerous psychometric, experimental and treatment outcome studies. The approach is a reasoning therapy that focuses on the resolution of the reasons for the initial doubt or obsession responsible for the client's symptoms. The therapy program is highly cognitive in nature often requiring a lot of attention from the therapist in correctly using the model taking fully into account the specific needs of the client. At the same time, there is also a great deal of structure in the current approach, and the accompanying materials are intended to benefit both the therapist and client in their collaborative work.

Step by Step

The idea of the stepped manual is that both client and therapist progress in small steps which simply follow on naturally from each other. The client moves from reflection on a point to intellectual acceptance, to personal and emotional engagement, to enactment. Along the way, metaphors are used to convey the natural nature of the progress and avoid the implication that major leaps out of the ordinary need to be made. In keeping with this 'natural flow' metaphor, the therapist should be careful to always locate him or herself and the client on the map of recovery. In particular the conditions to be met before transition from stage to stage are spelt out clearly.

Clinician's Handbook for Obsessive-Compulsive Disorder: Inference-Based Therapy, First Edition.
K. O'Connor and F. Aardema.
© 2012 John Wiley & Sons, Ltd. Published 2012 by John Wiley & Sons, Ltd.

We have tried to pinpoint the signs that reveal progress and of course how to deal with no progress.

Broadly speaking, the current stepped programme can be subdivided in three main parts– (1) Education and Foundation, (2) Intervention and (3) Consolidation, each of which consists of a series of different steps. Duration of treatment may vary from client to client, but in most cases, all steps can be provided to the clients in the course of 12 to 20 treatment sessions but number of sessions can be flexible. This allows the therapist to sometimes spend two treatment sessions on one particular step in treatment if the client experiences difficulty, or if further practice reinforcement is necessary before proceeding to the next step.

Each step in treatment includes accompanying worksheets that form the basis for the sessions covering the specific step in treatment. The worksheets are provided to the client after the session to ensure proper integration of the material. In addition, the client is provided with an exercise sheet and a training card as it pertains to each step in treatment. The exercise sheets and training card are intended to ensure the practical application of the material learned during the therapy, and form an essential part of the treatment. In addition, quizzes and cartoons are provided for further consolidation of learning, enhance understanding, and increase the overall complicity of the client and effectiveness of the treatment delivery.

The first part of treatment termed *Education and Foundation* primarily revolves around education and foundation and lays the foundation for IBT. Step one called *When Doubt Begins* shows the client how doubt is responsible for most of his or her symptoms. This step is intended to ensure a proper adherence to the model, as well as increase the client's awareness on the origin of his or her symptoms.

The crucial first step is identifying the doubt behind the immediate manifestations of OCD behaviour. The identification then permits establishing the origin and sequence of the obsessional chain ending in the self-sabotage of compulsions and safety behavours. Only later when the everyday doubts are resolved is the underlying self-doubting theme addressed. Why? Because the theme becomes more visible to the client at this point. Self-repositioning towards the authentic 'real' self is then easier and more likely to succeed than at the start of therapy. A key exception to this treatment sequence is where the doubting inference may already be close to the self-theme. This may occur in overvalued narrow mono-symptomatic obsession, 'I could offend the devil', or in existential ruminations largely centred on the self, 'I doubt who I am', or in hoarding, 'I could be nothing without my objects'. So the self-doubt can be addressed initially or in tandem with immediate obsessional doubts, if it is already visible to the person.

The next step of Education and Foundation termed *The Logic behind OCD* focuses on the reasoning preceding the doubt and is intended to show the client that the doubt or obsession does not appear out of the blue. Exercises are intended to increase awareness that there is reasoning behind the doubt rather than that the doubt is just 'happening' to the person.

The third step of Education and Foundation termed *The Obsessional Story* expands upon the previous step by showing how obsessional doubt gains its strength and reality value from a convincing narrative leading logically onto the doubt. This is the *narrative unit* giving credibility to the doubt and will be a primary focus in the course of therapy. The OCD narrative is constructed in collaboration with the client, utilizing the information on reasoning collected so far and filling in any gaps in the story. It is demonstrated to the client how the narrative leads to absorption into the obsession.

Finally, the fourth step of Education and Foundation *The Vulnerable-Self Theme* locates the OCD within a wider self-theme that makes the person vulnerable to create doubt in specific domains. The self-theme also throws light on the person's type and form of OCD. The vulnerability theme is the self the person fears becoming and is itself yet another OCD story. As noted earlier, the self-theme is derived from the obsessional doubts. This self-theme can be addressed right from the beginning of therapy, especially when the theme already forms a principal doubt in, for example, some ruminative doubts, or the theme can be introduced at a later stage when the person has already overcome doubts leading to more everyday compulsions. All of these four steps of Education and Foundation combine to form the fruitful ground for optimizing effectiveness of subsequent interventions.

The second part of treatment called *Intervention* attempts to directly change the obsession or doubt. It introduces the central tenet of IBT which is that obsessions are constructed and always occur without any direct evidence. Most crucially, in normal doubt there is always direct evidence or information that supports the doubt. No such direct evidence occurs in obsessional doubt. This concept is introduced from a number of angles in a series of distinct steps eventually resulting in an alternative non-obsessional narrative more in line with reality.

The first step of Intervention termed *OCD Is 100% Imaginary* establishes with the client that there is no direct evidence in the here and now, and so the OCD story is entirely subjectively generated. The client is shown that the doubt originates 100% from within the person rather than is fuelled from an immediate outside source. The purpose is not yet to invalidate the doubt. The main point to get across is that the doubt originates from the person as opposed to from reality in the here and now.

The second step of Intervention titled OCD is 100% irrelevant takes the point a little further and shows to the client that *if* the obsessional doubt originates solely from within the person rather than from the outside, *then* it is 100% irrelevant to the here and now. The crucial point here is that even though the doubt may very well be possible in the abstract, it is still irrelevant 'now'. Incomplete intellectual adherence to this idea should not prevent the therapist at this point from proceeding to the next step, but may negatively affect the effectiveness of future interventions. However, resolution of the obsessional doubt more likely in subsequent steps if the client intellectually grasps the idea that obsessions are irrelevant.

The third step of Intervention *The OCD Bubble* helps the client to identify the exact point where he or she crossed over to the imagination and left the world of senses. It is shown to the client that while inside of the OCD Bubble client contact with the physical senses and common sense is lost, and further compulsions only serve to fuel their imagination and rehearse the doubt, and so OCD makes them less secure.

The fourth step of Intervention termed *Reality Sensing* elaborates on how obsessional doubt is always a false doubt because it goes *against* reality. Reality sensing is simply trusting and going with the senses rather than doubting and going away from them. An alternative narrative is introduced that takes the senses into account leading to an entirely different conclusion than that which flows from the obsessional doubt. The client is encouraged to begin acting on alternative stories in combination with proper reality sensing. Potential problems with reality sensing are addressed, such as trying to do too much to 'get into' reality. The client may experience a void owing to a sense of not doing enough, and is taught how to sense reality without effort.

These four steps of the intervention form the basis for further consolidation of gains made so far in the course of treatment and to boost further progress.

The final part of treatment termed *Consolidation* attempts to further weaken the obsessional doubt by invaliding the obsessional story, strengthening the alternative story and encouraging the client to act upon this knowledge.

The first step of Consolidation is termed *A Different Story* where the client is encouraged to elaborate on the non-obsessional story in a natural and practical way. The person develops the art of story telling and how creating and telling stories about events and selves can transport emotions and perceptions and change beliefs.

The second step of Consolidation termed *Tricks and Cheats of the OCD Con Artist* familiarizes the client with the many tricks and cheats of the OCD that make it seem as if obsessional doubt has something to do with reality. Elements in the obsessional story of the client are addressed as specific devices used by the OCD to generate doubt. This is then followed up with teaching the client specific counter-strategies to trick the OCD con artist.

The third step of consolidation titled *The Real Self* highlights the selective nature of obsessional doubt as well as the vulnerable self-theme running through the doubt. The client is shown that the selectivity of the obsessional doubt only further invalidates the reality of obsessional doubt. A positive message is transmitted to the client to show that the OCD only affects a specific portion of the client's life, whereas functioning is often healthy in other spheres. Specific exercises are given to the client to strengthen awareness of this selectivity and in knowing the difference between their authentic and OCD selves.

The vulnerable self-theme underlying the OCD is also explored since this theme renders the person vulnerable to doubt in certain areas and not others. This OCD self is also a false self in the same way that the obsessional doubt is false. An important part of overcoming OCD is to find and recognize who the client really is ... the authentic self. The authentic self, since it is based in reality, is usually the opposite to the OCD self. The authentic self is the self which achieves constructive accomplishments in the world and was always there, albeit masked by the OCD.

The fourth step of consolidation termed *Knowing and Doing: Relapse Prevention* focuses on the translation of knowledge into action. The client is encouraged to act upon the knowledge that the doubt is false and to identify and correct any thoughts that keep him or her from acting 'sensibly'. This section addresses the split between knowing how to act and acting on it. Knowing implies behaving. It is not a leap in the dark but a natural progression of the same attitude. Every single thought and belief that still prevent the person from behaving in a noncompulsive way have to be specifically addressed as invalid *given* the lack of sense of information in the here and now.

Relapse prevention also addresses strategies to maintain gains, foresee difficulties and if necessary strengthen contact with reality with the authentic self and the senses and dispel imaginary doubts.

Finally, a trouble shooting and problem solving section covers technical problems in applying IBT, plus more general or conceptual queries from client and therapist.

Cartoon 1. The doubting dance.

Process Towards Integration

Emphasis is placed within the IBT model on the integration of the model into thought and action, and we illustrate the process by which contact with the IBT model can lead to full integration through a natural progression of accompanying steps.

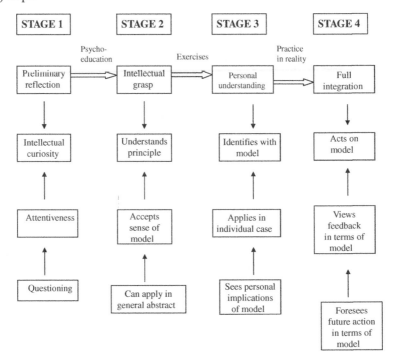

This cognitive schema, inspired by the well-known Prochasky and DiClemente's transtheoretical behavioural model of change, charts the progression from a preliminary reflection on the IBT model through intellectual and personal understanding to a full integration of the model. The therapist acts as guide through the stages combined with interventions designed to prompt insight and advance.

In stage 1, the person needs initially to show an openness and interest in the model. So, for example, psycho-education in the model and its account of aspects of OCD helps move the person along from a preliminary reflection to intellectual grasp. If the person does not show this initial interest, one might question readiness to undertake IBT.

In stage 2, intellectually, the person sees the utility and relevance of the model to OCD and how it can be applied generally. So the person may be able to describe how the model may apply to other people's OCD. In stage 3, in personal understanding the person is comfortable discussing their own obsession in IBT terms. The person begins describing their own symptoms in IBT terms, for example 'Here I realize I went over the bridge into imagination', or 'Yes, this doubt I experienced was definitely obsessional'. Finally, when integrated, the person uses IBT vocabulary to discuss all experiences. The person begins resolving their OCD experiences entirely in IBT terms. 'I see now how I need to catch the obsession before I cross over the bridge', 'I see that OCD was an illusion, making me imagine I needed to doubt and to check'. Ideally the person should be in between stages 2 and 3 for each of the specific IBT components when practicing this step. Typically the person arrives at stage 4 towards the end of the programme.

Treatment 'Resistance'

A word on treatment resistance. The term 'Resistance' is an unhelpful metaphor since it implies clients are actively fighting against getting better for all sorts of hidden reasons. In IBT, there is no treatment resistance, just different stages in an errorless learning process. The question becomes where and when the person is ready to take the next step. In following the programme, the person is always achieving and always somewhere on the map of progress, even if stuck for a while. The person can be succeeding even when standing still since they are doing the necessary reflections bit by bit to further progress. It is important throughout also to acknowledge and encourage even small steps since the person or family may consider them negligible. In fact, small steps are often the most important ones. A client not ready to progress to the next step may be still in reflection, may require more understanding or more answers, may be fearful or reluctant to progress or may have decided the programme is not for them.

In reality, the resistant person is often feeling lost, stranded, overwhelmed or misunderstood within the therapy-scape and needs guidance. In following the path of therapy, one foot step comes logically and naturally after the other, and if it doesn't, then for the client the passage from step to step no longer seems natural.

Chapter Two

IBT: Evaluation Tools

The following case provides an example of case conceptualization using the IBA model.

Mary

Mary (46) is obsessed about the possibility of being contaminated by blood, particularly other people's blood. She grows hostile and frustrated every time she sees a stain on a garment or a painting which is red – any shade of red – because she immediately imagines it could be blood, and if it is blood, then she will be contaminated. She gets angry at the people who would put this red in her way even if she doesn't touch it. She cannot use a multicolour carwash since she considers the red foam could be blood. She will not drive by a red slogan on the wall because it could be blood, or an advertisement in red for the same reason. If by chance she comes into contact with red, she is likely to throw out her clothes and insist her husband does likewise if he was near her. There is a seat in her car she has been unable to sit in for four years since a friend in a red dress who was menstruating sat there, and a room in her house is out of bounds to her and her husband since she once watched red ants on the television in the room and in her mind the red signalled blood and the blood could have seeped out of the television onto and into the furniture.

Halloween is her worst nightmare – red hands, masks, gloves, teeth. She curses the shops and children displaying these items. When asked whether she considers there is really blood on the Halloween items or in the carwash, she admits probably not . . . but there's a possibility. She read about a French artist who used real blood on his canvas. A guy put poison in the meat cans, so someone in a factory could put in real blood out of spite. How does she know it's not real blood? How can she or any one or even I, the

Clinician's Handbook for Obsessive-Compulsive Disorder: Inference-Based Therapy, First Edition.
K. O'Connor and F. Aardema.
© 2012 John Wiley & Sons, Ltd. Published 2012 by John Wiley & Sons, Ltd.

therapist, be sure it's not real blood? She gets very angry that the shops would prominently display these items. 'Have they no sense! These things are dangerous'.

Occasionally she will make enquiries to manufacturers or Google search to try to establish the content of red products, but far from reassuring her, these enquiries leave her even less sure. She has dismissed their reassurances in a couple of days with more doubt about the source. Once a doubt is implanted, then the story quickly chains off to a series of dire consequences in which Mary rapidly becomes emotionally engaged. Often she ends up neutralizing just to escape the emotional distress as much as the contamination consequences she is sure will follow.

Some of Mary's stories involve items contaminating other items and, for example, furniture, cushions and clothes have been in quarantine for years because they were in her car when she drove past some red. Ultimately now she cannot drive her car because the front seat was contaminated by driving too close to another red car. All this, of course, creates major obstacles to her family and her functioning.

When Mary came to the clinic for IBT she had already received exposure-based therapy and cognitive-behavioural therapy (CBT) based on re-evaluating her appraisals of the consequences of her obsessions. What she reported was that she was unable to get the initial stories about red contamination out of her mind and no matter how much she worked on minimizing the consequences by, for example probability calculations, the thoughts persisted. For example, although she knew that even if it were blood, her body defences would protect her, she couldn't get the potential doubt to go away. Whilst she accepted that some consequences were exaggerated, they were quickly replaced by new ones.

When her IBT therapist asked what she imagines will happen if she is infected, she is very vague about realistic consequences. But what she is particularly concerned with is the possibility of inadvertently, for no fault of her own, become infected.

Mary's case captures well the main points in IBT case conceptualization.

- Her problem begins with a doubt.
- The doubt is always about whether something which appears OK could be something else, in this case whether a red object is blood.
- The doubt goes against what her senses tell her that the redness is not blood.
- She becomes immersed in her obsessional story and acts on it, so giving it a reality value.
- The doubt is the problem and not her perception or her coping in reality with real blood.
- Mary already possesses the skills to deal with blood and is able to cope normally when encountering real blood. Interestingly, when faced, for example, with a sister's nosebleed, she rapidly helped her sister stem the flow.

In the following section discusses how to evaluate obsessions from an IBT perspective: the key dimensions to evaluate, how to use the clinical scales and in what way the scales inform the treatment plan. Evaluation forms an essential part of the treatment, and from the outset the client should understand that discovering the doubt and all its characteristics is essential to overcoming the obsession. Indeed, evaluation encompasses awareness which forms the building block to insight into the OCD.

Evaluation

Evaluation here covers factors specific to effectively applying IBT. It is assumed that decisions concerning standard diagnostic instruments will already have been made and Y-BOCS (interview or self-report), ADIS, SCID I & II and other clinical questionnaires such as family accommodation will have been administered (suggested references are provided in the bibliography at the end of this book). We also strongly encourage the use of process measures to monitor motivation, compliance, adherence, alliance and therapy and therapist evaluation to control for smooth running of the programme. Sample forms are given in the appendices at the end of this book and also referenced in the bibliography. Obviously, in the case of comorbid disorder, the clinician will decide which disorder to address in priority.

Comorbidity is only a contraindication to IBT when it detracts from compliance and adherence with the programme. IBT is a specialized treatment for OCD and does not apply to other anxiety or depressive disorders. We are currently adapting the programme for use with other related belief disorders such as body dysmorphic disorder (BDD) and delusional disorder. We have successfully administered IBT in the presence of comorbid anxiety, depression, tic disorders, body focused repetitive behaviour and attention deficit. Whilst IBT did not noticeably impact on the other disorders, the outcome results of decreased OCD symptoms in response to IBT were comparable to results with no comorbidity.

The main validation studies of IBT have included adult participants (18–65) of at least average intelligence, across all subtypes of OCD including hoarding (the OCD variant) and a range of comorbidities, and Axis II personality problems. So there are no contra-indications to administration of IBT other than the well-recognized obstacles to compliance: other stresses, severe personality issues, lack of motivation and lack of engagement in the therapy by either client or therapist.

Evaluations Particular to IBT

The IBT evaluation is particularly concerned to identify the primary obsessional doubts but it also takes account of anticipations, actions, consequences, avoidances and other safety behaviours. We recommend the following evaluations (described in detail below):

1. Inferential confusion (Inferential Confusion Questionnaire)
2. Hierarchy of efficacy in resisting the compulsive behaviour or neutralization

3. Content of and specificity of doubt domain
4. Force of the doubting inference(s)
5. Secondary chains deriving from the initial doubt (anticipated consequences and appraisals of self-judgement)
6. Conviction in need to neutralize (or extent of absorption) in and out of the OCD trigger situation
7. Vulnerable self-theme
8. Avoidance, accommodation or anticipatory behaviour
9. Situational or state triggers
10. Testing behaviour

1. Inferential confusion

Appendix 1 gives the Inferential Confusion Questionnaire. The Inferential Confusion Questionnaire is the instrument measuring degree of confusion between possibility, imagination and reality. It will give a good indication of the extent to which the client is immersed in OCD thinking. Essentially a score greater than 92 (1 standard deviation above the average score of nonclinical samples) implies a high degree of confusion more typical of OCD, but the therapist is encouraged to consult publications in the bibliography for more details on norms.

Are you inferentially confused?   We also suggest the therapist complete the ICQ and score it. There is nothing right or wrong to being high or low on inferential confusion, and no score bar limits or impedes using IBT.

Inferential confusion is a dimension and everyone has a bit of it (except the two current authors, of course!!!). In fact, having some degree of inferential confusion may even help empathize with the client's confusion. If the therapist does score high on IC, it is best on a 'know thyself' principle to be aware of the need to be vigilant when dealing with some of the steps of the programme. Particularly the transition stage from accepting that the obsessional doubt is a subjectively remote probability to understanding that it is essentially an imaginary possibility, completely irrelevant to the 'here and now' and actually in stark contradiction to the senses and common sense. In particular, strong inferential confusion driven arguments of the form 'Are you seriously telling me that microbes don't exist and there can be no invisible contamination on my hand?' can be difficult to circumvent if the therapist also subscribes to the inferentially confused thinking by drawing valid conclusions from what isn't there.

... And if the client is not inferentially confused?   In the evaluation we suggest administering the ICQ to clients. So what happens if the client with OCD scores low or even 0 the on ICQ? How can the therapist apply the IBT? Generally IC scores correlate with symptomatology and higher ICQ scores indicate higher severity of the OCD problem. So if someone scores low, they are a less severe case. Initially we worried that most people with OCD would score low on the ICQ since we assumed

that they are inferentially confused and so would not realize that they were confusing imagination with reality. But this did not occur and it seems most people with OCD may recognize the IC but feel it is justified or rest unaware of the implications. Numerous studies in North America, Australia, Europe, Turkey and elsewhere have now established the ICQ as a powerful discriminator of OCD from control and other anxiety disorders. So it's very unlikely that a client with OCD will score low on the ICQ if they are completing the same conscientiously and honestly. If the client scores very low and this score does not reflect subclinical or limited OCD symptoms, we recommend discussing the items with the client to ensure good comprehension. The client may have a very atypical OCD or be suffering from a related but separate OCD spectrum disorder (e.g., complex tic disorder or habit disorder) for which IBT is not recommended.

2. Hierarchy of self-efficacy in resisting compulsive behaviour and neutralization

Here the therapist can list with the client any and all compulsive behaviour and other mental or behavioural neutralizations performed by the client driven by obsessional thinking. The reason for starting with the behaviour is that the primary and secondary obsessions are usually derived from the compulsive behaviour in cases where they are not obvious. A broad definition of a compulsion includes any voluntary, effortful, cognitive or behavioural act that is directed at removing, preventing or attenuating the obsessional thought or the associated discomfort, or which attempts to change its presence or its content. The behaviour is described as it is performed by the client and the neutralizations listed must be independent of one another. So, for example, if a neutralization always entails a sequence of actions performed in the same order, it may constitute the same unit. The scale is anchored according to whether the client can absolutely resist the ritual (100) or never at all resist (0). The rating and list need to be repeated on two occasions prior to treatment to establish reliability and also allow the client to add or modify scores or neutralization units.

3. Content of obsessional thought

Content is important because it reveals the selective domain of the obsession. More importantly, it reveals the inevitable personalized nature of the obsession. The question of the subtyping of OCD is controversial, one reason being that the majority of people suffer more than one subtype. Another reason is that even within subtypes, each obsession is personal and idiosyncratic.

This point is important and deserves scrutiny since not only does attention to content fly in the face of conventional cognitive theory which prioritizes appraisal over content, but in addition it is a key argument in favour of the IBT since it clearly establishes the specificity of obsessions. The content of the obsession is usually idiosyncratic, repetitive and selective in its focus and based squarely on an idiopathic narrative and relates to a distinct context for each client. In IBT, the only way obsessions can be understood is through relating their content to the person's lived in context.

Why is one client preoccupied with their hands being contaminated by money but not with dirt, another with being exposed to invisible contamination but not to contamination by objects? One rather circular argument is that it is this thought to which the client accords importance because it is perceived as a menace. But although certainly such reactions may precipitate the imagined consequences and other sequels to the doubt, they cannot explain or predict the very selective nature of obsessional preoccupations. For example, a banker preoccupied with contamination from money may very well feel responsible about subsequent contamination of others. However he does not obsess about feeling overly responsible for the millions of dollars in the bank accounts he manages, or the expensive car he drives. If an over-developed belief in responsibility, threat or importance of thoughts were the core characteristics of OCD, why do not all concerns that involve responsibility or threat fuel obsessions? Appraisals are surely important in maintaining anxiety subsequent to the obsession, but there is no evidence that they are at its origin. So, for IBT, the origin of obsessions is in the initial doubt which impedes the rational appreciation and continuity of perceived reality. Capturing the idiosyncrasy of obsessional content is an essential part of IBT evaluation.

Even a contamination or verification 'subtype' will differ from client to client. This idiosyncrasy of obsessions underlines the need to understand the *content* and the *context* of occurrence within the person's life.

4. Force of the doubt

The force of the doubt is important also since asking the client to rate how strongly they believe in the likelihood of the initial obsessional doubt establishes it as an important variable. It allows the client the chance to realize that strength of doubt may fluctuate from obsession to obsession and from time to time. Furthermore measuring strength of probability emphasizes that the doubt takes the form of an inference (an arrived at conclusion) and not an intrusion.

The strength of doubt is normally distributed across the OCD population. It is effectively measured by asking the client to rate how likely the client considers the doubt as a real probability. It is important to cover all doubts since the client may strongly rate the probability of one doubt high but another as low. Clearly the rating of the doubt on the scale provided is important to plan with the client which doubt to target initially in the IBT programme. The reasons for the choice should include importance, prominence and frequency. We suggest that therapist and client begin somewhere near the lower end of conviction. There is in any case a generalization of effects over obsessions in IBT. Once the client has mastered one obsessional doubt, treating the others should be less difficult since the same strategies and insights apply.

It is important to measure the degree of doubt behind each compulsion since not only may the doubt be qualitatively distinct, but belief in its probability may vary. In more circumscribed, often over-valued ideas, there may be only one core doubt. However, most clients will tend to score on more than one 'subtype', and even in one 'subtype' the form of the doubt may vary form occasion to occasion. Very occasionally the client will hold the obsessional inference so strongly it will appear to be certain, especially since in such a case IC will be strong. However, in such cases, the primary doubt analysis remains identical. The client cannot be certain of something not actually present in the here and now. The client can be certain that something could or should be there. But if it is not objectively there. This forms an inference more about what should or might be rather than what is in fact there. Obstacles to identifying doubt are covered in Chapter 15 in the trouble shooting section of Chapter 15.

5. Secondary consequences

At the start of therapy it is important to measure secondary consequences in part to differentiate them from the primary obsessional doubt in the client's mind. In most cases the client will already be well aware of the secondary consequences following on from the doubt since these are often the major source of anxiety.

If my hands are dirty . . . then I'll contaminate my family, my town and kill people.
If I knocked down a child . . . then I'll be put in prison and lose all my friends.

Frequently there is not just one secondary consequence but a chain of them, one leading to another and another mostly up to a dramatic worst case endpoint. The client may create vivid images of the consequences and even be haunted by them. It is also possible that the consequences could change depending on mood or circumstance. It is also possible that there are no physical consequences but rather a subjective disequilibrium where the client feels an inner tension. Such may be the consequences in doubts of 'completeness' or 'not rightness'.

The secondary consequences are rated according to how realistic the client considers the consequences. Usually where the doubt is strongly held, the consequences are rated as strong. But the realism of the consequences is independent of the probability of the doubt. Furthermore, if the doubts *were* true, some of the consequences may appear reasonable. For example, if in the case of Mary she did come into contact with real blood when she herself was bleeding, then there could indeed be a realistic chance of infection. Rating the consequences also emphasizes the logical connection between the initial doubt and the consequences. If the doubt is eliminated, so by logic are the chances of the consequences. This helps in justifying the IBT emphasis on the doubt. Some examples of filled in forms together with case material are given later in the case illustrations.

Secondary consequences may chain off into several leaps. Here we are just interested in the most obvious direct consequence which will occur if the client does not do the ritual. The strength of belief in the reality of the consequences may also be variable. In some cases there may be no consequences, or the consequences may be rated low or high for individual obsessions within the same client.

6. Conviction in the need to neutralize in and out of the OCD situation

The dissociative quality of OCD often leads to the client knowing intellectually in the therapist's office that the compulsions are unnecessary but nonetheless becoming completely absorbed in the OCD behaviour in the OCD situation. This tendency to become absorbed in the OCD situation is an offshoot of inferential confusion and is dealt with in the programme. Hence it is measured in evaluation by noting conviction in the need to perform the OCD behaviour in and out of the OCD situation.

In the knowing and doing section of Chapter 14, we show how this discrepancy between conviction in and out of the situation becomes important. It is essentially a measure of how absorbed or immersed the client is in the OCD story, and how much they are still living in it. It is a measure of how successfully the client can distance the self and label the OCD as a story, both in and out of the OCD situation.

7. Vulnerable self-themes

The education section of part 1 of the IBT instructs the client on the sequence linking the obsessional themes to a central self-theme. This self-theme not only answers the obvious question of the client as to 'why do I have these obsessions?' but also makes the 'subtyping' clearer since the fact that the client has more than one type of compulsion can usually be traced to an all embracing self-theme. Examining in closer detail the self-theme and its false nature, and in particular changing the self-theme for a more authentic self, is dealt with in Chapter 6. At the evaluation stage however, it can be useful for the therapist to identify the self-theme on the basis of the thread connecting the doubts.

Examples of self-themes include 'I'm the sort of person to whom bad things happen inadvertently'. The self-theme is personal and usually complex and needs to be developed from the targeted obsessional doubts in collaboration with the person to refine all its components. 'I could be someone who isn't really as they appear and who is deceiving people'. Figure 2.1 illustrates how the nature of the obsessions and compulsions can be traced back to a self-theme. Where this is a

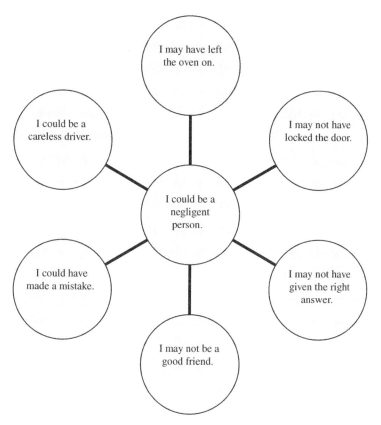

Figure 2.1 Relationship between individual doubts and self-theme.

circumscribed self-theme ('maybe I could be a dirty person'), the obsessional subtype is likely circumscribed. Where the self-theme is more general ('I could be a negligent person'), the obsessions and compulsions could be mixed 'subtypes'.

In other words, different doubts in distinct OCD situations may relate to a similar self-theme.

If the self-theme is at the centre of obsessional doubt, why not address this core feature first and do away with the need to address doubts one by one? The answer here is mixed. We do indeed suggest that in some mental ruminations and over-valued ideas, the self theme may be addressed first, if the self theme is already self-evident and clearly forms the focus of the obsession, e.g.: 'I'm the sort of person who could annoy God', or 'I could really be a reckless sociopath.' When we have adapted the IBT programme for use in ruminative and delusional disorders, we found it useful to identify and focus on the self-theme initially in therapy and make it clear that the obsessionally feared self-identity is inferentially confused. However, when the client is immersed in more ordinary doubts, we find it more useful to begin addressing inferential confusion in separate instances and then lead up to the self-theme. Otherwise, dealing with the self-theme can appear too overwhelming and perplexing.

8. Avoidance, accommodation and anticipation

Avoidance by definition is something the client doesn't do. So clients may not report avoiding since it is habitual and the client may need to be prompted. Also the therapist should be aware of any family accommodation where other members of the family may take on the compulsive behaviour to help out. Cognitive avoidance involves not facing certain information or facts or thoughts. It may also involve avoiding consideration of the OCD problem or certain aspects of the OCD. Avoidance can include things like: information, objects, activities, places, events, people, interpersonal relations, holidays, outings, family get-together, leisure pursuits and experiences. It is important to assess degree of anticipation shown by amount of vigilance towards the obsessions. The anticipation may take a number of forms. Typically the cycle develops as a consequence of rituals and avoidance playing a greater and greater role in life. The client may walk around in a constant state of vigilance, looking out for triggers. They may anticipate thinking a certain way. They may take preventative measures through safety behaviour. Anticipation is important to assess since too much anticipation or vigilance can upset or even go against dealing with thoughts in therapy.

If the client is continually anticipating obsessing, the client may end up in a state of continual vigilance, looking out for the obsessional thought and hence creating the likelihood of a self-fulfilling prophecy. The client lives in anticipatory fear of the obsessional thought appearing. Anticipation could be considered here as a kind of advance pre-emptive neutralization and so needs to be identified.

9. Situational triggers

OCD behaviour may increase or become more likely in different situational contexts. These contexts may be general (fatigue, stress) or more specific (visiting in-laws). It is useful also for the client to label the situations or states where OCD may become worse since these will become important in relapse prevention. This situational trigger form is filled in with the client and covers situations, states, events or activities likely to worsen or trigger the OCD. These situations are not triggers, thoughts or preoccupations directly linked to the OCD but rather contexts in which render the OCD more likely to appear. The form is useful in planning treatment and relapse prevention.

10. Testing behaviour

Testing behaviour is a particularly sabotaging type of compulsive behaviour. It typically occurs in ruminatory-type obsessions and impulsion phobia but can occur elsewhere. In a sense, it is another way in which the client accords the OCD a reality value. The client decides to check out whether an obsession is true by evoking the very event that the client fears will happen and that the obsession tells them could happen. In OCD speak, this self-fulfilling prophecy confirms the reality of

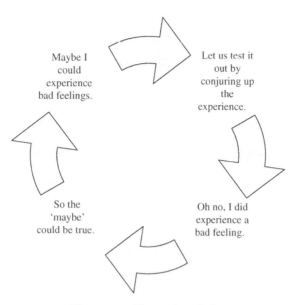

Figure 2.2 The testing circle.

the doubt: 'I undertake actions just to be sure', 'I produce images to test myself'. In fact, when people report their obsessions as disturbing images, it may be the result of such testing. The client thinks there is a possibility of thinking a blasphemous or other thought and so tries to think the thought to gauge their reaction. Testing may seem at first sight to be a kind of homespun exposure 'gone wrong'. But actually it is the very opposite and leads to more avoidance and intensifying of anxiety. Testing is driven by the OCD and is likely to confirm the worst obsessional doubts by seeking out signs which can be interpreted as proof that the obsession is grounded. Once the worst fears are confirmed, the client is even more haunted by the possibility of becoming or thinking what is feared and may increase the amount of testing. The client is trapped in a vicious circle (see Figure 2.2).

Testing examples:

1. A person who believes there could be S-rays escaping from the microwave and entering the brain places their head against a microwave to test out the feeling.
2. A person who believes they may be sexually oriented in an undesirable way visits a bar catering for this orientation to hang out and see if they are approached . . . which they are.
3. A person afraid of pornography conjures up sexually explicit images in his mind to gauge his reaction.

The question to ask in these cases is 'Has the person actively invoked or produced an event, image or feeling just to see if "it is really there"?' or to see ' if "I react to it in an abnormal way"?'

"Now, did I close the car door properly?"

Cartoon 2. Just checking to be safe.

The Inferential Confusion Questionnaire is given in Appendix 1.

Clinical scales and situational and avoidance forms, together with instructions, are found in Appendix 2.

Process evaluation forms are found in Appendix 3.

We recommend completing the forms pre-, mid- and post treatment to capture progress in the course of therapy.

Part I
Education and Foundation

Chapter Three

When OCD Begins

When OCD Begins

The goal during the first treatment session is for the client to learn that doubts are behind the obsessions and responsible for most of the OCD symptoms. In the majority of cases, the entire obsessional preoccupation of the client can be simplified tremendously by tracing it back to a few single doubts, and it is important to convey this notion to the client. In other words, as overwhelming, detailed and intricate as the OCD may seem to the client, there usually are only a few doubts by which most of the obsessional preoccupation stands or falls. A complete understanding that a doubt is the central problem also helps the client to lose some of his or her focus on the consequences and compulsive actions of the doubt. This is especially relevant among those with high anxiety and a strong focus and emotional submersion towards the secondary consequences of the OCD: it is also relevant for those who are exasperated by performing compulsive actions in a robotic fashion and who may have lost sight of the original reason for doing so.

What is Doubt... To be or... May be...?

So, firstly, what is doubt? How do we define it? Doubting is essentially a questioning of information, knowledge, assumptions or hunches one already possesses. The disciple Thomas was a 'doubting Thomas' because he doubted the received wisdom that Jesus was the Son of God. We use the word 'doubt' to denote that we are 'unsure' of some piece of information. Doubt then is not to be confused with

Clinician's Handbook for Obsessive-Compulsive Disorder: Inference-Based Therapy, First Edition.
K. O'Connor and F. Aardema.
© 2012 John Wiley & Sons, Ltd. Published 2012 by John Wiley & Sons, Ltd.

'uncertainty' or with 'lack of confidence'. We are 'uncertain' about events which have not yet happened or for which we do not have enough information. I may be 'uncertain' about what time a train from Ottawa arrives. I may be unsure about the capital city of Burundi. Uncertainty is used in the sense of being unsure as to the full facts. It hence can be resolved by seeking out the appropriate facts or accepting that the full facts are not available. There is a cognitive trait termed 'intolerance of uncertainty' where some people who suffer anxiety are unable to tolerate not knowing all the information. However, this trait is distinct from the cognitive statge of doubt as we use it in IBT.

Another related idea is 'lack of confidence'. People with OCD often seem to lack confidence in making decisions or undertaking actions, and may lack confidence in their own abilities to be effective. Many early experiments targeting memory and perceptual processes found lack of confidence in performance in OCD rather than deficient performance. Lack of confidence generally refers to beliefs about self-efficacy and outcome expectancies and is not related to our use of doubt here. Certainly someone who doubts their senses may subsequently engender feelings of uncertainty and lack of confidence in action. But these are subsequent to the doubt. The proof? Well, firstly, people with OCD only generally show these 'doubting' feelings in OCD-related situations. People with OCD can be very confident in some walks of life. Furthermore, scores on scales to measure OCD doubt differ from scores on scales of uncertainty or lack of confidence. The sequence of doubt creation is that the person's senses and common sense (if appealed to) sound no alarm. It is self-created possibilities following on from perception which create doubt.

Adjusting the Focus

The key is for the therapist to help the client identify the doubt as the first link in the OCD chain. It is important that the *client* identify it as such. It is not sufficient for the therapist to do it. Identification of the doubt usually comes as a revelation to the client. Chances are the clients are caught up in the consequences of the doubt and need to be guided back to the initial doubt. Generally speaking, the client will not have considered doubt as the origin of the obsessions for a number of reasons (an exception may be when the doubt applies directly to the self, e.g. 'maybe I don't exist').

Logical Template

In the majority of cases, establishing with the client that the source of the OCD is a doubt is fairly straightforward. The therapist should have a good idea of the form and content of the obsessional doubt before showing the client that doubt is the source of the problem. The therapist may need to help change the client's focus from fear of the consequences and how their fears spiral off into worst case scenarios. The adjustment can come naturally as the client talks of their problem and the therapist highlights key components of IBT in their own terms. The client with OCD may be preoccupied with consequences, emotionally distressed by images of outcomes. Often it is these images and their actions which appear problematic to the client, not the obsession itself. So one can establish the doubt by working backwards from the goal of the compulsion.

Three-Step Logical Template to Unravel Initial Doubt

1. What is the compulsive ritual?
2. What state of affairs would the client need to be sure of in order to not do the ritual?
3. So currently the client doubts this state of affairs.

This doubting provides the content of the obsessional doubt. The seven examples below illustrate how primary doubt can be identified. In the following two examples, the therapist works backwards from the goal of the compulsion to reveal the primary doubt.

Example 1

T: So what brings you to the clinic here right now?
C: Well, my washing is out of control. I'm now taking 3 hours to shower. It's too much. I need help stopping.
T: So you're showering too much?
C: Yes, cleaning, scrubbing, it's hallucinating. I even clean the shower head for half an hour, then I'm going over and over my nails.
T: So you must feel clean after all that?
C: Well, that's it. I'm not sure. I need some help, some rules to know when I'm clean.
T: So you feel you might not be clean? [Primary doubt]

Example 2

C: I obsess about what people say and I can't get it out of my head.
T: Can you give an example of a current obsession?
C: Yes, like now. My friend said to me he finds me a good friend and that he hopes I'll continue.
T: OK. So?
C: Well, why did he need to add the last bit? What did he mean?
T: Well, what do you think?
C: Well, I'm wondering maybe he's really thinking I'm not such a good friend.
T: So you're concerned about not being a good friend.
C: Well yeah, there's always the possibility [primary doubt]. It's important to me.

Note: In dialogue reported throughout the text therapist is abbreviated to (T) and Client to (C).

The following example elaborates on the role of the primary doubt.

Example 3

T: What would make you 100% certain for you not to feel any need to clean your hands?

C: If I could be sure my baby did not get contaminated I might be OK.

T: And what makes you think your baby might get contaminated?

C: Well, there might be bacteria on my hands [primary inference of doubt] that could make the baby ill [secondary consequence of doubt].

T: Any particular type of bacteria you worry about?

C: Not really. It could be anything.

T: So what if you would be 100% sure that your hands are not contaminated? Would you still feel a need to clean your hands?

C: Only if it's really 100%.

T: So, then it would be fair to say that if we can change the idea that your hands are contaminated, then you no longer would have any OCD?

C: I think so. But I don't see how it could ever be a 100%. It is well known there are harmful bacteria everywhere.

T: We will get to that. For now, I just want to ensure you fully understand that your OCD symptoms are preceded by an idea, or a doubt actually, namely that your hands might be contaminated. It's not just a feeling. It's not solely because you worry about your baby. It begins with the doubt that your hands might be contaminated. Would you agree with that?

C: Yes, I understand it begins there.

T: Of course, it may not always feel like a doubt. You may sometimes feel that it makes a lot of sense. But I'm talking about anything that 'could be' or 'might be'. This includes the idea that your hands might be contaminated. You *doubt* that your hands are clean, and we call it the primary obsessional doubt because everything else flows from it. You would not be anxious or worry about your child getting sick if it was not for the primary doubt. Is that correct?

C: Yes.

In the example below, the client with IC genuinely believes that the obsession starts with a fact or a valid perception.

Example 4

C: Well, I start obsessing when I see a doorknob in a crowded place.

T: Why does seeing a doorknob cause obsessions?

C: Well, because it's obviously contaminated by people touching it with their hands.

T: You're certain?

C: Well, come on, the probabilities are pretty high in a crowded place. People sneezing, picking their noses.

T: So you can't say for certain.

C: No, but I mean, it's common sense.

T: Do you see anything on the doorknob?

C: Well, occasionally yes, if you look hard, but even if not, I know if I had a microscope I would see all the bacteria.

T: OK, but mostly if I understand, you don't actually see anything on the doorknob.

...

C: Yeah, but even if I don't see anything, I know there are bacteria.

T: So you doubt it's clean despite what you see.

C: Right.

T: And your doubt is?

C: There could well be things I don't see and I'd better be safe.

T: So, it's not really seeing the doorknob?

C: OK, no, it's seeing the doorknob and doubting it's clean [primary doubt].

The client may be submerged in an emotion and so not able initially to clearly locate the doubt.

Example 5

C: I feel anxious all the time.

T: What do you feel anxious about?

C: I worry I could harm children.

T: And why would you harm children?

C: I might be one of those sex offenders [primary doubt].

T: And to what extent do you think that idea is real? Are you certain that you are a sex offender, or is it more like doubting yourself?

C: I guess it's more like a doubt. I don't really believe it, but it feels very real when I have the idea.

T: And what if you would be a 100% convinced that you are not a sex offender? Would you still feel anxious, you think?

C: No.

T: And would you still worry about hurting any children?

C: No.

T: That's why we call the idea that you might a sex offender your primary obsessional doubt. All your worry and anxiety stems from it. Without it, you would not have OCD.

Or the client may be caught up in vivid imagery.

Example 6

C: I'm really upset by these images of my mother dying.

T: What form do the images take?

C: It's really horrible. I see her like dying painfully and I love my mother.

T: You don't want her to die.

C: Of course I don't, but it's just these images. I can't tolerate them.

T: They arrive frequently?

C: All the time. I even told my mother about them. Well, she wasn't too happy and then I felt even worse.

T: How did they start?

C: Well, I saw this programme about someone dying painfully and I thought, 'Oh my God this could be my mother'. She's been diagnosed with cancer and it could be her.

T: So your original thought was 'Maybe my mother could die painfully' [primary doubt].

C: Then I thought what a terrible thought and then I thought maybe I really want her to die and I tried to get it out of my mind.

In the next example, a strong sense of ego syntonicity hides the primary doubt.

Example 7

T: So you feel obliged to rescue these objects from the neighbour's dump truck.

C: Absolutely. I feel good about it. I'm saving them. I can't believe people just throw these things away.

T: OK. So you have a use for them?

C: Well, not straight away.

T: I mean, these are not objects that you would necessarily want, need or use for yourself right now or in the near future.

C: No, no, that's why they end up on my pile. But I say to myself . . . one day someone will need them . . . I mean, *they could be useful* [primary doubt], I'd feel terrible if I threw them away.

T: So you think rather that you might have a use one day?

C: You bet.

The Primacy of Doubt

The therapist should always work with the client to show that OCD stands or falls with a single idea or doubt. This emphasizes to the client that their problems may not be as overwhelming as previously thought. Most clients readily agree that symptoms follow from the obsessional doubt, and as such, they are also able to recognize that initial doubt is a necessary precursor to symptoms.

Semantic objections (1)

Some clients may initially object to the term 'doubt', however, especially those who treat their doubts as facts. If the person objects to this term because they feel it does not reflect the factual nature of their OCD, then there is good reason to not accommodate the client in his or her choice of words. The main goal is for the client to understand that the obsessional doubt lies at the beginning of the OCD sequence. Whether this sequence is understood as starting with a doubt, a query or a possibility (from the client's perspective) makes no difference in terms of helping the client to understand that all symptoms follow from a single source.

Semantic objections (2)

Another reason why a client may object to the term 'doubt' lies in an incomplete understanding of what the term signifies. They may only think of it in terms of having difficulty about making up your mind about something. However, the definition of doubt as used in IBT is wider. Doubt designates an inference about a *possible state of affairs* in reality. In other words, any thought that includes a 'maybe', 'what if', 'perhaps', 'the possibility that', or 'could be' is considered a doubt ('I might be contaminated', 'I could have forgotten to lock the door', 'Maybe I murdered someone', 'What if I'm a blasphemer?'). Put in those terms, few clients will object to the notion of considering their OCD having its source in doubt.

Source of the Doubt

While showing the client that the OCD has its source in doubt, the therapist must, at this early stage, guard against getting too deep into the reasons behind the obsessional doubt. This problem may be exacerbated by a need on the part of the client to justify the doubt, and he or she may quickly volunteer all kinds of information to back up the doubt (e.g. 'Harmful bacteria are everywhere so my hands might be contaminated', or 'I might be a child molester because I have images about having sex with children'). These reasons are important from an IBT perspective, but it's important not to rush therapy. This applies to the therapist as well who may feel tempted to come to the rescue of a suffering client with too much information in one single session – information which will at this stage likely only feed into the obsessional cycle rather than be truly understood.

Intellectualizing the Doubt

The thinking about the doubt may be a compulsive activity in itself, where the client continuously weighs facts and counter-facts in order to find resolution to the obsessional doubt. Sometimes, the client may simply wish to get the therapist 'up to speed' regarding everything involved in his or her dilemma. For example, previous therapies may have included challenging the rationality of the obsession (which is to be avoided), and the client may wish to show the therapist that there is really no cure for OCD. Other times, the client is hoping for the therapist to offer some crucial new piece of information that might invalidate the doubt. Whatever the reasons, the therapist is best to say that all these topics will be addressed later in therapy. For now, the client needs to digest the idea that a single doubt, query or idea lays at the source of his or her problems, even though there may be further reasons behind the doubt. Slowing down and simplifying the OCD in this manner is quite beneficial for clients, especially for those who constantly analyze or reflect on their OCD.

Multiple Doubts

It is not unusual for the client to present with multiple obsessional doubts, especially if the client suffers from different subtypes at the same time, such as washing or checking. Even a client presenting with only one subtype of OCD may have several different primary doubts in one particular domain ('The door might be unlocked', 'I might have forgotten to turn off the stove'). These doubts can all be addressed following the same logical template in the first sessions. However, in the course of therapy, it might be preferable to focus initially only on the most preoccupying doubt. Addressing more than two obsessions will quickly become confusing, and may interfere with proper integration of what is learned during treatment. Some leeway is possible here, however. For example, if the client presents with many different doubts and they are all quite similar, they can sometimes be formulated as one single encompassing doubt such as 'I might have forgotten to check something in the house (stove, door, window, etc.)'. Otherwise, if obsessions are quite different, the therapist is generally better off focusing on only one or two obsessions at the time. It is not unusual in IBT that improvements in a specific obsession automatically generalize to the other obsessions not specifically addressed in therapy. If this is not the case, separate additional work may be needed with the obsessions that still bother the client. This can be assessed periodically or at the end of therapy. Usually, going through it for the second time, the client will be able to move a lot faster through the different steps in therapy.

Shameful Doubts

Finally, while assisting the client in identifying their obsessional doubt, the therapist should always be sensitive to difficulties with reporting if shame, guilt and another negative judgements and emotions are associated with the doubt. This is especially so if doubts about the self are involved or when the client suffers from obsessions about blasphemy, sexuality and aggression. If shame or guilt is present, the therapist can clarify and assure the client that it is OK to express such thoughts in therapy, and that these thoughts have nothing to with the client's real self.

Locating the Initial Base Doubt

The client may come out with a series of doubts, one following on from the other. 'Well I say to myself, what if the handle is contaminated and maybe there's invisible blood and it could be someone with AIDS touched it and . . .' The primary doubt is the point where the client leaves the world of perception, goes away from reality into a doubt. In the case of the examples above the base doubt is: 'What if the handle is contaminated?'

Normal . . . But Not Normal

Keep in mind that unlike most other cognitive therapies, the message of IBT is not that these doubting thoughts are 'normal' and occur to everyone. The content of the obsession may very well be normal, in the sense of a content commonly experienced. But the key message of IBT would be that the manner and context in which the client with OCD arrives at these doubts are not entirely normal. They are in effect false ideas or doubts about reality (or the self). As such, the therapist could reassure the client that the obsession does not reflect a true state of affairs, even while of course the client initially obsessively doubts this fact.

Phobic Doubts

Another area requiring sensitivity on the part of the therapist is to be aware that the consequences of some obsessional doubts may elicit phobic reactions. The client may be afraid of the consequences of even thinking about their doubts or obsession, let alone talking about it. For example, an obsessional doubt such as 'I might die if I say the word 'death'' is difficult to report by the client. The therapist can expect a lot of cognitive and behavioural avoidance in these clients, which may have to be addressed first before IBT can even commence. However, once the client has grasped the inferential confused motive behind a less threatening avoidance, they may feel more able to loosen other avoidance.

Decision Chart

Proceeding to the Next Stage of Treatment

- The client is aware that the primary obsessional doubt is central to their symptoms.
- The client is aware that consequences, distress and compulsions logically follow from the doubt.
- The client is able to identify all aspects of the obsessional sequence.
- The client is able to explain the model to the therapist.

Client Worksheet 1
When OCD Begins

Obsessive-Compulsive Disorder (OCD)

OCD has two main components: obsession and compulsion. The most well-known compulsions are checking and washing, but there are many other types of compulsions as well that are not so easily identifiable. For example, if you have the obsession 'I might be a dangerous person', then you may frequently *mentally* check yourself to ensure you might not be harming others. So here, even though it is invisible to others, the mental checking is the compulsion.

What is an Obsession?

In the majority of instances, an obsession is no more than a doubt about what is there. Often such doubts take the form of a *possibility* such as a 'what if . . .', a 'might be . . .' or a 'could be . . .' For example, if you check the door, then there is a possibility or doubt that motivates you checking. Perhaps you believe that you may not have properly locked the door, or that the lock might be damaged and therefore not properly locked. This is the doubt or possibility we are talking about.

Compulsions Always Start with Obsessions

If you do not have the obsession, then there would be no need to do the compulsion. Likewise, if you did not have the obsession, then you would feel no anxiety or discomfort either. For example, if you have the obsession 'I might have left the stove on', then you may begin to worry about all sorts of possible consequences such as that the house might catch fire, or might worry about being responsible for harming others. You would get anxious, and will then begin to check the stove to reassure yourself that everything is OK. But none of these actions would take place if was not for the obsession.

The Consequences of the Doubt Follow on from the Initial Doubt

For example, using the above door checking example, a worry about someone breaking into the house is not the primary doubt responsible for your anxiety. This is only a consequence of the doubt, where you feel you *might* not have locked the door correctly. Without the doubt, you would not worry about anyone breaking in, and this worry is not where the problem starts.

Obsessional Doubts Do Not Come Out of the Blue

There may also be triggers for the doubt. For example, just walking past the door can be a trigger for the doubt that it might be left unlocked, in the same way that touching a metro pole could trigger the doubt that you might have been contaminated. You also may have all sorts of reasons why you believe the doubt to be realistic enough to act upon in the form of a compulsion. So it's not like there is nothing that precedes the doubt, which is an important aspect of obsessional doubt you will learn more about in therapy later on.

Almost All Your Symptoms Follow from the Doubt

This is a very important point to understand. And if you did not experience the doubt, you would stay firmly grounded in reality, in the here and now. You would not get anxious and would not feel forced to do the compulsion. So the doubt is the source of the problem. This is good news, because once you begin to change the doubt, you will change everything that follows from it as well. It does not matter which kind of OCD you have (see Figure 3.1).

Cartoon 3. The door prize.

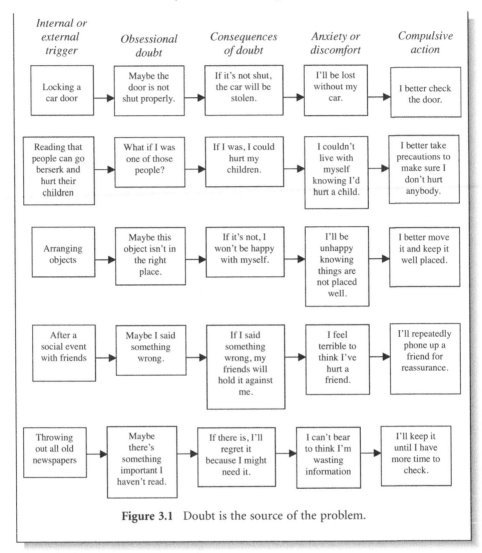

Internal or external trigger	Obsessional doubt	Consequences of doubt	Anxiety or discomfort	Compulsive action
Locking a car door	Maybe the door is not shut properly.	If it's not shut, the car will be stolen.	I'll be lost without my car.	I better check the door.
Reading that people can go berserk and hurt their children	What if I was one of those people?	If I was, I could hurt my children.	I couldn't live with myself knowing I'd hurt a child.	I better take precautions to make sure I don't hurt anybody.
Arranging objects	Maybe this object isn't in the right place.	If it's not, I won't be happy with myself.	I'll be unhappy knowing things are not placed well.	I better move it and keep it well placed.
After a social event with friends	Maybe I said something wrong.	If I said something wrong, my friends will hold it against me.	I feel terrible to think I've hurt a friend.	I'll repeatedly phone up a friend for reassurance.
Throwing out all old newspapers	Maybe there's something important I haven't read.	If there is, I'll regret it because I might need it.	I can't bear to think I'm wasting information	I'll keep it until I have more time to check.

Figure 3.1 Doubt is the source of the problem.

Client Exercise Sheet 1
When OCD Begins

The Sequence

During the therapy session, and as explained in the accompanying worksheet, you have learned that your symptoms follow naturally from a particular doubt. The manner in which OCD evolves, and how you eventually end up at the feeling that you have to engage in compulsive behaviours, we call the 'obsessional sequence'.

The Trigger

The obsessional sequence is usually set in motion with a trigger. This trigger can either be internal, or it can be external event. For example, if you suffer from doubts that you might hurt someone, this doubt might be triggered just by thinking about an argument you had with someone else a few days ago. Then, once the doubt has a hold on you, you may worry about the consequences, feel anxiety, and engage in some sort of compulsive behaviour, such as trying to block the thought out of your mind. The trigger elicits the doubt and the OCD begins with the doubt.

Your Own Personal Doubt Sequence

The specific obsessions and doubts of people with OCD can be very different, but the obsessional sequence is always the same. So if you are unaware of the obsessional sequence, it may be difficult to recognize yourself in other people's OCD. But by looking more closely at your own OCD, and applying it to the obsessional sequence, you will see it really is all the same. There is a trigger, a doubt, and everything else flows from there. Nothing makes this clearer than applying the obsessional sequence to your own obsessions.

David

Below, you find an account from a client describing his obsessional thinking. Try to identify the following:

1. The trigger
2. The obsessional doubt
3. The anxiety or discomfort
4. The compulsive action

David has recently begun to feel anxious each time he is in the car, especially when he gets out of the driveway. The problem started 2 months ago. He had read about someone killing a child on the driveway, and shortly after Dave began to wonder whether something like that could not happen to him. Dave has even begun to avoid driving his car and now often takes the metro to work. Why risk ever to be thrown in jail and having to live with killing a child? Besides, it simply takes too long to even get out of the driveway. He is jittery and has a sinking feeling in his stomach. Each time, he would get out of the car, and check everywhere to make sure he did not hit anyone. He even checked under the car and behind the wheels, and still doubted whether he had maybe missed something.

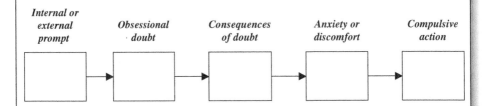

- So using the form below, slowly trace out and identify the obsessional sequence for one or two obsessions that have recently been bothering you the most:

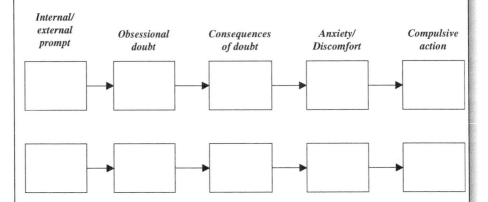

Now, do the same for an obsession with which you may have been preoccupied in the past, but that has not been bothering you for a long time:

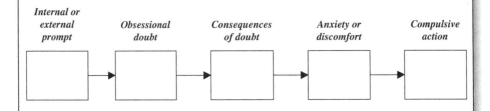

Lastly, try to come up with an obsession that another client with OCD might have, and yet means nothing to you.

Internal or external prompt	Obsessional doubt	Consequences of doubt	Anxiety or discomfort	Compulsive action

Bring the exercise sheets with you for the next session to discuss your answers with your therapist. Write down below anything you consider important about what you have learned or that you wish to comment on. Also note down any questions you have.

_____

_____

_____

_____

_____

Creative Exercise

Creating doubt through doubting. During the day, think of any action you performed during the day and ask yourself, 'Did I really do that?' Keep repeating the question and reflecting on whether you really did do it properly.

Example 1

You've just said goodbye to a friend on the phone, and both of you have hung up in a normal fashion. You ask yourself:

'Did I really say goodbye just now?'
'Maybe I thought I did, but it got distorted on the line'.
'Perhaps that's why he hung up. Maybe unwittingly I insulted him'.
'Maybe I've done this before without realizing'.
'How can I be absolutely sure I didn't say it?'

How is your doubt level about how you ended the call? More, less or the same?

Example 2

You turn off the television set and you see the light go out. You ask yourself:

'Am I sure I'm sure I turned the TV off?'
'Maybe I didn't really turn it off'.
'Maybe it looked like it was off, but it wasn't really or it came back on?'
'Maybe I should check it just to be sure'.

How is your doubt level about turning off the TV? More, less or the same?

Example 3

You've just been invited to a party by a friend. You say:

'Maybe s/he doesn't really want me there'.
'Maybe s/he felt obliged to invite me'.
'Maybe s/he is just embarrassed by me'.
'S/he could be hoping I don't turn up'.

How is your doubt level about being wanted at the party? More, less or the same?

Example 4

You're thinking of a close friend or relative you really like.

1. How sure are you that you like the person? Sure or unsure? Now rehearse the following doubts.

Rehearse the following statements:

'Maybe I don't really like him/her'.
'Maybe I just think I like him/her'.
'Maybe subconsciously I hate him/her'.
'Maybe I really want him/her to do badly'.

How sure are you now that you like the person? Sure, less sure or unsure? Do you see how doubting creates more doubt? **yes or no?**

Client Training Card 1
When OCD Begins

Learning Points (Front)

- A doubt is about a possibility – a thought about what 'could be' or 'might be'.
- Your symptoms of OCD begin with doubt.
- Consequences, distress and compulsions logically follow from the doubt.
- Without the doubt, you would remain firmly grounded in reality without any symptoms of OCD.

Daily Exercise (Back)

Over the next seven days, three times a day, when you are engaged in a compulsive activity, try to identify the obsessional sequence leading up to the activity, including the trigger, the doubt, the consequences and the anxiety. You may find it useful to discover components by slowing down the sequence and slowing down your progression from one thought to another. Then ask yourself what would remain of the obsessional sequence if the doubt was not true. Imagine for a moment what it would be like if the doubt was false. Do not try to debate the doubt in your mind. Just ask yourself the question, 'How much OCD would remain if the doubt was incorrect?'

Client Quiz 1
When OCD Begins

(Please check all answers which apply)

1. OCD begins with . . .
    - ○ a feeling of tiredness.
    - ○ a doubt.
    - ○ seeing something wrong.
    - ○ none of the above.
2. A doubt is about . . .
    - ○ a need for control.
    - ○ a possibility.
    - ○ lacking confidence in life.
    - ○ none of the above.
3. Thinking you will get ill if you might become contaminated is . . .
    - ○ a sign of being ill.
    - ○ a consequence of a doubt.
    - ○ the primary thought responsible for your symptoms.
    - ○ none of the above.
4. Without obsessional doubt . . .
    - ○ you would not feel anxious.
    - ○ you would have no compulsions.
    - ○ you would have no other OCD symptoms.
    - ○ all of the above.
5. The thought that you hurt someone if you ran over the person in your car is
    . . .
    - ○ Irrational.
    - ○ a sign that you worry too much.
    - ○ realistic *if* the initial doubt 'maybe I ran over the person' is correct.
    - ○ none of the above,
6. In which of the following subtypes of OCD does obsessional doubt play a
    crucial role?
    - ○ Checking
    - ○ Washing
    - ○ Symmetry
    - ○ Obsessions about harm
    - ○ Hoarding
    - ○ All of the above

Please check your answer by referring to the Quiz Answers Sheet.

Chapter Four

The 'Logic' behind OCD

The key points to convey in this chapter through explanation, illustration, exercise are:

(1) There is reasoning behind the obsessional doubt.
(2) The reasoning justifying the obsessional doubt seems logical and credible.
(3) It is not the content but the context of such reasoning which is problematic, in other words the relevance of the reasoning process.

The Reasoning Behind the Doubt

This step in treatment aims to increase the client's awareness of the thoughts and beliefs which precede the obsession, and familiarize the client with his or her reasoning behind the doubt. This identification of reasons behind the doubt should be carried out in an exploratory fashion without necessarily labelling those reasons as the *cause* of the problem. In fact, it is emphasized to the client that the justification can appear quite logical. The main reason for this apparent 'logic' behind the obsessional doubt is that the arguments supporting the doubt are not necessarily incorrect in isolation from the context in which they occur ('People do die from germs', or 'There is always the possibility of making a mistake'). In other words, it is often not the logic which renders the justification of the doubt 'invalid'.

The justification behind the doubt often presents itself in a logical fashion, and emphasizing this point with the client avoids unhelpful arguments between the client and therapist. Moreover, it removes the client from the assumption that the OCD can be resolved through internal dialogue recounting arguments for and against whether or not the doubt is valid.

Clinician's Handbook for Obsessive-Compulsive Disorder: Inference-Based Therapy, First Edition.
K. O'Connor and F. Aardema.
© 2012 John Wiley & Sons, Ltd. Published 2012 by John Wiley & Sons, Ltd.

Increasing awareness of the precursors to the obsessional doubt also has the benefit of putting the therapist and client on the same footing. Both client and therapist can agree that the point can be made that if the justification behind the doubt presents itself in a logical and credible fashion, then the source of the problem is elsewhere. Hence the client can already be made aware that it is not the particular content of the justification behind the obsessional doubt that is important here, but rather, that there are some peculiarities with the relevance of the reasoning behind the doubt.

There are reasons to be doubtful. In order to show that there is reasoning behind the doubt, the client is invited to generate reasons as to why his or her doubt might be valid. This might require some probing with the clients, but the therapist needs to keep in mind that any sort of compulsive behaviour implies that the client believes that some state of affairs might be wrong, harmful or undesired and that such possibilities invariably require some sort of justification.

What is Reasoning?

Reasoning is how we make sense of the world, how we arrive at inferences or conclusions about the world. Our reasoning literally allows us to be sure of concluding this is this or that is that. Our everyday reasoning is not necessarily logical or rational. Reasons can be emotional, wrong footed, rhetorical, acquired and (sub)cultural. But for us when we use them, they make sense to us and seem to us 'reasonable'. It is very rare as humans that we do not feel the need to give reasons to justify our conclusions or actions.

Occasionally we may invent reasons or genuinely not know why we do an action. But if we do not know why, the fact that we feel we should know why confirms the important role of reason as a basis for our thinking and planning.

Even an apparent nonreason for an act, like 'Well, I just felt like it' or 'An urge overtook me', are reasons in that behind them is a story about how it's OK to be guided by feelings and intuition, to give in to 'urges' now and then.

This also underscores another important point about reasoning: that it is not more complicated than the stories we tell ourselves about ourselves. In fact, if we didn't have a story of who we were and how we got where we are, we would be worried. Of course, we can have different rationales at different times and changing stories changes our perspectives on ourselves.

The use of the *reasoning categories* as provided on the accompanying worksheet may help facilitate this process by assigning the reasons within the categories 'rules', 'abstract facts', 'hearsay', 'personal experience' and 'it's possible'. In addition, the client is asked to repeat the same exercise with an obsessional doubt that is neutral to him or her. Contrasting the reasoning behind both doubts should illustrate how both obsessional doubts are equally plausible in terms of their reasoning logic. Thus, the point can be made that all obsessions contain an element of reason, and that the client's own doubts are no different in form from others people's obsessional doubts.

Prompting the Reasons

If the client has difficulty acknowledging or reporting any sort of justification for the obsessional doubt, then the therapist should proceed to resolve this lack of awareness. Often, a role playing exercise is useful to put the client in a more receptive state of mind, and increase his or her understanding of the OCD such as the following:

"I understand that the thought seems to be coming from nowhere, and that it very much upsets you that these thoughts seem out of your control. However, there is a reason for these thoughts. They do not come out of nowhere. Part of you believes in it – even if it's only a small part. So instead of telling me that the thought makes no sense, and that you cannot figure out why you have the thought, let's do a little exercise. For the next 5 minutes, I want you to talk for the OCD alone. Act as if you were defending the obsession, while I will act as if I were you and try to counter the OCD. So tell me, speaking for the OCD only, why could you be a child molester?"

Usually such prompting leads to an uncovering of the reasons behind the obsessional doubt. This suggests that even when people with OCD may sometimes have difficulties with providing reasons for their obsessional doubt, they are not deeply buried in the client's mind.

So it's important to bring the response down to a normal conversational level. Clients might enjoy the exercise as a chance to allow the OCD to speak freely for the first time. A typical interaction may constitute the following: In this example the client expresses doubts about child olesting.

T: So, tell me, why could you be a child molester?

C: Well, I don't know, it's always possible . . . no?

T: What makes it possible?

C: Well, how well do we really know ourselves? We might have urges – the kind of urges that make a person a child molester.

T: Okay. It's possible in a general sense as you say. That's a reason. And what if I would say it does not apply to you? How would the OCD respond?

C: Well, I do have these thoughts and images about molesting children. They must be there for a reason.

T: So you have thoughts and images. So one of the reasons you could be a child molester is because you have thoughts and images about molesting children?

C: Yes. Well, not really. I get confused. It's not like I really want to.

T: That's you talking now. Not the OCD. So let me ask that question, 'It's not like you want to. So how can you be a child molester if you don't want to?'

C: But a lot of child molesters try to resist their urges. Perhaps if I don't want to, it means I might be even more like them.

T: That's a good one. Sounds like you're really beginning to talk for the OCD. Okay, so you might be a child molester because you don't want to be.

C: I know it sounds stupid.

T: No. Speak for the OCD.

C: Well, I once watched this programme about child molestors and what kind of people they were like. All their psychological characteristics and what made them the way that they are even as they resisted their urges. And I started wondering, what if I was one of those people? And I started comparing myself to them, and did notice similarities. And I began to worry.

T: Ok, tell me more about that. In what other ways were you similar?

The reasoning can be bizarre or mundane, and in the telling the person may be aware of the idiosyncratic nature of the belief. However the point is not about challenging the OCD. The client already has plenty of practice with resisting the obsessions put forth by the OCD, and challenging the content of the obsession in order to effect a change is likely to be counter-productive. Prompting the reasoning is about creating an environment where the client feels comfortable with speaking up for the OCD. Any counter-arguments of the therapist should rather be queries and serve to elicit a more in-depth response so that the client will become more familiar with the reasoning process behind the obsession. The following example describes a bizarre justification.

C: OK, well, you're going to say this is weird. I know it sounds wacky but the OCD tells me contamination can travel across oceans and barriers. I mean locusts do. So the wind brings along invisible dirt and it can spread like ants getting into cracks and get to me.

T: OK, but how can this happen?

C: Well, it just can. It's like science fiction, but I saw a film where a cloud spread. I mean there is stuff going on and we have no idea about it.

T: So why does it get to you and not everyone else?

C: Well, I'm unlucky that way. I mean if there was one person to catch it in a thousand, it would be me. I catch cold easily. I was told I've got a low immune system.

T: So for you this travelling contamination idea is reasonable.

C: Yeah, I don't think others know about it like I do.

Issues in Teaching the Client to Reconnect with the Reasons for the OCD

In general, the client will usually volunteer reasons for their obsessional doubt. In some cases, however, the client may have difficulty in reporting the reasons behind the obsession. So far, we have identified several processes that may limit the client's awareness of the reasoning behind the doubt.

'Automatisation'

Many clients have experienced OCD for years, and a certain level of automatisation has begun to set in, where the reasons for engaging in compulsive behaviours have been lost, and the person simply goes through the motions. At one point or another, people with OCD may have been aware of the justifications behind the obsession, but now experience difficulty with reporting the reasons behind it. They may even report there is no good reason behind the obsession, and that it is simply happening without rhyme or reason. Difficulty in reporting the justification behind the doubt may also occur among those with strong investment or over-valued ideation, where there is a strong conviction in the real probability of the doubt. Here the doubt forms the taken for granted and unquestioned starting point for compulsive behaviours, while the reasons behind it have been forgotten.

Most commonly, those reasons are simply covered up by secondary concerns about losing control of themselves or misconceptions about the exercise. The client may feel you are asking them to come up with deep seated reasons as to why the client has OCD . . . in other words, do your job for you. The person may feel overwhelmed and unable to comply: 'Well if I knew the reason why I doubt, I wouldn't be here, would I?'

Level of Aversion to the Doubt

A different albeit interrelated problem that may influence the client's awareness of the reasons behind the obsessions, is a high level of aversion to the doubt. The client may treat the doubt as an affliction, rather than being the result of reasoning. Such clients tend to be quite upset with the perceived uncontrollability of the thought, sometimes even more so than with the particular content of the thought itself. They may act as victims of their mind while being unable to recognize that these thoughts are always arrived at through reasoning. They may exclaim, 'I don't understand why I have the thought. I just can't get it out of my mind', or 'None of it makes any sense. What is wrong with me?'

Imaginative Processes

Another influence that may hamper awareness of the reasons behind the thought lies in various imaginative processes associated with the OCD that make it more difficult than usual to retrieve the reasoning behind the OCD. Obsessions are highly absorbing occurrences that contribute to a subjective sense that the thought comes out of nowhere. Antecedents to the obsessional doubt are easily lost in such a dissociated state of awareness. It may be necessary to wind the person back step by step to where the dissociated bubble was entered and hence where the doubt began.

Decontextualization

Obsessions often occur in situations that are only remotely related to the actual events in the here and now. Clients may already be aware that their obsessions are very subjectively generated, and this may add to a person's sense that there is no logic to the OCD. If the therapist finds that the client is unable to reconnect with the reasons behind the obsessional doubt due to an excessive focus on its decontextualized (i.e. situationally inappropriate) occurrence, then it should be clarified to the client that this is indeed an important characteristic of obsessions. However, this does not mean that there are no reasons that make the client give probability to the doubt. The focus on the decontextualized occurrence of their doubts usually only serves to emphasize the uncontrollable and senseless aspects of the OCD, without understanding the implications of the idea that obsessional doubts come about in a very subjective manner. The main point to make at this stage in the therapy is that the obsession does not come out of the blue and has a certain type of logic behind it.

The crucial point is that the client connects with a personal justification for the doubt. So the client realizes the doubt arrives as an inference based on reasoning appealing to personal logic. The client should not feel here that the logic is invalid or that they need to confront the logic.

Decision Chart

Proceeding to the Next Stage of Treatment

- Person understands that there is a reasoning behind the OCD.
- The reasoning justifies the doubt somehow.
- The doubt does not come from nowhere but is a reasoned conclusion.
- Client accepts and understands reasoning as the basis for the doubt.

Cartoon 4. A clean break.

Dialogue Illustrating Awareness of OCD Logic

T: We saw last week the reasoning devices that OCD uses to distance you from reality and the world of the senses. Do you recall how the devices affect you?

C: Yes, they're all ways of creating confusion between reality and imagination. They are like salesman tactics to make you buy a product you don't really need.

T: Exactly. OCD functions like a salesperson. It uses all sorts of tricks to try to sell you, not a broom or a tie, but a doubt that is irrelevant to you.

C: I realize I don't need to buy the doubt, but the OCD is very convincing.

T: That's the problem. But if we identify the OCD tricks, it is easier to uncover the OCD and not be taken in.

C: And buy doubts only when they are real and justified.

T: Now let's take your OCD and we'll try to identify the reasoning strategies that OCD uses to make you believe that you're attracted to men.

C: OK. Well, one of the OCD arguments is that in the presence of men I'm sometimes nervous and uncomfortable and for me it's a sign that I could be attracted by them.

T: What makes you believe that?

C: Well, when I'm really attracted to a woman, I have the same sensations. I have butterflies in the stomach, my heart beats fast and I'm hot. If I experience all the same signs with a man, then it means I'm attracted to him.

T: So the OCD is creating a link between type of sensations and attraction.

C: Yes, and up to there, it's not wrong.

T: You're right. There are sensations present when one is attracted to someone. But there are equally many other factors to consider. In the presence of a woman who attracts you, apart from feelings you described, what else occurs?

C: I have the desire to get close physically, to touch and embrace. Imagining having sex gives me pleasure. I really have the desire to do it for real.

T: And what about when you are with a man?

C: Well, for sure no!

T: So you feel nervous, your heart beats fast and you get flushed in the presence of a man, but there is a 'necessary ingredient' missing to label this sexual attraction.

C: Effectively yes. Without this 'ingredient', one could as easily say I'm anxious rather than attracted.

T: Exactly so. The OCD tries to make you treat the two states as one and the same but it ignores the differences. Only your senses can naturally provide all the relevant information to discriminate anxiety from sexual attraction.

C: So we have here a 'category error'. The OCD is mixing up two concepts which don't go together: anxiety and attraction.

T: Can you identify other category errors in your OCD story? Can you say which ones?

C: Well, when I'm having fun with a friend, we enjoy ourselves. I feel good. The OCD tries to mix this up with attraction.

T: Would you make this confusion with a woman who really held no attraction for you?

C: No. I would be able to say it was only friendship, a good feeling of togetherness.

T: So this confusion applies just in the presence of a man.

Client Worksheet 2
The Logic Behind OCD

The exercises of last week were intended to help you understand the obsessional sequence. You should now be able to identify your own doubts that lie at the core of your OCD. Being able to recognize and identify your doubt is important, since we will address in many ways in the course of your therapy.

Reasonable Doubt

It is also important to understand that doubt does not come out of the blue. You can not have obsessions or doubts without reason. There is a certain kind of logic and reasoning behind obsessional doubts. For example, if you doubt or worry about the possibility that you might hurt someone, be contaminated or make a mistake, then there is a reasoning process behind these ideas. At the very least, you consider the doubt to be possibly true for some reason or another, since if you really considered it to be impossible, then you would not have the doubt.

Reasoning categories

Below you see some of the categories that are often part of the reasoning by which most people arrive a doubt.

1. Abstract facts and ideas
2. General rules
3. Hearsay
4. Personal experiences
5. It's possible

For example, if you have the doubt that you might have accidentally run over a child after driving out of the driveway, *abstract facts* might say tell you accidents do occur, *rules* that you should be careful when driving, *hearsay* that you read recently about someone driving over a child and *personal experience* that you once hit the garbage bin when driving out, and after all it is always *possible* you might have a accidently hit a child even when not seeing that you did.

OCD Sounds Pretty Reasonable!

Another example would be the doubt that a person might have been contaminated with dangerous germs. The justification behind the doubt might take the following form:

1. Germs exist. (Abstract facts)
2. Surgeons are obliged to wash their hands too. (Rules)
3. I heard of someone getting ill after visiting a bathroom. (Hearsay)
4. I once got ill after eating unwashed salad in the Caribbean. (Experience)
5. There is always a chance of anybody contracting illness. (Possibility)

The point of all this is to show you that there is reasoning behind the doubt, and that doubts can present themselves in as a 'reasonable' way. This is not to say that these doubts are 'correct'. There are a number of other crucial ingredients which render your obsessional doubts invalid for different reasons. In the course of the therapy we hope to show you why they are always false. But we are getting ahead of ourselves. For now, it is important to understand and identify the justification behind your *own* obsessional doubt.

Client Exercise Sheet 2
The Logic Behind OCD

Finding Your Reason

In identifying some of the reasons behind your own obsessional doubt keep in mind that there are *always* reasons behind a doubt. You may or may not be very familiar with those reasons. Some people with OCD, for example, when asked why they believe what they do, come up with lots of reasons why the doubt might be true. Others will say that have no idea how their doubts come about and experience their doubts as extremely unlikely and even as nonsense. Yet, these two groups of people are not so different. Both groups feel that they must act upon their doubt even though it might be experienced as unreasonable by one person and reasonable by the other. No matter if you believe your doubts are unreasonable and extremely unlikely, there are reasons why you doubt *your* particular doubt that *you* believe in. If you did not, you would not act on the doubt. There would be no obsession.

Be Reasonable

To find the reasons behind the doubt, you only need to ask yourself the question why you think your doubt could be possible, even if only to the slightest extent. What are the reasons you think you *might* have left the door unopened? What do you do think that the papers *might* not have been placed correctly? Why do you think your hands *might* be contaminated? What is it that makes you think it is possible, even if the chances of it being true are only 0.0001%?

First, to identify the reasons behind your own doubts, write down below the two obsessional doubts that bother you the most.

1. _____

2. _____

Next, write down any justification you think of in the corresponding category (abstract facts, hearsay, personal experience, etc.). Take your time with filling in the form, and try to write down the reasons as they occur to you while you are actually having your doubts. Let the OCD speak its mind. What does the OCD tell you?

A. Abstract facts
   1. _____

    2. _____

B. Rules
    1. _____

    2. _____

C. Hearsay
    1. _____

    2. _____

D. Personal experience
    1. _____

    2. _____

E. It's possible
    1. _____

    2. _____

F. Other reasons
    1. _____

    2. _____

Example

Doubt: I could be contaminated by waves coming from mental objects.

1. Abstract facts could include 'There have been reports of nuclear factories leaking radioactivity.'
2. Rules: People in contact with metals are obliged to wear gloves.
3. Hearsay: I've heard of people suffering from metal infections.
4. Personal experience: My hands smell and feel funny after I've touched a metal object.
5. It's possible that metals give off contaminants that they haven't discovered . . . like with Asbestos.
6. Other reasons: hot metal glows when it's warm; heat rises and could give off toxins.

Now, put yourself in the mind of another person with OCD, and try to come up with reasons behind the following obsessional doubts:

1. I might go suddenly crazy and hit another person.

2. There might be broken glass in the meal I prepared for my children.
    A. Abstract facts
        1. _____

        2. _____

    B. Rules
        1. _____

        2. _____

    C. Hearsay
        1. _____

        2. _____

    D. Personal experience
        1. _____

        2. _____

    E. It's Possible
        1. _____

        2. _____

    F. Other reasons
        1. _____

        2. _____

Try to compare the reasons you have come up with those of your own doubts. Are they any different, and if so, how are they different? Write down below anything you have what you have learned, wish to comment on, or that you have questions about.

_____

_____

Client Training Card 2
The Logic Behind OCD

Learning Points (Front)

- Obsessional doubts do not come out of the blue.
- There is 'logic' behind obsessional doubts.
- Doubts arrive due to prior reasoning.

Daily Exercise (Back)

At least four times a day, try to identify the doubt that motivated you to carry out compulsions or made you feel anxious, and rephrase the doubt in the form of statement of what could be or might be. Next, identify the reasoning you have applied to justify the doubt or statement. If you are not immediately aware of any thoughts before the doubt occurred then ask yourself, why does the doubt seem real? Or use the categories of abstract facts, hearsay, general rules, personal experience or mere possibility to help you identify the justification behind the doubt. Remember to slow down your thinking so you dwell on the validity of each component of your thought and how one presumption leads on to another.

"Make sure we don't invite him again next year".

Cartoon 5. Just to be sure.

Client Quiz 2
The Logic Behind OCD

1. Obsessional doubts are . . .
   - always correct.
   - preceded by reasoning.
   - sometimes realistic.
   - none of the above.
2. Obsessional doubts . . .
   - have justifications behind them.
   - come out of the blue.
   - ask normal questions.
   - all of the above.
3. The reasoning behind obsessional doubt . . . .
   - is sometimes based on possibilities.
   - follows a logic.
   - makes the doubt seem likely.
   - all of the above.
4. The reasoning justifying the doubt may come from . . .
   - abstract facts.
   - general rules.
   - hearsay.
   - all of the above.
5. The difference between normal and obsessional reasoning is that
   - obsessional reasoning is more logical.
   - normal reasoning is about the here and now.
   - normal reasoning concerns more dangerous topics.
   - none of the above.
6. Obsessional doubts are relevant because
   - they are possible in the abstract.
   - they are based on valid reasoning.
   - they are telling me new facts.
   - none of the above.

Please check your answers by referring to the Quiz Answers Sheet.

Chapter Five

The Obsessional Story

The Obsessional Story

The client will now be familiar with the reasoning behind the obsessional doubt. In this chapter the aim is to show how this reasoning in everyday life is connected up into the form of a story or narrative. The therapist helps the client to see how the obsessional doubt obtains its strength and reality value from a convincing story which leads the person logically to the doubt. This is the *narrative unit* giving credibility to the obsessional doubt, which will be a primary focus in the course of therapy. The narrative unit comprises both *reasoning* and *rhetoric*.

Narratives

The therapist and client should already have identified several reasoning devices in the narrative, but care must be taken to identify personally relevant elements behind the obsessional doubt, and not solely those that have been primed in the context of an exercise. During the session, the therapist explains how our thoughts weave a story that leads us to believe in certain things. The story gives the obsessional doubt credibility. The point to be made is that although it is isolated thoughts and ideas that provide the reasons for the obsessional doubt, it is how this reasoning is built up in a dramatic way into a story which renders it captivating and absorbing and creates a lived-in realistic possibility.

Clinician's Handbook for Obsessive-Compulsive Disorder: Inference-Based Therapy, First Edition.
K. O'Connor and F. Aardema.
© 2012 John Wiley & Sons, Ltd. Published 2012 by John Wiley & Sons, Ltd.

Telling the Story

The identification of the story behind the obsessional doubt should be carried out as a collaborative effort with the client. The previous sessions and exercises should have made the client comfortable with relating the reasoning in detail without fear or shame, and without fear of immediately being challenged by the therapist. Some prompting might be required, but in general the story is fairly easy to access. Previous information from the first two sessions can be used to dig more deeply into the overall storyline leading up to obsessional doubt. In addition, questions such as 'What makes you think the handrail is dirty?' or 'Why do you think the door could have been left unlocked?' may help to reveal the story behind the obsessional doubt. Sometimes the story is volunteered spontaneously. In the following example the story containing the reasoning behind the doubt flows naturally.

Example

T: So you don't handle the mail when it arrives?

C: I saw the postman dragging his bag on the ground and when I look at the people delivering circulars, I can see they are not clean. The person who sorts the letters doesn't wash – why would he – they don't get a chance – I was at a sorting office and it had no facilities – there was paint peeling of the walls; I mean touching all those sorts of objects, one after another, then the letter gets put through the same letter box as the circulars and I've seen the person who delivers the circulars, scruffy dirty, and mail drops on the mat.

T: Do you check to see if it's dirty?

C: Well, no, it's obvious it's dirty. I just know it is.

A Tall Story

In addition to the reasoning devices noted in Chapter 4, the OCD narrative is peculiar in interposing associations, bridging, assumptions, generalizations and hearsay and according all equal legitimacy to arrive at the inference that what is not there is, in fact, there. In the following example, the person is convinced to wash their hands just by recounting a narrative. 'So I say to myself: Well, my kids were playing outside and like I know it's dirty outside, I've seen the dirt and I think well maybe they touched something dirty, like picked up something from the street, dirty paper or shit, and then I say well if they're dirty then I'm going to be dirty and I'm gonna make the house dirty, and so I go in and wash and I can't stop, you know, it's like a voice in my head, saying over and over again, you're dirty, you're still dirty . . .'

The hallmark of such narratives is the weight accorded to 'maybes' – that is, to hypothetical possibilities. In reasoning terms, essentially, the narratives convincingly replace confidence in the senses (and the self) with a doubting inference based on remote possibilities, and/or lead the person astray from a commonsense approach, where interacting with the situation is congruent with goals and perceived task demand towards adopting irrelevant and unrealistic criteria. The following illustrates the power of the possible over the actual in OCD.

T: You've been married 10 years with three children; you've never had a homosexual affair or been attracted to a same-sex relation. What makes you doubt whether you are heterosexual?

C: Well, I had a close girlfriend when I was 14 and sometimes when I slept over we shared a bed, and soon after I saw a film where a man was married all his life and came out as gay, and then there was a live show featuring all these couples who had came out in late life and the impact on their families and children, and then since I got married young, I'm asking myself maybe I could not really know my sexuality and maybe I'm in denial and . . .'

Recording the Narrative

While identifying and writing down the narrative unit, the therapist should stay as close as possible to the wording and experience of the client. The narrative could start with connecting the justifications from the previous step into a more flowing personal story. Care should also be taken to include as much detail as possible to fill up any potential gaps in the story that the client takes for granted. The narrative unit is the engine behind the obsessional doubt logically arrived at through the power of its reasoning and rhetoric on its own stream. We do later address a more general vulnerable self-theme underlying the narrative unit, but not in the form of a single core belief. The rhetorical strength of the narrative resides exactly in its narrative form, a form not attained by itemized thoughts.

Outing the Story

After the obsessional narrative has been identified by the therapist, it may be useful to read out the entire story to the client while inviting further comments from the client. The proper attitude from the therapist is here to encourage the client to speak for the OCD as carried out previously in identifying the various separate reasoning justifications behind the obsessional doubt. The therapist should refrain from any attempts to challenge the story, which will prove to be counter-productive. Besides, the therapist should be aware that the thoughts and ideas that make up the story are not necessarily incorrect, and that it is not the correctness of these specific thoughts and beliefs that is addressed in IBT, rather their relevance in the here and now.

The Power of Narrative

The narrative is the unit of thinking and reasoning about ourselves and the world. We like good stories. It's unusual for humans to reveal motives, meaning, through discrete words or phrases. If you ask yourself how you came to be sitting here, reading this book, you would probably recount a narrative, with a past and present and maybe future. 'I saw the title and it seemed relevant so I ordered the book and then it arrived, so I put it aside and decided to read it today'. It's unlikely you would say, 'Saw book, ordered it, read it', unless you were deliberately aiming for a staccato sound-bite.

Live-in Stories

Narratives are important because they have a lived-in feeling. They literally transport us from one event to another; they position us in our histories and give room for nuance, attitude and emotion; they seem real. For this reason, they are also credible and convincing.

Rhetoric and Reason: Rhetorical Devices

The power of the narrative unit or story in OCD comes partly from the reasoning but from a variety of *rhetorical devices* which make it come alive and seem absorbing.

The language of the story and the way you connect up the story contribute enormously to its sense. In addition there are a number of devices from rhetoric which can boost elements in the narrative to transport is further.

Rich in detail

Part of the immersion comes from absorption in details of the story. The richer and more nuanced the details, the more credible the story becomes.

Smooth transport

The second is the transporting nature of stories which seem to take the person along with them on a journey. OCD stories travel from A to B on a seemingly credible route.

The person is along for the ride

The third element is that the person features in the stories. It's not just a third person narration like listening to a voice book read by a famous actor. The personalization of the happenings in the story centres events around the person, so that the key transition points are dramatic and meaningful, and touch the person emotionally.

Believed-instories

Narratives are used traditionally for mood induction to induce role-play and compliance, and are great vehicles for imaginative and magical thinking. But it is important that clients practice and discover the effects for themselves. In particular, the way believability gets stronger, the more minor the details, the more credible and the more the person is trapped in the twists and turns of a rich scenario.

Doubt creating stories

Recognizing the power of the OCD story is a crucial element to resolving the doubt, since the story creates the doubt. In one sense, a trick of the story is to be so convincing and immersing that the person doesn't realize that it is a story and takes for granted that it is obviously founded. The best way to illustrate the power of the story is through exercises. Again you can be creative and use your own variations, but a favourite is the pen story.

Creative exercise – the magic pen

Take an ordinary visible clean pen and ask the person if they feel able to hold it. Usually the person will comply. Ask the person if they consider the pen clean. Then recount a story of how the pen was found outside in the mud, it was covered in mud and dog poo. You previously saw a couple of dirty people holding, sucking it and wiping it under their armpits. It was lying in the dirt and a dog peed on it. But you thought it was a nice pen so you rescued it and wiped it off but you haven't had a chance to sterilize it properly. Now, ask the person if they are happy to hold it. Usually the response is an empathic NO. So the punch line is 'Why? What has changed, the pen or the story?' Answer: the story.

This story is not quite the same as an OCD story. Firstly, it is coming from an outside source (you, the therapist) and not the person, and seems to be recounting events that happened rather than remote possibilities. However, it does demonstrate how a story can trump sense information. The person's senses say all is OK, and with no story they would happily touch the pen. If it looked, smelt and felt dirty, the normal common sense reaction would of course differ.

Counter Stories

We now turn to the person's own OCD through use of a counter story, and here the aim is to temporarily resolve it through changing the story to eliminate the justification for doubt. Example:

OCD story: Well, there could be something wrong with the lock. I read about locks not working, and I'm not too mechanical so it could be something is not clicking and I don't know what. I once broke a watch trying to wind it up. If I was burgled, I'd be very upset and ashamed.

Counter-story: I've locked the door many times; there has never been a problem. I locked doors, boats and ladders all the time; I never made a mistake. I know exactly how to use a lock, and my senses give me feedback. What happens to others or what I did with a watch is irrelevant to a lock.

The counter-story is built up with the person so that all aspects of the OCD story which could induce doubt are countered by more reality-based alternatives. It is important the alternative story employs the rhetorical devices noted earlier. Usually, after immersion in the counter-story, the person will agree that the doubt has reduced or even disappeared . . .' at least temporarily. The success of the story may be qualified by the client with 'But how do I know your story is true?' or 'Well, I still believe the OCD story'. This is fine because at this stage you are showing that (1) the OCD and the counter are both equal stories; (2) the OCD story is the less realistic one; and (3) you're demonstrating rapid, if very temporary, resolution of the doubt through changing a story. Creating an alternative story more systematically is dealt with later on.

Decision Chart

Proceeding to the Next Stage of Treatment

- The client is aware that the justification behind the obsessional doubt takes the form of a convincing story.
- It is the story that gives the doubt credibility.
- The client is aware of all the elements in the obsessional story leading up to the doubt.

Dialogue illustrating rhetorical power of narrative from a client convinced he may be poisoned by white powder he found while cleaning behind his stove.

T: So, we had the fear of poison from a filler story about the idea of poison and everything poison means, that comes from common knowledge but not from what was actually in your situation at that moment, that scared you and became a filler that allowed you to jump over that gap where there was no sense-based justification. You then went to the narrative and you used it to Photoshop the gaps where the sequence in the senses just wasn't there [see Figure 5.1].

C: Right. And I even knew I was doing it.

T: This is very common with absorption into the obsessional narrative. The emotion of fear pulled you further into the story and farther away from reality. But that awareness is an important part of this battle. And at this point in treatment, being able to see this is a goal and we will take it. In the next steps, you will be better able to see the doubt doesn't come from the here and now situation you are in.

C: Yes, I can see that.

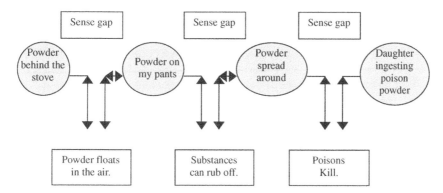

Figure 5.1 Narrative justifications that are irrelevant to the here and now.

T: What do you think would need to happen for you to be able to hold back on neutralization, for you to be able to tolerate this discomfort?

C: I would have to know that it was not dangerous.

T: Well, that would involve you trusting your senses. Now, intellectually, you were halfway there. You knew intellectually that you did not see anything on you or the clothing that your daughter would come in contact with; but the narrative was too emotionally compelling and washed over. But even though you didn't see it, you can't believe that it is really not there, right? And what made this so difficult?

C: So as I said, rationally when I went through the drill of what we have been talking about, if I had just washed my hand and taken off my shirt, that should have been enough.

T: Well we could go back even further and ask if you are really going with your senses would you really need to change your shirt, until after you had finished being in work mode?

C: But isn't it just common sense that if you might be handling a poison, before you touch a baby to wash your hands?

T: Yes, if you were working with what could reasonably be a poison and you were then going to touch your baby, yes, washing your hands would be reasonable. But that is not what was happening here. You didn't just touch a powder and head over to touch your daughter. You went through all these sequences of washing and changing when you saw nothing and you weren't even picking your daughter up.

C: No, that's true, I could have stopped right there, but that is where I crossed the bridge. It is too easy to just neutralize and go on with my life.

T: I would add that it was too scary not to neutralize.

C: Yes, I agree, too scary.

T: You were too pulled in. As you get better at seeing the difference between what you generate internally, the stories you construct and what is actually out there and as you get better at understanding how you come up with justifications to support what you construct, it will be easier to trust what you see, what is actually there and not act on what the narrative wants you to do. That will get easier. Tolerating not acting on that narrative will get easier.

C: Right. I can see this. I am just not there yet. But I feel I am getting closer.

T: Yes you are. This is tough work. You are doing great, you really are! You are at a point where you have one foot in the bubble and one out. But if you continue to work at it and take in the model and stay grounded to the 'what is' would, this will get easier. Let's talk about tasks for the next week. . . .'

Client Worksheet 3
The Obsessional Story

Feeling Real

Why do doubts (or obsessions) *feel* so real? To answer this question, you will first have to understand why it is that something can feel real to us in the first place. For example, take the activity that you are engaged in right now, the reading of this page. Why does it feel real to you? It feels real not only because of the information that comes through your senses but also, far more importantly, because there is a story attached to this activity with a past, present and future.

Appealing Stories

Ask yourself, how did you come to read this page? Almost immediately a whole story will start to unfold that reads like a novel. You may see yourself in the past struggling with OCD, how you decided to seek help, your trips to the therapist office, the conversation and questions, the work you did at home, and the hope to overcome your OCD in the future. Imagine for a moment you would be engaged in reading this page without the above story? How much would remain of your sense of reality in reading this page?

Listening to Your Own Novel

In a way, listening to your own thoughts is like reading a novel. This is not merely coincidental, but is part of how we organize our opinions and feelings about ourselves and how we experience the world around us. While we are engaged with the world around us, a story is unfolding, and we add elements to this story which makes the world around us seem real and convincing, whether you are on your way to the grocery, going to work, conversing with friends or family or obsessing. So in a way, we go through life being storytellers, and the stories we tell ourselves have an important effect on our experience, what we believe in, and how real these beliefs feel to us. In the same manner, obsessional ideas also come about and appear real to us through the stories we tell ourselves. They have a history and a story attached to them, which make them feel very plausible and real.

We're All Storytellers

Aside from all being storytellers, we also reason, and weave our stories in a generally logical and coherent way. So in the story there are all kinds of seemingly logical and rational reasons behind the obsessional doubt. In fact, you are already quite familiar with the story behind your own obsessions and doubts. After all, in previous sessions, you have identified a lot of thoughts that appear to justify to obsessional doubt. However, all these bits and pieces of information that you have considered so far are really part of a more compelling story – the story you tell yourself when you think about why your doubt might be true. We also sometimes call it the *narrative unit* of your OCD. It is this narrative that makes the OCD feel so real.

Client Exercise Sheet 3
The Obsessional Story

Identifying the Story

During the last session, together with your therapist, you should have come a long way towards identifying the story behind your obsessional doubt. This story is likely to change over time, as there are likely important elements not yet included in the story. In the course of therapy, you can expect to become increasingly aware of the story behind your doubt, including all sorts of reasons that give the doubt credibility. This story will be addressed in many different ways in the course of therapy. This is why it's a good idea to start writing down your story, and to add new elements to it as you become aware of it.

Your Own Story

For now, write down your OCD story below. The story is composed by joining up the reasoning you identified in chapter four which justifies your obsessional doubt. You can use a separate piece of paper if you need more room:

_____

_____

_____

_____

_____

_____

_____

_____

_____

This is the story behind your own personal doubt. Other people with OCD have similar convincing stories. For example, consider the following two OCD stories:

I can't go too far from home, or the city that I live in, because I don't know how panicky I might get. I might go really crazy and do something to myself. Who knows what is really wrong with me? One of my family members has schizophrenia, and I might have some serious disturbance also. I could be crazy enough to cut out my tongue. When I'm anxious, I can 'see' myself doing it, using a knife to cut it off. It feels I could actually do it. Then I'll be in the middle of nowhere without help. Then when I'm found I'll be sent off to a psychiatric hospital somewhere that I don't know, and they'll lock me up.

I have to check my stove each time I leave my apartment because I know I am an absent-minded person and that I can forget things. It even happened once that I forgot a pot on my stove; it could have set fire to my apartment. Also, I heard that a fireman forgot a pot on a stove right at the fire station and it set fire to the station. It is reasonable to think that if a fireman forgets pots on stoves, it could happen to anybody and especially to those like me who tend to be absent-minded.

Relating to Stories

The degree to which you can relate to these stories probably depends on whether they lead to a similar conclusion as your own story. For example, if you yourself have doubts about contamination, then all manner of reasons that warrant the idea of the contamination story may make more sense to you, while the other story will make less sense to you. Still, in both cases, there is an equally valid story that leads up to these doubts. They are not really different, and one is not necessarily any more or less valid than the other.

Creative Exercise

Using your creative abilities, now we want you to make up a story for a different type of OCD, one you wouldn't normally obsess about. Pick a theme from one of the following: 1) park benches are contaminated; 2) you can never be sure you really posted a letter; 3) people could easily misunderstand you on the phone.

Illustration

List the reasons supporting the doubt. What would happen if you wove the reasons you wrote down there into a convincing OCD story? Try to use the devices to make the story as credible and real, and write the story down below:

_____

_____

_____

_____

_____

_____

_____

Now, compare your own OCD story with the one you have come up with. How are the stories different? How are they similar? Write down below anything you have learned, wish to comment on or have questions about.

_____

_____

_____

_____

_____

_____

_____

Client Training Card 3
The Obsessional Story

Learning Points (Front)

- Doubt is experienced as real because there is a credible story behind it.
- Your own OCD story is no more or less valid than any other OCD story.
- The story becomes real when you act on it.
- Change the story and you change the doubt.

Daily Exercise (Back)

Invent stories both positive and negative about objects you encounter during the day, and experience how these stories change your experience and attitude towards the object. For example, what if this mug was used by a beautiful woman who cared for it well and washed it regularly? What if this same mug belonged to a writer who kept his pens inside? When your OCD doubts appear, stop before plunging into them and recall the story behind them, and how repeating this story convinces you of their validity.

Client Quiz 3
The Obsessional Story

1. Behind every obsession there is . . .
   - ○ a core belief.
   - ○ a story giving credibility to the doubt.
   - ○ a phobia.
   - ○ none of the above.
2. The story determines . . .
   - ○ the credibility of the obsession.
   - ○ the truth of the obsession.
   - ○ how I act in general.
   - ○ the real facts.
3. An obsession can be created by
   - ○ asking someone else to repeat a story.
   - ○ you creating a story.
   - ○ suppressing the story.
   - ○ changing the situation.
4. The story takes the form of a narrative because
   - ○ a narrative can be lived in.
   - ○ a narrative paints a convincing context.
   - ○ a narrative flows along.
   - ○ all the above.
5. Individual thoughts can be converted into narrative units by
   - ○ placing the words together.
   - ○ a magic formula.
   - ○ telling a story connecting them.
   - ○ saying the thoughts out loud.

Please check your answers by referring to the Quiz Answers Sheet.

Chapter Six

The Vulnerable Self-Theme

The Vulnerable Self-Theme

In the evaluation section, we touched on the idea that behind the client's individual doubts and neutralization is a common self-theme which binds them together. We have already noted that the OCD theme is selective. It does not cover all aspects of the client's life domains. We know also that the OCD, even if it falls within a larger subtype, is idiosyncratic. No two obsessions or their triggers are identical from client to client. Also clearly the doubts that the client expresses are selective because they are meaningful to the client and the client alone. In other words, your self is in some way relevant to your doubts.

In this section, we carry this idea further by developing the idea of a central self-theme which renders vulnerable to experiencing a particular selective bag of doubts. Essentially the argument is that OCD has convinced the client that s/he could become someone s/he really doesn't wish to become. As a consequence the client is vigilant about making mistakes, becoming contaminated, and so on . . . because OCD has convinced him/her that s/he could become this sort of person if s/he did not watch out and protect himself or herself through neutralization.

The client needs make this extra bit of effort which others do not since s/he is particularly vulnerable to be lacking here in care, attention, thoughtfulness or whatever the OCD self-theme dictates. Hence the self-theme, since it is the underlying conductor joining up the individual doubts, can in turn be identified by grouping up doubts and looking for common concerns.

The theme can be complex, but it will encompass all individual OCD doubts. So, for example, a man who is convinced he could be someone who could expose

Clinician's Handbook for Obsessive-Compulsive Disorder: Inference-Based Therapy, First Edition.
K. O'Connor and F. Aardema.
© 2012 John Wiley & Sons, Ltd. Published 2012 by John Wiley & Sons, Ltd.

himself to danger inadvertently and not be aware of important consequences might develop obsessions about a variety of past actions where feasibly he could have missed out on details of potentially risky events. A mother whose vulnerable theme is that she could be negligent develops obsessions about not harming her children in a number of ways through negligence.

Who Am I?

A common discourse of people with OCD is a lack or emptiness of self. It is true this can manifest itself as ambivalence, such as 'I'm not sure who I am'. But it is frequently more pointedly an authentic feeling of not being anyone. Let's look at two narratives.

This is Frank (43), who performed washing rituals since the age of 7.

"It's now such a part of me I just can't think of who or what I would be without the rituals. I say, well at least you've got your rituals . . . that's who you are. When people make comments, 'Frank, oh you mean Mr Cleaner than clean', I say, 'Yep . . . that's me, that's who I am'."

This sense of nonbeing gets stronger as the client becomes more invested in the obsession. This is Jane (56), a hoarder: 'I find myself in my objects. Without them I just don't know who I would be I shudder to think. They're my whole life. They're protecting me but at the same time they're part of me, they're me and my world'.

Misplacing the Self

The client may displace self onto objects or rituals which temporarily reassure that the client is there. However, in accordance with IBT, the actions are not driven by who the client thinks they are but who they believe they could be or become. In other words, it is not so much that the client is divided into one person wishing to do the rituals and another not willing to. Rather the client gets absorbed through inferential confusion into douibting who s/he 'could be'. The clients are living the possibility that they could really be a negligent mother or otherwise undesired person that the self is not as it appears and they must take special precautions. In other words, for people with OCD, their central self is about who they do not want to be rather than who they really are.

A Selfless Doubt

This point is very important since it has a strong explanatory power over a number of self-related OCD thoughts and actions. The conception is contrary to the common idea that OCD actions are driven by a perfectionist self constantly seeking to complete or not complete actions to an unrealistic degree, or constantly striving to be absolutely certain when certainty is not possible. In fact, the client is not going towards any goal at all. Rather the goal is to escape and protect themselves from becoming someone he or she is not and does not want to be, and will never be, since it is an inferentially confused OCD-created self-doubt about his or her real identity.

Is that (really) You?

Joan is a good enough mother. She cares for her children's welfare. She's attentive to their needs. She's always on hand to take her kids to school or drop them off at friends'. But she feels guilty because she's convinced she could do bad things to her children, smother them, strangle them. She watches her hands and tries as much as possible to avoid hugging or touching them. Whenever she hears a report on the television about a mother assaulting or maltreating children, she becomes alarmed and thinks to herself, 'That could be me!' Joan's story illustrates well the dilemma of the OCD self. All her actions and her wishes align with the self-concept that she is a good mother. But the OCD doubt convinces her she could be another person who she really fears becoming. The point is that she fears becoming a possible self that she is not, but *could* become if she doesn't take precautions. So in protecting herself from the feared self, she disrupts the functioning of the self she actually is. . . . It's a lose-lose situation.

Joan's Theme

Joan's vulnerable self-theme (that is, her feared self or feared identity) is that she could be a child abuser or batterer. Where did this theme come from? Clearly not reality, since all her actions, sentiments and behaviour describe a good mother, responsive to her children's needs. But if we ask her to justify this feared self, she comes up with a narrative.

"Well, I read somewhere that deep down we all have two sides . . . you know Dr. Jekyll and Mr. Hyde, and that often what we are on the surface is the opposite to what we really feel. I sometimes am just not sure all the time of my motives and people can just flip like that. Many murderers appeared to be nice people on the outside. So I could be the opposite to who I think I am. I could be fooling everyone."

Detecting Obsessional Elements

The reader will by now easily identify this narrative as an obsessional one, with all the similar obsessional reasoning which is creating doubt in other areas. Joan also related this view of herself to an experience in early childhood where she was taught to distrust her view of herself and her talents by disparaging remarks from her parents.

Joan: I really like playing hockey.
Mother: No you don't... it's a dirty game... you can't like that.

It will rapidly become obvious that who the actual person differs widely from who the OCD says they could become. In other words, there whatsoever what so ever that the person even vaguely resembles who the OCD says they could be. Of course, OCD, trickster that it is, will try to weave around this with something like 'Well, it's because you're OCD vigilant that it doesn't happen'. However, the client can relate this OCD talk to the other obsessional doubts already identified, and also the narrative revealing the baseless story behind it. The therapist can say, 'Well, remember when you explored the story behind the doubt about your door perhaps not being locked? Do you see similarities? Does the self-story show the same reasoning devices?'

Centreing Doubts Around the feared OCD self

In most cases the subjective doubt of the obsession is nurtured by a more encompassing vulnerable self-theme. We can say that at the root of all our concerns is our self-wellbeing. It's our bottom line, and any threat to our self will merit priority attention. However, again the benefit of IBT is that finding this self-theme is logical and follows logically from the doubt. So, for example, it seems very reasonable to conclude that someone obsessed with being contaminated considers themselves the type of person who could be contaminated. If not, why become preoccupied with this and not another possibility, say for example, with making a mistake? Similarly, a client preoccupied with the door being left unlocked considers themselves the type of person who could leave a door unlocked. This recentreing of the obsession around the active personal agency is the first crucial step to uncovering the self-theme. So, in other words, from 'This doorknob could contaminate me', we shift to 'I'm a person who feels especially at risk of being contaminated'.

The next question to ask is what type of person would léave a door open, make a mistake, get contaminated? The client may reply 'A person who is inattentive, careless, caught off guard'. The further question is 'Are you this type of person?', to which the answer is usually 'No ... but I don't wish to become one'. In other words, the person is driven not by a sense of who they are (e.g. 'I'm a perfectionist so things must be perfect', or 'I'm a responsible person so I should act responsibly'), rather they are driven by fear of who they might become. Obviously, such a negative self cannot develop. Several writers have drawn attention to the importance of imma-turity and ambivalence of the self in the OCD field. But crucially, in the IBT model we are proposing that it is doubt about the self the client could become which determines the multiple manifestations of obsessional doubt. These doubts may cut across different domains but will nonetheless reflect the same self-theme consistently.

For the therapist, the first step to discovering the OCD self-theme is to go back with the client to the clinical sheet listing the client's obsessions and ask what theme they all have in common. The self-theme should be established collaboratively with the client to ensure credibility.

Confused Selves

When we introduce obsessional doubt into the debate about self-doubt as with other doubts should make clear why the client can never be sure of the self because the client is continuously rehearsing the doubt that they could be someone they are not. Therefore in the same way that everyday obsessional doubts maintained by belief are about remote possibilities, so the feared OCD self is driven by possible selves, not real ones.

From Self-Theme to Self-Story

Once the self-theme is established, it will be apparent that the self-theme is a doubt about who the client *could* be or become (not who she or he actually is). So if it is a self-doubt, then it is an obsessional self-doubt which means there is a reasoning story justifying it.

So, on the basis of the theme, what is the client's self-story?

_____

_____

_____

Does the client see reasoning errors in the self-story comparable to the reasoning errors in the individual doubting stories? Specify.

_____

_____

_____

Dialogue Eliciting a Vulnerable Self-Theme

In the example below, the client's OCD behaviour (3–5 hours per day) included multiple verifications at home, at work, such as checking doors, wallets and the alarm system for errors in its technical designs, and safeguarding electronic documents. He also had washing rituals when showering, bathing his children and cleaning teeth, and frequently avoided contact with household objects, so he wouldn't become dirty particularly after showering. After discussion of the theme running through his different obsessional doubts, the client concluded that all he could think of was that they all related to the fear of being careless or irresponsible. He noted that he would never forgive himself for certain errors, particularly if there were grave consequences.

C: So ... I would never forgive myself for forgetting to lock my car door if it was robbed.

T: OK. Any other examples of unforgivable errors?

C: All errors which touch work or home. As I said, I'm super-responsible.

T: But if you know you are super-responsible, why would you consider yourself at risk 0 accidents?

C: Well, if it was an unforeseen accident, probably I could forgive myself. But not an error I could have avoided.

T: So you're afraid of becoming the type of person who could make avoidable mistakes.

C: No. I don't think so. I look out all the time. I always watch carefully and I assure myself that all is done as it should be. I've been like that a long time, since junior college I would say.

T: How would you describe yourself before junior college?

C: I know when I was a kid I didn't care for school. I never completed my homework, and I was placed in a class for difficult children in secondary school. That hurt my self-esteem. I know also my father didn't like me making errors and he never stopped severely reprimanding me.

T: Can you give some examples of errors that your father would reproach you for?

C: Yes [laughs]. I remember once I broke the snow blower because a piece of metal in the snow got stuck in it. I didn't see it because it was covered with snow. My father was really cross and said I should have seen the metal. The same thing happened with other things which I don't remember, but frequently he would say, 'You should have known that would happen'.

T: Do you think these experiences with your father led you to view yourself as the type of person at risk of not foreseeing errors?

C: Well, at the time I was upset. But now I say, well those things were really unpredictable and well my father was my father and I shouldn't take it all so seriously.

T: Ah, so I see, you've succeeded in distancing yourself from your father for these past accidents. But I'd like to know if there were situations where you considered you were unforgiving to yourself.

C: Yes. It's true, I can become intransigent sometimes. For example, if I have workmen in the house, I verify their work and if I see things may be botched, I become nervous. I begin to identify with the worker and I feel like I've done hard work just like him. One could say it's as if in everything I do, I'm also a botcher. I know in reality I work well. But it's as if I fear to become like him, to be a botcher, which for me is the worst thing possible.

T: OK. To resume, then, you say you know you are not a botcher, that in fact you are a meticulous worker. However, after seeing some botched work, you begin to fear that you could be a botcher. Is that right?

C: Yes, it's bizarre but that's how it is.

T: Could we say that you fear becoming a botcher, that is, you fear becoming this type of person in particular?

C: Yes, exactly. In some way I know I'm a good worker but still I'm afraid of becoming a bad worker who could do things all wrong, even if in reality I know it makes no sense.

T: What then are the reasons justifying that you could be this type of person?

C: Well. [Silence] When I was young, for example at primary school, I remember feeling not at all on top of the teachers' requests because I was frequently in detention ... the same in secondary school ... and this is how I feel still today. To be correct, I need to do more than others. [Silence] I need to watch myself because I had a tendency to go off in the wrong direction and find myself off track and not at all doing what was expected. Now I have a good job because I took myself in hand at junior college. I have a house and a family, and it's important for me that they are looked after. But I've got to be careful because I could go astray. I could go back to who I was in the past. ...

Client Worksheet 4
The Vulnerable Self-Theme

The worksheet in this section covers:

- How to discover your vulnerable OCD self through decentreing your everyday doubts around you.
- Understanding how the self-theme may dictate the type of everyday obsessions you experience.
- Understanding how the OCD is not a real self but an illusory self arrived at on the basis of inferential confusion.
- In other words, it is a possible self you are convinced you could become and who you do not wish to become, but are convinced you could become on the basis of an absorbing story.
- Your real self is exactly the opposite of the OCD feared self you fear could become.

Looking at the doubts listed on the clinical scale, perhaps we see:

- Doubt that I checked the stove.
- Doubt that I wrote the correct number.
- Doubt that I said the right word.
- Doubt that the car door is locked properly.
- First question to ask: 'What do the doubts share in common here?'

Answer: The first obvious point in common amongst the doubts is checking to see if everything was fine.
- The second question: 'What does this checking action tell us about your's self-construct?'
Answer: The client fears that she or he may have made an error, mistake or gaffe.
- The third question: 'What sort of person would do this?' introduces the self-theme.
Answer: A person who is clumsy, prone to gaffes, inadequate or careless.
- The self-theme is idiosyncratic and can be quite complex. It is important to cover all the options of self-themes with the client and include all components.
- Your doubts reveal your OCD self, since you only doubt obsessionally in areas where your self-theme says you would be most likely to doubt. For example, a person who is constantly checking to see if the lights in the house are off clearly considers he is a person likely to leave the lights on. At the same time he does not constantly check whether the car is

parked correctly when the client goes out to a car park, clearly does not consider it any more likely than anyone else to find the parked incorrectly.

- The OCD self-theme plays an important part in determining the type of OCD you experience. Hence it is important to know it. In other words, the self is not a real self that you can identify with real positive attributes. It is rather a non-existent self which you are afraid you will become. Or, more precisely, you think *maybe* you could become. Rather, it's another obsessional doubt and follows all the reasoning errors that make your obsessional doubt believable.

  Good news: you will readily identify all the imaginary and illusory tricks by which the OCD convinces you that you could become a self you fear, and don't want to be.

- Bad news: the OCD has done a really good job of convincing you that this illusory self is a real possibility.

- The OCD self is actually the complete opposite of who you really are, and in a later chapter we will cover how to replace the OCD feared self with the authentic self you really are.

- Obviously, knowing and changing this theme comprise a giant step in helping you overcome your OCD. Why? Well, because if this theme makes you vulnerable to doubt in the way you do, then repositioning you towards a more solid self will make you far less vulnerable. You will begin to base your self-evaluation on who you really are and what you are really likely to do, not on a self that OCD says you might possibly, one day, become.

So now let's counter your OCD self-story with an authentic self-story.

Client Exercise Sheet 4
The Vulnerable Self-Theme

Steps to Discovering your Theme

- Joe doubts constantly that he has locked his car door properly. So recentring this doubt around Joe gives us: Joe believes he's the sort of person who could leave car doors unlocked.
- Joe also needs to check several times that he closed the lights before leaving his lab at work. So recentreing *this* second doubt around Joe gives us: Joe believes he's a person who could leave the light on.
- Finally we have a third obsession where Joe becomes preoccupied that he might have forgotten some important detail of this work. So recentring this doubt gives us: Joe thinks he could be a person who leaves out important details in his work.

If we combine all three doubts to arrive at a common theme, we could say Joe is a person who thinks he could be someone who forgets to do important actions.

So look at John's series of obsessional doubts:

_____

_____

_____

_____

What do these doubts have in common? Well, they all involve John and all involve cleanliness. Anything else?

What about order? Clearly John gives a lot of importance to being clean, being surrounded by an orderly environment. Assuming the doubts listed are exhaustive of John's OCD, what is he not obsessionally concerned about?

_____

_____

_____

_____

Well, a number of OCD domains: making errors, hurting people and saying bad things, to name a few. So John obviously considers that he doesn't need to concern himself so much with these areas. But why not? Isn't he just as likely to experience problems in these areas? Yes, in everyday life we can encounter problems in any area. But John doesn't obsess in these other areas. So why not? Well, the answer, according to IBT, is because his self-theme does not make him vulnerable here. John considers himself the sort of person who could become unclear or could live in an unclean, disorderly environment which he does to wish to become. His extra obsessional concern is to prevent himself becoming such a person or a person who lives in such a state. John has never actually been such a person or ever lived in such a state, but OCD has convinced him he could become such a person if he doesn't obsess about it and perform his OCD rituals. In fact, when we ask John how he lives so cleanly, he will reply because he's obsessional and spends hours cleaning. Is he right? No, he's not. The OCD *as we know* has installed doubts in his mind which make him continuously fear he hasn't done enough or isn't clean enough. But these doubts *as we know* are based on an unreasonable story full of reasoning errors. In fact, doing the rituals simply reinforces and increases the doubt that he could become the person he fears he will. So he lives in a vicious circle where doubting produces more doubt which produces more rituals which reinforce the doubt and make real the real doubt seem real . . . so round and round the mulberry bush we go!

So where does the self-theme come from? Well, in the present, which is what concerns us here, the self is created and maintained by a story which bears all the hallmarks of an OCD doubting story. It draws on remote possibilities, abstract out-of-place facts and irrelevant events to make a convincing justification.

John's self-story was 'Well, my father was always forgetting to wash, he wouldn't change his clothes, and you inherit your father's traits. I'd help my mother clean up and she'd say, "Don't become like your father" '.

But how did this self develop in the past? We're not completely sure, but research suggests that people with OCD may have a tendency to compare themselves negatively to others and ignore their own needs and self-attributes. However, the important point is that we can change all this in the here and now without the need to look back to the past. It may be in working on your self-theme, you will recognize the origin of your story in a childhood experience. If so, fine, but the goal here is not to interpret the self-world but to change it.

Now repeat this exercise with your own doubts. List doubts, and then explore a common theme.

———————————————————————————————————

———————————————————————————————————

———————————————————————————————————

———————————————————————————————————

So obviously you consider yourself the sort of person who also could be:

_____

_____

_____

_____

This is your OCD theme, the person you are afraid you might become:

_____

_____

_____

_____

What is the evidence for this OCD possible self? Why are you so convinced you could become such a person that you need to invest so much time and effort to make sure you do not? Obviously the con trick of the OCD is to say to you, 'It's only because you do your rituals and are ultra-vigilant that you do not become your feared self'.

   So now, justify your conviction in the OCD possible self. What convinces you?

_____

_____

_____

_____

Do you see the OCD reasoning here? Compare the reasoning related to self-doubt with the reasoning about your everyday obsessional doubts.

_____

_____

_____

_____

Client Training Card 4
The Vulnerable Self-Theme

Learning Points (Front)

- My OCD self is a possible self I'm afraid I could become if I don't perform my compulsions or rituals.
- The OCD self is based on a story.
- The OCD self is against my authentic self who I really am.
- My fear of becoming who OCD says I am or could be fuels my everyday OCD doubts and the OCD precautions I practice.

Daily Exercise (Back)

Become aware of how important a role your OCD feared self plays in motivating your specific OCD thoughts and actions. Would you be so driven if you possessed another self?

Monitor your actions every day, and from these actions (whether good or bad) build up a picture of the attributes you've shown during the day. How do your attributes and accomplishments support/not support, you becoming your feared OCD self? For example, Mary's feared self is that she will inadvertently commit or expose herself to danger. But actually, she is known to her colleagues as someone to consult if they foresee a problem. She is often invited to participate in forums to troubleshoot problems.

Cartoon 6. The hot spot.

Client quiz 4
The Vulnerable Self-Theme

1. My OCD self-theme is . . .
   - a personality trait.
   - the same for everyone.
   - a true story.
   - about who OCD says I could become.
2. My OCD self-theme . . .
   - is who I really am.
   - determines the theme of my obsessions.
   - can't be changed.
   - helps me be someone.
3. My OCD self-theme:
   - is all I've got.
   - cons me into doing rituals.
   - tells me the truth.
   - needs to be taken seriously.
4. My OCD self:
   - is based on doubt.
   - is how others perceive me.
   - is realistic.
   - should be the basis for my actions.
5. I'm basically empty, so:
   - OCD fills me up.
   - OCD gives me a true identity.
   - I could be nothing without OCD.
   - OCD hides my true self.
6. I can find my OCD self theme by:
   - reading a novel.
   - noting the common thread to my daily OCD doubts.
   - meditating.
   - asking other people.

Please check your answers by referring to the Quiz Answers Sheet.

Part II

Intervention

Chapter Seven

OCD Doubt is 100% Imaginary

OCD is Imaginary

The person has already accepted that obsession is subjective, and that it is not reality-based but imaginary. In this section we home in on the key targets for intervention in IBT. Firstly, we explore in more detail the imaginary nature. In particular we underline how the obsessional imagination contradicts reality and perception; how it joins up distinct events, objects, activities into a common association; and how the imagination can make the non-existent seems only too real.

The most crucial element of inference-based therapy, which the therapist may wish to spend more than one session on, is to establish with the client that obsessional doubt is entirely generated from the imagination. More precisely, the justification behind the doubt (the narrative unity) does not contain any direct evidence in the here and now to support the doubt. In other words, the obsession originates not only entirely from *within* the client, but from within the imagination.

Doubt is 100% Subjective

The entirely subjective generation of doubt is an important characteristic of OCD which differentiates it from other anxiety disorders. For example, in spider phobia, the person may encounter a spider, and overestimate the likelihood that the spider will jump on him or her and bite. Yet, a spider is present in this case, and some spiders do jump and bite. In contrast, in the obsessional case, there often appears to be a *complete* lack of objective justification for any particular threat. The source of threat is inferred and rarely perceived directly.

Clinician's Handbook for Obsessive-Compulsive Disorder: Inference-Based Therapy, First Edition.
K. O'Connor and F. Aardema.
© 2012 John Wiley & Sons, Ltd. Published 2012 by John Wiley & Sons, Ltd.

What do we Mean by 'Imagination?'

Imagination is the opposite of perception. Both are cognitive faculties that are very useful but for distinct purposes. The term 'imagination' here is a useful catch-all to cover any ideas or intuitions that are subjectively generated. The imaginary contrasts with perception by which we see what is in front of us with our senses. So here we use the term 'imagination' to label any idea, inference, impression, image, sentiment of what could be that is subjuectively generated in the absence of direct perceptual support from reality in the here and now.

Possibility Versus Reality

After introducing the idea that the obsessional story does not contain any justification in sense information from the here and now, the therapist continues to dissect the OCD story with the client to establish whether it indeed lacks any direct evidence from the here and now. In our experience, it always does. Of course, the story may contain all manner of facts, possibilities and ideas that *could* be true ('germs exist', or 'perhaps the door was left unlocked'), but there is never any *direct* evidence in the here and now to support the obsession ('seeing dirt on your hands', or 'seeing the door left unlocked'). This is also the case for obsessions without over-compulsions, where there is also a lack of direct evidence from the here and now, both in terms of information coming from the 'outer' senses, but then 'inner' senses as well. For example, an obsession such as 'I might hit someone' occurs without the client *actually* being angry or upset, and as such, there is no evidence or justification in reality that the obsession might be true. Our common sense tells us what is most likely given our perceived environment. For example, common sense might help us decide what clothes to bring along on a hot summer's day. Common sense might dictate an umbrella but not a fur coat with snow boots.

Direct Evidence Versus OCD

The therapist should also have a firm grasp of what constitutes direct evidence in the here and now. For example, a client may justify washing their hands continuously by pointing out the possibility of an epidemic breaking out. None of this is factually incorrect, but it still occurs without any actual evidence in the here and now. On the other hand, if such an epidemic is inspired by an immediate threat (i.e. an actual epidemic having broken out), then of course precautions are not really obsessional. Likewise, washing hands while inside of a hospital is not obsessional. It is appropriate to the situation and contextually linked to being from the outside world. Frequent signs encouraging people to wash their hands for sensible reasons. There have occasionally been outbreaks of flu requiring precautions in public. But although clients may attempt to wheel in such an event as outside proof of contamination, it is of course never the origin of the OCD behaviour.

At the intervention step stage, the therapist should only try to show the client that there is no direct evidence for the doubt. The obsession is not directly challenged, although the client may sometimes experience it in this manner. They may argue, for example, that the fact that there is no evidence from the here and now for the obsession does not make the obsession impossible (e.g. 'Yes, I agree, but it might still be possible'). This is indeed true, and not really the point. The client only needs to come to an understanding that there is no direct evidence for the obsession in the here and now. It can be conveyed to the client that this idea has implications, which will be addressed in later sessions, but it does not mean the obsession is impossible. How many times has the client's obsession been proved correct?

Imaginary Doubt

Once the client agrees that there is no direct evidence in the here and now for the obsessional doubt, the therapist is able to show that the obsession comes from within or, more accurately put, from the client's imagination. This can be formulated broadly as follows by the therapist in his or her own words:

So now that we see that your OCD story has no basis in the here and now (even though it might be possible), the question is where does the obsession come from. It does not come from the outside, since there is no justification for it there. So that can only mean one thing, which is that it comes from inside of you. In fact, it is generated 100% by your imagination. And with imagination I mean anything that you come up with that is not directly related to the here and now. Imagination is a normal faculty. We all use our imagination to conjure up possibilities and think about things that do not directly come from evidence in the here and now. But in the case of your OCD story, it is *entirely* based in your imagination. Would you agree with that? In fact, it trumps your senses.

Few clients get offended with this formulation, and most readily agree the OCD comes from their imagination. Clients may wish to discuss the implications of this idea in trying to prove that its imaginary nature does not make the obsession impossible. At this stage, this kind of discussion is to be avoided. Once again, the client only needs to agree with the idea that the OCD story and the ensuing doubt originates from the imagination (as opposed to reality) *regardless* of the implications of that idea. If there are objections, most of these are resolved as the therapist begins to present a more elaborate model of perception and the imagination on which inference-based therapy is based.

In order to properly establish with the client that the obsessional doubt is generated subjectively, the therapist needs to use the terms 'imaginary' and 'imagination' in a constructive way and not in a manner that might be interpreted as derogatory by the client. 'Imagination' encompasses creative personally generated ideas. The use of these terms has wider implications than just telling the client 'It's all in your head'. In fact, the terms are better introduced only after the client has grasped the idea that there is no direct evidence for the doubt in the here and now. This idea can initially be introduced to the client as follows:

'We have now established that there is a story behind your doubt. And we have also established that this story can contain all kinds of information that seems to logically lead into your doubt. But I now want to propose another to idea to you, which is that even though the reasoning behind the obsessional doubt appears to be quite logical, there is something very peculiar about obsessional doubts. It is something that makes the doubt *obsessional* as opposed to ordinary doubt. And this peculiar something is that obsessional doubts always come about without any direct evidence or justification from the here and now. I mean anything that you can really *sense* in the here and now to justify the obsession, nothing you can smell, see, touch, hear or feel. This is the case for everyone with obsessional doubts. Let's have a look at your story for example, and see if you agree it applies to you as well.'

Perception and Imagination

The presentation of the model is initially a simplified explanation of the interaction between imagination and perception. The client is simply shown that as we come to conclusions about what might or could be there, people vary to differing degrees as to how much they rely on perception and the imagination. The following diagram (Figure 7.1) and formulation can be used to explain this to the client:

The important lesson to be drawn from comparison of imagination and perception is that (1) imagination and perception are separate faculties performing separate functions, (2) we are aware when we are using imagination and when we are using perception and (3) the problem arises when imagination trumps perception.

Normal Versus Imaginary Doubt

Following an explanation of Figure 7.1, the client is given various different examples that show how obsessional doubt differs from normal doubt. Normal doubt always occurs in an appropriate context and with a certain amount of sense information from the here and now. Obsessional doubt always occurs without such sense information. Of course, there are *triggers* for obsessional doubt (for example, seeing a stove and wondering whether it has been left on), but if the doubt is obsessional there is no real sense information to support the doubt.

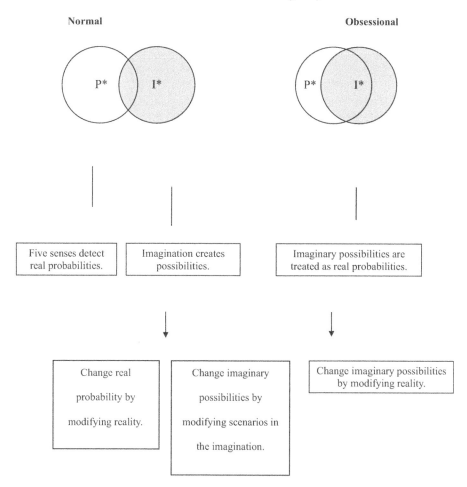

Figure 7.1 Inferential confusion and obsessive behaviour. *P = Perception; *I = imagination.

Vive la Difference!

The following examples can be used by the therapist to help the client understand the difference between direct and indirect evidence for the doubt, as well as to teach to client to begin making a distinction between perception and imagination.

The therapist can illustrate the difference between obsessional and normal doubt by asking the client to look at the examples above and indicate whether the doubt is obsessional or normal, as well as to argue why this is the case.

You're about to cross the street. Your look to your right and left and see no traffic. Then, you think the sun might have been shining into your eyes while you were checking for traffic. You begin to doubt and wonder whether it might not be a good idea to check your right side once more. Is this a normal or obsessional doubt?

Which sequences were imaginary?

1.

_____

2.

_____

3.

_____

How Imaginary Thoughts Become Real

OCD inferences are entirely imaginary, yet they feel real. How so? Well, by acting on the thoughts through rituals they seem real. The thoughts can also get blended with reality through association, a possibility can be confused with reality. We review here a series of processes: inferential confusion, thought-thought fusion, blending, and neutralizing and _____ behaviour.

Inferential Confusion in OCD

Inferential confusion occurs when a client mistakes an imagined possibility for a real probability. This confusion may occur briefly under conditions of perceptual ambiguity where imagination may overlap with perception (Figure 7.1a). However, inferential confusion becomes pathological when the client crosses over from the real into the imaginary, treating the imagined possibility 'as if' it were real (Figure 7.1b). We suggest that inferential confusion is a process characterising different extents of obsessive-compulsive disordered thinking, and that as a process it may account parsimoniously for a variety of 'fusion' experiences, particularly wherein the imagination plays a decisive role in rendering non-existent events or feelings more probable.

Inferential confusion process

This inferential confusion process starts with the client inferring a possible state of affairs, such as 'This object might be contaminated', or 'I could kill my child'. This possible state is only postulated, not actual, but the client then acts 'as if' the possible event or impulse was actually likely to occur. Imaginary possibilities are distinguished from real probabilities not necessarily by their content but by their inferential context wherein plausibility is inferred not from an objective assessment of probability but entirely on the basis of a subjective narrative. The inferential confusion, which is at the heart of the inference-based approach to therapy, proposes that there is a critical point when the client with obsessive-compulsive disorder crosses over from the real world of perception into the imagination. This cross-over point is identifiable and is reported by clients as a transition from reality to nonreality, sometimes accompanied by different amounts of derealization. This cross-over point represents the start of the obsessional process since the obsessional anxiety springs from this metacognitive confusion. The subsequent compulsive rituals, neutralization and coping strategies also result from a confusion that acting in reality can change imagined consequences (Figure 7.1b).

Imagination, as we noted, is considered here to be an autonomous faculty that operates in parallel with perception with some normal overlap (see Figure 7.1b) but that processes possibilities rather than reality. An imagined thought or event has no value. Whereas real probabilities are finite, imaginary possibilities are infinite. So the client who confuses the imaginary for the real is likely to be trapped in a spiral of interminable 'maybes', chaining on one from another, but with no reality check, since imagination has replaced reality (see Figure 7.1b).

Explanatory value of inferential confusion

In inferential confusion, obsessions are experienced as ego-dystonic since people with obsessive-compulsive disorder unknowingly act as if they have produced unwanted effects. In fact, in some cases, they are merely imagining the general possibility. Because such clients are unaware of this metacognitive confusion, they cannot do anything else other than take these thoughts seriously and act on them as if they were real (see Figure 7.1b).

Inferential confusion also readily explains the repetitive nature of the compulsive ritual, or other neutralization, and the arbitrary stopping rules (relying on counting, repeating a phrase or having a feeling that the time is to end the ritual) since the client is trying to change reality on the basis of what is only imagined. Doubt is likely to be increased through carrying out rituals, since such action only reinforces the imagined possibility. The impact of new information is attenuated since the client is focussed on an imaginary not a real world and so feedback from any real action never definitively resolves the doubt. As part of the absorption in the imagination, the client may begin to experience physical sensations congruent with living 'as if' the event was occurring (e.g. feeling bloated and fat, feeling guilty and experiencing sticky hands). The client starts with a possibility such as 'What if I appear fat after eating?', or 'What if my thoughts make an accident more likely?' and then lives 'as if' the possibility were plausible. In all such cases, imagination trumps perception and the client lives an imaginary story as though it is real. The inferential confusion model would also propose that a fusion experience reflects greater absorption in imaginary possibilities than in other nonfusion experience. However, this does not represent a separate subtype since this absorption is a continuum.

Thought-thought fusion

A special case of inferential confusion may be termed 'thought-thought fusion', where the client confuses the possibility of experiencing a thought with actually experiencing the thought. There is a distinction between entertaining an abstract idea of what is possible and formulating a motivated intention. For example, a client had frequent thoughts that she might think of cheating on her boyfriend. While putting on makeup or dressing in an attractive way, she thought this might mean she could consider cheating on her boyfriend. Anything slightly associated with female attractiveness or sexual desire became evidence that she might want to cheat on her boyfriend. However, the actual intention to cheat on her boyfriend had never occurred. Another client confused thinking about the possibility of experiencing sexual thoughts with the sexual thoughts themselves. Every time the client was in the company of women, he considered the possibility of having sexual thoughts and that these thoughts might in some way leak out and be noticed and produce an aversive response. In fact, he never experienced any sexual thoughts but reacted uncomfortably 'as if' the sexual thought had occurred, so confirming the anticipated aversive effect of his thoughts. In other words, he confused possible imagined sexual thoughts with actual thoughts.

Mental rituals are likely to be provoked by thoughts such as 'I should not think this particular thought', 'I have to avoid thinking of this particular thought' or in the case of monitoring one's own mental content 'I might think again of this particular thought'. Mental rituals such as effacing or replacing the thought reinforce the potential presence of the thought that the client wants to avoid. But if, in fact, the actual thought did not occur, then neutralizing activities consist of client attempts to not have a particular thought that has not been experienced. Since trying not to have a possible thought reinforces the possibility of having the thought, the client is caught in a perpetual cycle. The thought that one could think again of a particular thought that one wishes to avoid implies its potential presence and could easily be confused with the actual occurrence of the thought. Thus, inferential confusion does not necessarily always revolve around a confusion between outer and imagined events, and in the case of discrete obsessions can also involve a confusion concerning an actual and imagined cognitive state of affairs.

Factors producing inferential confusion

The inferential confusion process in OCD clients may be a product of a low threshold for imaginal absorption and an over-reliance on inductive reasoning. For example, clients are more likely to change intensity of conviction on the basis of self-generated possibilities than either anxious clients or nonpsychiatric controls. The initial inference about the imagined possible event or thought occurring seems supported by a narrative which leads the client to believe that 'Maybe I could really do or think

X' or 'X could really happen'. The narrative typically confuses distinct categories of events, draws on irrelevant memories, associations or hearsay, misapplies general facts to personal context and creates purely imaginary sequences. In particular, the narrative dismisses actual evidence and sense information in favour of a hypothetical reality in an attempt to say more than what is there. A client, asked to explain how his negative attitude could influence a relative's distant job interview, admits there is no logical physical explanation but appeals to 'waves, invisible forces we don't yet know about, as to how thoughts get transmitted'.

Examples of the above inferential sequences are identified in brackets in the following client's thought-shape narrative:

I was feeling comfortable like I'd lost some weight, my jeans and pullover felt loose, then I weighed myself and saw on the scale I'd gained 2 pounds, so I began to think I can't feel OK since I must look really fat [dismissing sensory evidence in favour of an hypothetical reality]. I thought about the pizza slice I'd eaten earlier in the week and had the same sense of fullness [purely imaginary sequence]. Fat people have their stomachs sticking out [irrelevant association] so I thought if my stomach is sticking out, people will look and point at me as well [misapplying facts to personal context]; I felt I'd better hide my stomach, so I ended up feeling really fat and hating myself.

Figure 7.1a illustrates the normal relationship between perception (P) and imagination (I), and Figure 7.1b the much greater overlap experienced during obsessional compulsive experiences of 'fusion' due to inferential confusion. The confusion between imagined and perceived inferences leads the client with OCD to believe she or he must act 'as if' the imagined was real and so modify reality rather than the imagination.

Blending

Blending is a process by which one concept becomes blended together with another concept with distinct meaning. In blending, the person imagines that distinct categories, events, activities, are identical and hence merit identical reactions.

In OCD, people often blend their OCD thoughts and behaviour with other terms which on the face of it seem to make the OCD not only acceptable but even admirable and desirable. Here are some examples:

Sara likes things 'well done'.
John describes himself as a 'perfectionist'.
Mathew is devotedly 'religious'.
Brenda is 'more ecological than others'.
Mike just likes to go 'that extra mile that others won't'.
Harriet saves cats from being 'abandoned'.

On the face of it, those sentiments seem fine. Who doesn't want things 'well done'? Who is going to argue against the virtue of 'going the extra mile' or being 'devotedly religious'? But of course, what do people mean by these terms? What activities are included? And is the meaning consensually shared?

So for Sara scrubbing her counter 50 times with bleach so that the patterns and material disappear is the meaning of 'well done'. For John, hanging his trousers always in the same way spaced equally apart in his wardrobe is perfectionist. For Mathew, being devotedly religious means praying 30 times per day in his place of worship to the exclusion of other duties. For Brenda, 'ecological' is hoarding broken appliances in her living room which one day he will fix . . . maybe . . . one day. For Mike, the extra mile is showering 5 hours a day to make sure all the dirt is washed off his skin.

Apart from using these terms in a nonconsensual way, the client in performing the OCD ritual is actually acting in opposition to the term they are blending with the OCD. In other words, hoarding is not ecological, it is wasteful. Praying 30 times per day is not being over-religious, it is actually ignoring the rules of the religion. Hanging trousers equally is not perfectionist since the trousers will become oddly creased and unwearable. In other words, all these people are doing the wrong jobs, using the wrong terms but convinced they are right through the imaginative blending.

It is a bit like saying I'm a better chef because I put 3 lbs of sugar in the cake recipe when it only said $1/2$ lb, or I'm a more careful driver because I always stop 10 yards before the line at traffic lights. In both cases, what appears to be better is actually worse. The blending terms are at the best irrelevant to the claimed behaviour, and at the worst they represent the complete opposite and sabotage the intended goal.

Harriet says she cares so much for her 20 cats that if she finds one of her cats a home, even a very good one, she feels she is abandoning the cat and this is intolerable to her since she reports that she felt abandoned as a child. In her narrative, when children are passed from home to home, it means they are abandoned and nobody wants them. In reality, in finding the cat a better home and a better quality of life, she is caring for the cat, not abandoning it. Harriet is blending 'caring' with 'abandoning', opposite terms which, when blended, seem to justify the dysfunctional behaviour.

Blending with perfectionism

Perfectionism occurs often in clients with OCD and it deserves a special mention since it involves attaching a desired value to the OCD thought and action. A good example here is perfectionism. Perfectionism exists as a trait with several sub-dimensions, and pathological perfectionism is also a trait in OCD. However, people with OCD will often blend their OCD thinking with perfectionism as a way of explaining and justifying their OCD. 'Well, it's true, I'm too perfectionist. What can I do? I guess it's a personality trait. I just need to be perfect'. Here an OCD task is undertaken on the basis of confusing a remote and irrelevant approach with the immediate task demand, and the confusion is blended with a commonly understood notion of perfectionism, which then, in turn, becomes its rationale. How so? After all, we all admire perfection, and who will argue against the virtue of being perfect? The client may also score high on a perfectionism scale with the conclusion, by both therapist and client, that the client simply needs to be less perfectionist. Perfectionism can be indeed modified through laying out realist achievable options and goal management. However, where OCD is manifested, apparent perfectionism masks the fact that the client is applying irrelevant criteria to a task in the here and now from another time, job and place and through inferential confusion, not through perfectionism.

A client who spends an hour writing a cheque with evenly spaced letters considers himself a perfectionist. But he considers cheques must be written in this manner since his uncle was a sign writer. He is confusing writing a cheque with sign writing and he always felt that space signaled neatness, and guaranteed the legibility and durability of the writing. A client who spaces coat hangers equally in the cupboard with trousers always creased in the same spot is blending the job with a meat-hanging factory where hygiene is paramount. A client who needs to replace objects or clothes always in the same place in the same position is blending clothes hanging with organizing objects in the family antique shop where it was considered important that objects not be moved unnecessarily because of their great value.

Blending with negligence

Blending with the term 'negligence' also deserves special mention. The blending can take the form of imagining that a harmless activity is synonymous with a negative term such as negligence. A client may blend negligence with an activity such as not replacing objects in their exact same places, which would not be included in a standard dictionary definition of negligence. A client with OCD feels negligent if papers are not arranged or there is a speck of dust on the floor. For another client, wasting time or space is classified as criminal and she literally imagines receiving punishment as a consequence.

Blending metaphor and literal meanings

Finally, the therapist will be aware that some clients blend a metaphysical experience with a literal experience. Client may blend a metaphorical with a literal experience. There is also a tendency for people with OCD to translate such blending or even more habitual metaphors literally. So common throwaway expressions such as 'No rest for the wicked', 'Look what the cat brought home' or 'You look like you've been dragged through a bush backwards' might lead the client with OCD off on a spiral of imagined scenarios of how exactly the client did end up in a hedge and hence fuel the possible at the expense of the actual. Again here the imagination is in play with an 'as if' metaphor blended with a lived scenario.

De-blending

An important task in IBT is for the therapist to help the client with de-blending. The sequence of the blending process is as follows:

1. An association is made between two usually opposing terms, such as one is blended together with the other as inseparable.
2. The client acts and lives 'as if' the two terms were one and the same.
3. Emotions, cognitions and behaviour are aligned with the blending so that the client reacts as if the two terms were the same.

De-blending:

1. Awareness of inappropriate reaction to blended terms
2. Rehearsing appropriate labelling for OCD action
3. Subsequent acting as if the terms were truly separate

De-blending involves (1) pointing out the blending of incomparable terms and the confusion of past task with present task requirements, and so replacing irrelevant with relevant rules, terms and criteria; (2) establishing realistic criteria for functioning in the here and now; and (3) rehearsing the proper task with feedback on functional performance in the here and now. An example is given later in the case series.

Neutralizing and Testing Behaviour

A key way in which the imagination becomes real is through the rituals and neutralization which permits the imaginary OCD to have a real effect on the world. Performing neutralization confirms that something needs to be done, as the OCD says. The real impact and feelings generated by the compulsive act then generate their own ex-consequentia justification in reality. 'If I acted just now, it must mean I needed to act'.

Another way of making the imaginary real is through testing behaviour. Here the client with OCD deliberately tries to realize the obsessional doubt by placing themselves in a situation which the OCD doubt says will test whether they are or can do what the OCD doubting says.

Examples of Testing Behaviour

A man who is uncertain of his sexual orientation visits certain bars to see how he feels. A boy who fears he could be inappropriately aroused by his auntie stands or sits close to her and plays with himself. A woman who is afraid she may have rays coming into her head from the microwave puts her head close up to test any sensation. A client afraid they might have pornographic images . . . conjures up such images to see how she reacts. As noted earlier, the testing seems like homegrown exposure but actually increases anxiety and credibility of the doubt, since this kind of testing is driven by the obsession.

Decision Chart

Proceeding to the Next Stage of Treatment

- Client distinguishes between perception and imagination.
- Client is aware that the reasoning behind the doubt is 100% based in the imagination without any direct link to reality in the here and now.
- Client is able to tell the difference between obsessional doubt and normal doubt.
- Client is able to link obsessional doubt with the imagination and how imagination trumps perception.

Cartoon 7. An offer to refuse.

Client Worksheet 5
OCD Is 100% Imaginary

Lack of Direct Connect

One of the most important characteristics of obsessional doubts is that there is never any direct justification for the doubt in the here and now. Consider the following examples of obsessional doubts: 'The door might be unlocked', or 'I might have been contaminated with something dirty'. You may have just stepped outside and locked the door, or you may have just touched a metal pole in the metro or bus. But was there anything in the here and now that actually justified these particular doubts? Did you actually sense anything that supported the doubt? For obsessions, the answer to this question is always no.

Obsessional Doubt and Reality

This is even the case for obsessions that are not entirely related to what is around you. For example, you might have an obsession such as 'I might hit someone' or 'I might be a child molester'. There is no real information in the here and now that supports these doubts, not even the reality that is *inside* of you. For example, do you every *actually* feel angry at someone when you have an obsession like 'I might hit someone'? Once again, if it is an obsession, the answer to this question is always no. The obsession is never supported by reality, and this includes your own *inner* reality and common sense.

In one of the cases discussed later, the distinction between obsessing about the possibility of committing an impulsive act and the real impulse to act is traced to the lack of any real identifiable intention or desire. A client who doubts their sexual orientation typically has no desire related to this doubt, only an anxious reflection on its possibility. The genuine sexual arousal all points away from the doubt.

Doubts Go Against Reality

Obsessional doubt never has anything to do with immediate reality in the here and now. It is what makes your doubt an obsession. It is almost impossible to over-estimate the significance of this fact. It is the basis of all your symptoms.

Creative Exercises

Ask yourself the following questions for your own obsessional doubts the last time they occurred:

1. Was there any information in the here and now to justify the doubt?
2. Did the doubt go beyond objective (inner) sense information?

Reality of Doubt

You may readily agree that your doubts have no basis in reality, yet you may also wonder why this is so important. After all, even if obsessional doubts are not always supported by 'immediate' reality, this does not mean they are impossible. You might feel, for example, that just the fact that you have no direct evidence for the door being unlocked does not mean it might not have been left unlocked. This is certainly true. All manner of things are possible. But this is not the point. The reason why it is important that there is never any direct evidence for an obsession is because it tells us a lot about where the obsession originates from. It tells us it originates from inside of you. And because it has nothing to do with reality in the here and now, it can actually only come from your *imagination*.

Imagination

Keep in mind that we use the term 'imagination' here to refer to anything that does not directly relate to reality in the here and now. We know that people with OCD rely a lot on their imagination when coming to conclusions about reality. They seem to very easily come up with possibilities. And these possibilities never ever seem to directly relate to reality, including their own actual inner reality. For example, in the case of a doubt about not having properly locked the door, this may include ideas like 'Doors are sometimes accidentally left unlocked', 'Perhaps I do not remember correctly locking the door' or 'What if the lock broke when I was turning it?' In the case of an obsession without overt compulsions, it may include ideas like 'I might offend God', 'Did I just swear?', 'What if I would spit on the bible?' or 'What terrible things could I think of to offend God?'

Imagination and Reason

Of course, we all rely on imagination during reasoning to some extent. It surely would be a strange world to only ever have thoughts about only those things that exist in the here and now. For better or worse, imagining is a very human trait. However, what is particularly peculiar about obsessions is that they are generated on a *purely* imaginary basis. There is no direct evidence for the obsession in the here and now. It originates for a 100% from your imagination, which is exactly what makes your doubt obsessional.

Distinguishing Doubts

The difference between normal and obsessional doubt is that there is always direct evidence in the here and now for the doubt. It does not have to be a whole lot. It can be very little. But as long as there is direct evidence, then the doubt is a normal doubt. In that case, there is always *some* overlap between reality and imagination during reasoning. Such normal doubts occur with specific evidence or information for the doubt. They occur in an appropriate *context*. For example, you may have plans to spend the next day outside, or you noticed you were running late for an appointment. Also, these doubts are quickly resolved (e.g. check the weather report, or do a simple calculation on how much longer the journey will take).

However, in obsessional doubt, it almost seems like the doubt comes out of nowhere. And it often feels like that too! Because, in reality, these is no justification for the doubt! In fact, reality and imagination are completely disconnected from each other. Imagination does one thing, while reality does the other. Perhaps, then, it is not so surprising that your obsessions so often feel like they are out of your control.

Client Exercise Sheet 5
OCD Is 100% 'Imaginary'

Perhaps you already intellectually accept the idea that your obsessional doubts originate 100% from the imagination. And with imagination we mean that there is *never* any direct evidence for the obsessional doubt in the here and now. It is what makes your doubt obsessional as opposed to it being a normal doubt.

For example, take the following normal doubts (or questions):

1. Will it rain tomorrow?
2. How long will the journey take?

Such normal questioning occur with specific evidence or information for the doubt. They occur in an appropriate *context*. For example, you may have plans to spend the next day outside, or you noticed you were running late for an appointment. Also, these doubts are quickly resolved (check the weather report, or do a simple calculation on how much longer the journey will take), and from a commonsense point of view you would be convinced all had been done.

Now, take the following obsessional doubts:

1. Did I shut the stove?
2. Did I read that word correctly?

If these doubts are obsessional, they will occur without specific evidence or information. You would check without having direct evidence or information that the stove was still on or that you didn't read the word correctly. The doubt would arise in a situation without having any real indication that the stove is left on. Such doubts are not so easily resolved if you do not realize there is no real evidence in the here and now for the doubts. Even if from a commonsense point of view you would know you have checked enough, the compulsive urge to check would continue.

Being able to determine whether something is a normal or obsessional doubt can make a real difference, especially with respect to your own OCD doubts. First, however, we'll put the idea into practice with some OCD stories other than your own. To do so, try to determine whether the stories written down lead into an obsessional or normal doubt. Remember, if there is no direct link to reality in the here and now, the ensuing doubt is nearly always obsessional.

Creative Exercises

Story 1

A woman checks the front door five times on leaving to go to work and looks back several times to see if her cat has escaped. She also looks and fixates on the door when in her car for a few minutes. The cat has escaped once before in the summer when she was gardening and left the back door open. However, it has never escaped at the moment she leaves for work.

What is the doubt in the story?

_____

_____

Is this doubt obsessional?   ☐ Yes   ☐ No

If yes, what makes it obsessional (or non-obsessional)? Please be specific in your answer.

_____

_____

Story 2

A pharmacist recounts the number of pills when she gets distracted during her count. She believes the recounting is justified because it's important to be careful when it comes to people's health. Yet, she never has made any mistake with counting pills. However, she did once make a mistake in labelling the bottles.

What is the doubt in the story?

_____

_____

Is this doubt obsessional?   ☐ Yes   ☐ No

If yes, what makes it obsessional (or non-obsessional)? Please be specific in your answer.

_____

Story 3

A girl is preoccupied that she might unwittingly hit a passerby in the street as she walks along. This has never happened, but she often feels very angry at people. She once knocked someone down in a supermarket when someone was getting in her way all the time. It really feels to her that she could do it with even less provocation the next time.

What is the doubt in the story?

_____

_____

Is this doubt obsessional? ☐ Yes ☐ No

If yes, what makes it obsessional (or non-obsessional)? Please be specific in your answer.

_____

_____

Story 4

A man checks the clothes in his wardrobe for ants, believing ants will lay eggs and eat and destroy them like moths do. His clothes have already been eaten once by moths. He once saw an ant on the towel in the bathroom and another climbing up onto the plant. They are small and could get in and ruin anything like moths.

What is the doubt in the story?

_____

_____

Is this doubt obsessional?   ☐ Yes   ☐ No

If yes, what makes it obsessional (or non-obsessional)? Please be specific in your answer.

_____

_____

Now, let's turn to your own OCD story. You already have it written out from a previous exercise. Try to determine whether there is anything in your OCD story that has any direct link in reality. Keep in mind that even though some ideas and facts are often *about* reality, this does not mean they have a *direct* link to reality in the here and now.

   Did you find any direct justification for your own doubts in the here and now?

☐ Yes   ☐ No

If yes, write down below if you found anything in your own story directly relating to reality in the here and now:

_____

_____

Is there anything currently not part of your OCD story that makes you feel your doubt directly relates to the here and now?

_____

_____

Write down below anything you have learned from this exercise or wish to comment on, or that you have questions about.

_____

_____

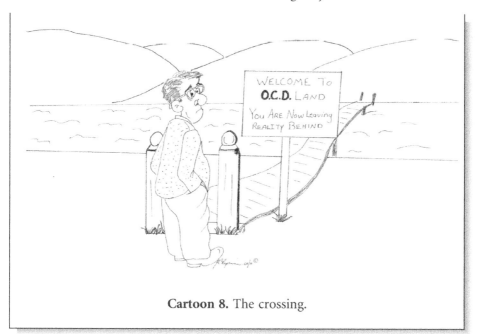

Cartoon 8. The crossing.

Client Training Card 5
OCD Is 100% Imaginary

Learning Points (Front)

- Obsessional doubt comes from within you. It has nothing to do with reality.
- Obsessional doubt occurs without direct evidence in the here and now.
- The reasoning behind obsessional doubt is 100% based in the imagination.

Daily Exercise (Back)

Each time you have an obsessional doubt, ask yourself whether there is or was any direct evidence or information that justifies the doubt. If you think there might be, write it down to bring with you to the next session. Try to compare what the doubt says 'could be' with information coming from your senses, perception and common sense.

Client Quiz 5
OCD Is 100% Imaginary

1. The phrase 'OCD is 100% imaginary' means that . . .
    o   you do not perceive correctly.
    o   there is no direct evidence in the here and now.
    o   the doubt is not possible.
    o   none of the above.
2. 'Direct evidence' always refers to . . .
    o   what your physical senses tell you.
    o   what you can actually perceive.
    o   your real bodily reactions.
    o   all of the above.
3. The fact that there is never any direct evidence for the obsessional doubt tells you that obsessional doubt comes from . . .
    o   relying on remote possibilities.
    o   your own subjective reasoning.
    o   relying entirely on your imagination during reasoning.
    o   all of the above.
4. A doubt is obsessional when . . .
    o   it is too intelligent.
    o   it makes you do things you do not want to do.
    o   it occurs without any direct evidence or justification from reality.
    o   it makes you very scared.
5. Relying solely on the imagination during reasoning . . .
    o   is adaptive.
    o   is positive.
    o   takes you away from real perception.
    o   all of the above,
6. Relying solely on the imagination during reasoning *about what might be there in reality* makes you . . .
    o   phobic.
    o   more profound.
    o   have obsessional doubts.
    o   less intelligent.

Please check your answers by referring to the Quiz Answers Sheet.

Chapter Eight

OCD Doubt is 100% irrelevant

This chapter continues with the implication of the obsessional doubt as a 100% imaginary by making three further points 1) the doubt is impossible precisely because it goes against the senses; 2) it is 100% irrelevant to reality; 3) with the realization that the obsessional doubt is 100% irrelevant, the OCD and its cognitive and behavioral sequences are resolved.

Doubt and Possibility

Before progressing to the next step, the therapist should ensure that the client fully agrees with the idea that there is no direct evidence in the here and now for the doubt. Utilize any information the client may have written down from the training card exercise of the last session. If the client feels there was evidence for the client's doubt, then likely the notion of no direct evidence has not been fully understood, and situations where the client felt there was direct evidence need to be discussed and clarified.

Irrelevantce

Once any ambivalence regarding the idea of no direct evidence for the doubt has been resolved, the therapist can proceed to the next stage, which is a crucial step in treatment. During this stage, the therapist attempts to show to the client that the lack of evidence for the obsessional doubt and it's imaginary nature makes it 100% irrelevant despite the fact that the doubt might be possible. As such, the next step in treatment focuses primarily on the *implications* of the idea that there is no direct evidence in the here and now for the obsession.

Clinician's Handbook for Obsessive-Compulsive Disorder: Inference-Based Therapy, First Edition.
K. O'Connor and F. Aardema.
© 2012 John Wiley & Sons, Ltd. Published 2012 by John Wiley & Sons, Ltd.

Implications of Obsessional Doubt

There are many ways to convey these implications to the client, which are ultimately aimed at a complete resolution of the obsessional doubt. Over time, as your level of comfort with IBT increases, you will find your own way of conveying the irrelevancy of obsessional doubts to clients. Until then, one way of helping the client understand the 100% irrelevancy of obsessional doubts can be done by largely following the text on the accompanying worksheet below:

"You hopefully now agree with the fact that nothing about your obsession is supported by anything in the here and now. Yet, you might also feel this doesn't mean the obsession is entirely irrelevant. After all, people do become contaminated and ill even though there was nothing in reality to indicate that might happen. Likewise, people do forget to the check that the door is loched, and their home is broken into, often completely unexpectedly and without warning. So it seems that the obsession might still be possible even if it is imagined and there is no justification in the here and now. But do you really believe that just the fact that something is possible is a real justification for anything? Does it justify your checking, washing, worrying and everything else the OCD has put on your plate?"

Impossibility of Obsessional Doubt

Here, the therapist has introduced the idea that because there is no direct evidence for the obsession in the here and now, the obsession or doubt is entirely irrelevant even though it may be possible. After all, stoves are indeed left on, and fires do start as a result. Likewise, doorknobs sometimes do have germs on them, and people do get sick. However, the imaginary nature of the obsession does not refer to impossibility. IBT does not rely on convincing the client of the improbability of the obsessional inference (whether 0.01%, 0.001% or 0.0001%). Instead, it highlights the 100% imaginative nature and lack of sense data in the here and now that could justify the obsessional inference even is a remote possibilities. In turn, the IBT approach stresses that that the lack of sense data in the here and now makes the obsession completely arbitrary and irrelevant to the situation at hand. This is the essence of *inferential confusion* where the client believes that obsessional doubt is a real probability instead of an imagined possibility with no relevance to the here and now. Specific examples such as given below can be used to drive home the point that the lack of evidence in reality does indeed make the obsession entirely irrelevant.

The therapist might use an example such as this:

"Let's say, to use a ridiculous example, that I have an obsession about a meteor falling on my head. I constantly check the sky to ensure that nothing is falling down. The fact that there is really nothing in the here and now to support the idea that there is a meteor around doesn't convince me. Here, you would probably agree that the mere possibility of a meteor landing on my head provides no real justification for me to start worrying about meteors falling down even though it might be possible. But how is this different from your own obsessions? You don't have any justification for your own obsession in the here and now either. The fact that your own obsession might be less of a rare occurrence than a meteor falling down makes no difference. Again, it's not about how possible something is on a chance-by-chance basis. The problem is that you rely on possibility to begin with when in the here and now to support the obsession. For example, when it would make sense to start worrying about a meteor falling down on my head? What would have to happen in reality for such a doubt to be relevant?"

Establishing Irrelevance

Posing the question 'What would make a doubt relevant?' inevitably leads to the requirement that there has to be evidence in the here and now for such an event to be relevant, even if highly unlikely. In the case of the meteor such evidence might be something along the lines of meteor storms having been predicted, or actually seeing a meteor falling down. Only then can we say that the possibility about meteors falling down on your head is not entirely imagined. It is important for the therapist to remind the client that most of his or her own reasoning in non-OCD spheres of life already operates in this particular manner. The following prompt might be helpful.

'In reality, you already agree with the idea that there has to be evidence in the here and now to take a doubt seriously. In most aspects of your life, you never just rely on possibility. For example, do you worry about a car running you over after you checked the street before crossing? You don't, because you trust what your senses are telling you. You have this trust in your own senses or self in almost every other aspect of your life that has not been affected by the OCD. Yet, in the OCD situation you suddenly reason and act differently. There, you believe that only the possibility that the door might be unlocked is already enough to justify you checking it. The fact that you have seen it lock seems to make no difference. Or, alternatively, you might worry about being contaminated without actually seeing anything on your hands. In other words, your reasoning is very selective when it comes to OCD. You do not really trust yourself in these situations.'

It is worth introducing at the stage the comparison point of how the person decides on relevant information in other spheres of life. What information does the person take into account when making a decision on whether to buy a home, or to fix a car or to form an opinion on someone. Does the person create imaginary possibilities using all the reasoning devices to create a story?

Anatomy of Obsessional Doubt

Understanding the nature of the obsessional doubt is the key to the IBT approach. So it is absolutely essential (no 'maybes') that the client and therapist grasp the principle that immersion in OCD begins with entertaining and giving credibility to obsessional doubt. This doubt is unlike normal doubt because:

1. It is generated subjectively remote from the here and now.
2. It cannot (ever) be resolved in the way normal doubt can be resolved.
3. It goes further and further into the doubt, under the impression that this will solve the doubt, which is the core of the obsession.

This is quite a lot of information to establish with the client. However, from experience, this step is essential to progress. It needs to be established step by step, and reasonable objections need to be faced and answered. If there is a subsequent block in progress, it is frequently due to a failure to fully integrate this initial step. If necessary, as the therapist may need to return to this step several times to ensure the integration of gains.

The therapist should continue to provide examples until the client is able to apply the difference between obsessional and normal doubts in different situations. At the end of the session, the accompanying worksheet is handed out to the client as well as an exercise and quiz to reinforce what has been covered during the session. The therapist can also use these examples to hint at the resolution of obsessional doubt such as what would be the required information to resolve the obsessional doubt in the second example (e.g. to check whether there is sun shining in your eyes to begin with). Also, the client is given a training card to help him or her practice in recognizing the difference between normal and obsessional doubt. The main criterion for progressing to the next stage is an understanding on the part of the client that the doubt originates from within him or her, that is, from the imagination rather than from the senses.

Doubt Dialogue

T: OK. So you doubted if what the salesperson had told you was correct.
C: Yeah, that was after I'd signed the contract.
T: So what did you do?
C: Well, I went back and checked the contract.
T: And?
C: So basically it was true, I had the warranty.
T: And then what?
C: Er . . . you mean about the doubt . . . well, it went away.

T: Now let's look at obsessional doubt.
C: So you mean when I doubt if whether I'm capable?
T: Yeh.
C: Well, I just get the idea I'm no good. I could fuck up and be nothing. I mean well and good.
T: What's the proof?
C: None, but I keep turning over in my mind the past times when I had the same idea.
T: And?
C: Well, it reinforces my idea.
T: So the more you doubt, the more you're going to the doubt. . . .
C: The more it gets stronger, the idea won't go away.
T: So what's the difference between normal and obsessional doubt?
C: The obsessional doubt won't go away. It's never over.
T: And the normal doubt?
C: You resolve it, you find out.
T: and with obsessional doubt?
C: Well you can't . . or rather you resolve it by not giving in to it . . . by ignoring it.

Resolution of Doubt

IBT differs from other therapies in that it aims for complete resolution of the obsessional doubt. It tries to convince the client that if there is no evidence in the here and now, then the obsessional doubt is 100% irrelevant. In effect, the obsession is *false* and *wrong* because it came about on a purely imaginary basis. This will be a central topic in subsequent sessions. For now, the main criterion for progressing to the next stage is at least a partial intellectual adherence to the notion that the obsession is 100% irrelevant. In a manner of speaking, this can be viewed as having been successful in injecting a healthy dose of doubt into the appropriateness of the OCD reasoning.

Decision Chart

Proceeding to the Next Stage of Treatment

- Client agrees at least partially that the imaginary nature of the obsession makes the obsession entirely irrelevant.
- Client understands that something being possible does not automatically justify the obsession or make it relevant.
- Client understands that under ordinary non-OCD circumstances, his or her reasoning has some basis in reality rather than solely relying on possibility.

Client Worksheet 6
Doubt and Possibility

Imaginary Nature

You hopefully now agree with the fact that nothing about your obsession is supported by anything in the here and now. It originates entirely from you rather than the outside. It comes from the *imagination*. But what does this mean exactly? Are there any implications to this idea?

Possible Versus Probable

On the surface, the idea that there is no direct evidence for the obsession seems to make little difference. After all, people do become contaminated and ill even though there was nothing in reality to indicate that might happen. Likewise, people do forget to check whether the door is locked, and their homes are broken into, often completely unexpecting and without warning. So it seems that the obsession might still be *possible* even if there is no justification in the here and now. But that is exactly the problem with OCD! It thrives on possibility and doubt! So before saying that the obsession might still be possible even if it comes from your imagination, let's have a closer look at that argument. Does something merely being possible really provide a justification for anything? Does it justify your checking, washing, worrying and everything else the OCD has put on your plate?

Keep in mind that we are not debating here whether your obsessional doubt is possible or not in the abstract. Most obsessions are indeed possible in a very abstract and generalized sense. So this is not what we are arguing here. What we are looking at right now is whether *making* the argument that something is possible in the here and now is justified by an abstract or remote possibility. Or is it impossible because it's irrelevant?

Example

Let's start with something that is really possible even if it's a small possibility. Let's say, for example, that I have an obsession about a meteor falling on my head. I constantly check the sky to ensure that nothing is falling down. The fact that there is really nothing in the here and now to support the idea that there is a meteor around doesn't convince me. I feel I have to worry about it without any sort of real justification. Here, you would probably agree that the mere possibility of a meteor landing on my head provides no real justification for me to start worrying about meteors falling down even though it might be possible.

In Your Own Case

But how is this different from your own obsessions? You don't have any justification for your own obsession in the here and now either. The fact that your own obsession might be less of a rare occurrence than a meteor falling down makes no difference. Again, it's not about how possible something is on a chance-by-chance basis. Rather the problem is relying on possibility to begin with *if* there is nothing in the here and now to support the obsession.

Selectivity of Doubt

And ironically, whether you know it or not, you already agree with the idea that there has to be evidence in the here and now to take a doubt seriously. In most aspects of your life, you never just rely on possibility. For example, do you worry about a car running you over after you checked the street before crossing? You don't, because you trust what your senses are telling you. You have this trust in your own senses or self in almost every other aspect of your life that has not been affected by the OCD. You don't confuse stories that import facts and possibilities from elsewhere as though they are happening now.

Why Act Differently?

Yet, in the OCD situation you suddenly reason and act differently. There, you believe that only the possibility that the door might be unlocked is already enough to justify you checking it. The fact that you have seen it lock seems to make no difference. Or alternatively, you might worry about being contaminated without actually seeing anything on your hands. In other words, your reasoning is very selective when it comes to OCD. For whatever reason, you do not really trust yourself in these situations.

Realizing Irrelevance

But none of this changes the fact that you can realize right now that your obsession is 100% irrelevant to the here and now. It is irrelevant since just because something is possible provides no justification for anything in the here and now. It is exactly the same as worrying that the ceiling might come crashing down. These things are possible, but you do not worry about them without direct evidence. It would only make sense to worry or doubt if you see sudden cracks in the wall, hear loud and strange noises above your head or something along those lines. There would be sense information in the here and now to justify the doubt; if there is sense information to support it, it would be a non-obsessional doubt.

Applying the Principle

Do not get hung up on the fact that these examples may seem a little far-fetched. If you look at it carefully, you will see that the same *principle* applies to your own obsessions. You treat a mere possibility as if it is a realistic probability. You can come to this realization by applying this knowledge to your own OCD. And when you fully realize that this reasoning is incorrect you can indeed completely get rid of your OCD. You only have to *apply* it.

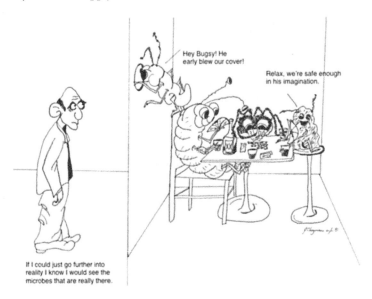

Cartoon 9. Going beyond reality.

Client Exercise Sheet 6
OCD doubt is 100% irrelevant

Credibility

Sometimes people with OCD look at each other in disbelief when they hear about the other person's obsessions. They can't believe that anyone would doubt in these situations. Just think of an obsession you have read about before or during this treatment that made absolutely no sense to you. There are probably several you can think of which you do not find credible at all. Write down below a couple you can think of right now.

Obsessions which I find not credible:

1. _____
_____
2. _____
_____

As unlikely as these obsessions may seem, they are not really different from your own. They are in fact very similar, because ALL obsessions occur without direct evidence in the here and now. In other words, your own obsessions are as irrelevant to reality as the ones you have just written down.

Seeing your Own Obsession Differently

Being able to see how your own obsession is irrelevant to reality is important. Once you do, your doubt will lose a lot of its credibility, and you will feel far less need to act on it. You might even begin to look at your own obsessions with the same level of disbelief as you feel towards others' obsessions. But to be able to do so, you need to fully understand how the OCD is able to make something incredible seem credible by introducing a lot of possibilities that have no direct link to reality. It is those possibilities that make it *seem* like the OCD has something to do with reality in the here and now.

Exercise

The exercise for this week is to pick a situation that is very *neutral to you*. It should have no importance to you whatsoever, and be an area where you experience no problems whatsoever. You could even pick a situation related to the obsessions you wrote down earlier. Then, once you have picked the situation, we want you to *make it* obsessional. That is, you think of all the reasons why a particular situation might not be safe, and why a situation that would normally be neutral when you look at it in a non-obsessional way becomes a problem. For example, if you were to make the neutral act of crossing the street entirely obsessional, it could look something like this:

"It is not safe to cross the street. I heard about an accident happen to someone who was always very careful. So accidents can happen just like that whether or not you pay attention. No one takes any notice of pedestrians anymore. So now when I cross the street, I do not look twice or three times to my left or right. Instead, I stand there for half an hour looking to see if there are any cars coming. Even if I don't see any car, one could come out from a corner suddenly. Or it might be a silent car that I cannot hear, since there are even electrical cars now. So I often decide not to cross the street. It just doesn't feel safe even if I don't see any traffic."

Now, write down below a different situation you picked that is ordinarily completely neutral to you:

_____

_____

Next, make this situation obsessional by introducing a lot of possibilities on why it could be dangerous or unsafe:

_____

_____

_____

_____

_____

_____

Creating OCD

As you can probably see, a situation that initially did not seem very believable became a lot more credible simply by introducing a lot of possibilities. Of course, it won't have such a big impact on you as your own OCD story. It was a neutral situation to you to begin with. But how would you go about disconfirming the story you just wrote down? Would you argue with the specifics of the possibilities you introduced? Or is there something else that makes the story irrelevant?

Write down below what is wrong with the story:

_____

_____

And how does this apply to your own OCD story?

_____

_____

Write down below anything you have learned from this exercise or wish to comment on, or that you have questions about.

_____

_____

_____

_____

On the basis of what you have now learned about OCD doubt and its role in obsessional sequences and behaviour:

Do you see how your OCD can be resolved?

Yes ☐   No ☐

How confident are you? (0–100%)

How do you think you can best resolve your OCD?

_____

_____

_____

Client Training Card 6
OCD doubt is 100% irrelevant

Learning Points (Front)

- Obsessional doubt is completely irrelevant to reality.
- Just something being possible does not make it relevant.
- Normally when you reason, you never entertain possibilities that have no basis in reality in the here and now.

Daily Exercise (Back)

Each time you have an obsessional doubt, ask yourself whether there is or was any direct evidence or information that justifies the doubt or possibility. Next, think of an example in your daily life where you would never consider a similar possibility because it is irrelevant to the here and now. Without debating with the OCD, try to *see* each time how this makes the obsessional doubt irrelevant.

Client Quiz 6
OCD doubts are 100% irrelevant

1. Possibilities that justify a particular obsessional doubt are . . .
   - impossible.
   - not relevant.
   - relevant when they are facts.
   - none of the above.
2. Obsessional doubt is completely irrelevant . . .
   - because there is 0% justification in the here and now for the doubt.
   - because the doubt originates 100% from the imagination.
   - because the doubt comes entirely from you rather than reality.
   - all of the above.
3. When reasoning about a practical state of affairs in reality, possibilities should be considered only when . . .
   - you want to understand ultimate reality.
   - there is at least some basis in the here and now to justify the possibility.
   - you feel creative.
   - none of the above.
4. Your reasoning about situations unrelated to the OCD . . .
   - shows that you reason differently from the OCD situation.
   - involves possibilities as well.
   - includes possibilities that have some justification in the here and now.
   - all of the above.
5. Which of the following is true?
   - All is possible, so I should consider all possibilities.
   - Inventing possibilities keeps me safe.
   - The possible and the real are all the same.
   - None of the above.
6. Obsessional behaviour can be completely resolved if:
   - I challenge the rationality of my obsession.
   - I resist ritualization.
   - I distract myself.
   - I realize that the doubt is irrelevant and dismiss it.

Please check your answers by referring to the Quiz Answers Sheet.

Chapter Nine

The OCD Bubble

The OCD Bubble

Clients with OCD often refer to the feeling of OCD as being inside of a 'bubble' sometimes accompanied by mild feelings of detachment and derealisation. This is not surprising, since by giving in to obsessional doubt, the client enters unreality on the basis of a purely subjective narrative that has nothing to do with the here and now. They 'cross over' from reality into the imagination where they are either cut off from the reassuring influence of the physical senses (e.g. they have concerns about checking, contamination) or they are disconnected from their real self (e.g they have concerns about sexuality, aggression and blasphemy).

This chapter which covers step 7 in therapy continues to explore the idea that resolution of the OCD follows from realization that the initial obsessional doubt is irrelevant. The key points covered by the therapist are: (1) identifying the precise cross over point when the client leaves reality; (2) exploring the experience of dissociation as the client enters the OCD bubble; (3) understanding how the OCD bubble is divorced from reality and how it sabotages interpersonal contact and safety.

Dissociating with OCD

The extent to which it is tempting for the client to engage with an obsession by trying to solve the problem posed by the obsession should not be underestimated. The OCD exerts a strong pull on the client even where there is some level of understanding that the OCD may be incorrect. Often, however, this awareness regarding the falseness of the obsession is only partial, and if delved into deeper with the client, all manner of possibilities and justifications will be provided by the client as to why the obsession may be real and credible. This problem is further exacerbated by various imaginative processes that appear to operate in OCD. For example, recent evidence appears to suggest that a tendency towards absorption and imaginative immersion may be an important element in the production of symptoms of OCD. The exact manner in which absorption or imaginative involvement contributes to symptoms is currently unknown, although it seems reasonable to suspect that it may increase the intensity and reality value of both the narrative and the resulting obsession.

Disadvantages of Living in a Bubble

The problem with being absorbed in a bubble is that the client environment and awareness shrink to the boundaries of the bubble. The client becomes highly self-absorbed in the OCD world to the exclusion of contact with the real world. The real world seems opaque and distant through the bubble. This results in a lessening of contact and vigilance about real events and real problems going on around. This deadening of contact can lead to serious physical and interpersonal problems.

Explaining the Bubble

The current step in treatment explains the OCD Bubble to the client as well as helps the client to identify the exact point of cross-over into the imagination. This cross-over point can be identified as it is initiated by thoughts that lead the client away from reality and remove them from what they can actually see or sense. Clients becomes aware that there actually is a point where they can choose to either engage or not engage with the obsession by utilizing their knowledge regarding the nature of obsessions they have learnt so far in treatment.

. . . That OCD Feeling

At the beginning of the session, the client can be asked what it *feels* like when they are completely into their OCD. Often, the client will be very happy to answer this question, since it ties in very closely with their subjective experience of the OCD where focus narrows and the client becomes oblivious to reality. The ensuing conversation can subsequently be used by the therapist as a springboard to explain the various features of the OCD Bubble to the client followed by identifying the cross-over point with the client. These features of the OCD Bubble should be explained in detail during this 7th step by the therapist with diagrams. The client worksheet 7 at the end of the chapter covers the same material.

Reasoning in a Jam Jar

Conceptualizing the obsessional reasoning as living in a bubble provides the client with a global overview of the resolution of OCD. It lets them know that as long as they learn to refrain from falling into the OCD Bubble, they will be OK. It is crucial therefore for the client to learn how to recognize when he or she is about to enter the OCD Bubble. Typically, this cross-over point can be identified by thoughts that take the client beyond the senses or the self (i.e. 'I see it's clean, but maybe…' or 'I never molested anyone, but maybe …'). Specific examples of situations which have occurred in recent days should be discussed with the client, along with how these thoughts consequently led them into the OCD Bubble. The obsessional sequence can be used to pinpoint the exact moment that the person is about to enter the OCD Bubble, which is usually immediately following the trigger and thoughts that lead the person to a distrust of the senses or the self. Another way to identify the cross-over point with the client is to conceptualize it as the moment when the urge to engage in compulsive behaviours comes to the surface. Once the client has a good grasp of identifying the cross-over point, the therapist can proceed to explain the exercise and worksheet for this step.

Self-Sabotage: How OCD Keeps me Unsafe

Most cognitive behavioural approaches to OCD emphasize how OCD compulsive rituals and other neutralizations reinforce and maintain the obsessive compulsive cycle. IBT works with the additional idea that compulsive rituals self-sabotage. Most people carry out OCD rituals under the impression they are helpful or at least preventive. An important element in IBT is for the client to understand that not only are the compulsive rituals unhelpful, but also they actually sabotage the very goal the person wishes to attain, and ultimately lead them to act against their values. Examples include:

- Checking a doorknob to see if it's loose to the extent that the doorknob becomes loose.
- Hoarding articles on the obsessional basis that they may be useful to the extent that they deteriorate into uselessness.
- Washing hands repeatedly to safeguard against infections until the epithelial layer of protection is washed away, exposing the person to infection.
- Repeatedly requesting reassurance from friends that the client did not offend or alienate them to the point that the same friends become alienated.
- More subtle examples could include: getting into danger in reality because the client is ignoring reality in the OCD Bubble.
- A mother who gives up her children since she's afraid of hurting them.
- A teacher who gives up his job because he's afraid he might molest children.

- Someone who stares at their locker, afraid it will be robbed, and so attracts a robber's attention.

The therapist can share the above examples with the client and maybe solicit other example from the client. At the same time the therapist can go over with the client the non-OCD criteria for deciding when and how a job is performed and how OCD in a small or big way sabotages the goal.

Decision Chart

Proceeding to the Next Step in Therapy

- The client is aware that they cross over from reality into the imagination.
- The client is aware that OCD doubt increases the more you go into it. It removes you further away from reality into bubble.
- The client is aware that OCD makes you less secure, not more secure.
- The client is aware that trying to resolve obsessional doubt with compulsions makes them more stressed.

The following transcript is provided to demonstrate identifying the client's the cross-over point into the OCD bubble.

C: My concern is I was sweeping a pesticide and that is what it is because when I pulled the oven out the first time, there was a white powder.... I have seen that in other places around our house where you would put down pesticide.

T: So where did you go from there?

C: My wife asked if I would just sweep out behind the oven and that is when I noticed the white powder. I was concerned that my daughter was taking a bath right there or it would get airborne and or that it would get on my clothes and I did my usual neutralization and it was pretty self-contained [referring to the fact that he did not go onto further elaborate neutralization]. Life is so easy when you just neutralize, yeah?

T: When you say 'neutralization', what did you do?

C: I mopped the floor, took a shower and changed my clothes.

T: So let's go back. You mopped the floor because you saw white powder. The mop got the white powder. But you weren't satisfied there?

C: Yes, because, when I was sweeping, the white powder could have gotten on me.

T: Could have gotten on you? That is what your doubt was saying to you? When you start with white powder, you can see with your senses that there is white powder. But when you wipe up the white powder you can no longer see anything, right?

C: Well, I didn't wipe up the white powder.... I swept where the white powder was, but I didn't sweep up all of it. So then I was concerned that some of the powder could have gotten dragged out, so I mopped the entire kitchen floor.

T: And what did you see then?

C: Nothing.

T: So you saw nothing, but where did your mind go to then?

C: My mind went to when I was sweeping, it could have gotten on my clothes or my skin. So I changed my clothes after and took a shower.

T: So when you say that. . . it could have gotten on your clothes, are you basing that on anything that you could see or for which there was any direct evidence?

C: Yeh, because I was sweeping it up.

T: Right, you were sweeping up, but as far as it being on your clothes?

C: Yeah, because with a broom sweeping up a white powder it is going to get a little bit airborne so, yeah, I was worried.

T: Could get a little bit airborne. Yes, powders can get airborne. But then you said that it might be on your clothing? Because that was your concern, right?

C: Yes.

T: Well, did you see any on your clothes?

C: No.

T: So you didn't see any on your clothes?

C: No.

T: But you were concerned that it was on your clothes even though you did not see any on your clothes?

C: Yes.

T: OK. Where did your mind go to justify that concern at that point?

C: So, my mind went to if it is a pesticide, it's a poison and now it is on my clothes and I'm holding my daughter and her hands get on it and it gets in her mouth and that it could be very dangerous.

T: So that is your narrative, your story that you came up with, which is a very scary story. But the facts are that you start with white powder, you mopped that up, you see that, you are still in your senses, but then something else happens. At what point do you feel that you leave your senses behind? Because when you don't see anything, you are no longer in your senses.

C: I go to 'It's contaminated'. If I just changed my shirt and wash my hands, that would be a more reasonable response.

T: Well, certainly washing your hands if you are touching something you could see on your hands. But when you thought it was on your clothes although you did not see anything, is that where you could have left your senses behind?

C: Well, I think legitimately it could have been on my sleeves and my shirt because sweeping like that it could get there.

T: But this comes down to whether you saw any powder on you? Did you?

C: No.

T: So at that point your senses did not tell you that anything was on you and you didn't see anything on your pants. This is really a question of is it there or not?

C: No. That is where I guess I crossed the line.

T: Yes, I agree. This is where you crossed over and ignored your senses. So you didn't see anything, but then your mind went to what?

C: That it could happen.

At this point, the client has understood the cross-over point.

Client Worksheet 7
The OCD Bubble

It may not seem obvious at first, but you would be surprised how much your OCD is about going beyond the senses. In fact, the *only* way for the OCD to make a convincing case is to come up with possibilities that make it seem *as if* the doubt has something to do with reality around you. More importantly, these possibilities make it seem as if reality does not really matter.

Let's say that you worry about certain dangerous germs on a particular object. Yet, there is no evidence in reality that these germs are present. It looks clean. There is no smell. The object has been used before without incident. On the basis of what reality and your senses tell you, there is nothing to worry about. Yet somehow, the OCD is able to make an obsessional doubt relevant by going *beyond* the senses: For example:

1.   Germs are too small to be seen. . . so there might still be germs on it.
2.   Who knows who else has touched it. . . so there might still be germs on it.
3.   People never clean enough. . . so there might still be germs on it.

All these possibilities may not necessarily be impossible, yet they do not originate from sense and common reality around you. In other words, obsessional doubt is *never* kept alive by reality, but *only* by what your imagination can come up with. And because OCD is such an *all-or-nothing* disorder that originates 100% from the imagination, there is an exact point in time where you enter the world of the imagination. It occurs with the first thought that you have that takes you beyond the senses. Like this:

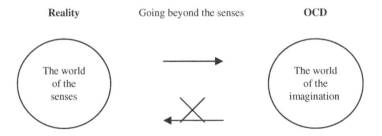

| **Reality** | Going beyond the senses | **OCD** |

| The world of the senses | | The world of the imagination |

When it comes to OCD, reality and the imagination are really two separate worlds. And you are entering the imagination with that first thought that gets you beyond the senses. The worst part, however, is that as soon as you cross over into the imagination, it is very difficult to get back to the world of the senses, or reality. This is often described by people with OCD as being in a bubble, or a circle. There is this sense that you are sucked into something from where there is no escape no matter how hard you try. And you are indeed sucked into something.

You are sucked inside the world of the imagination – welcome to *the OCD Bubble.*

The following sections describe what the OCD Bubble is really about.

The OCD Leads You Beyond Reality into More Doubt

Obsessional doubts never have any direct link to reality, which means they always come from your imagination. The story leads you to believe that maybe there is something wrong in reality and that therefore you should act in reality to overcome it. But the doubt is only a story. So when you give in to the story, you are only encouraging more doubt. Which is why the more you perform the ritual, the deeper you go into OCD, and the less you are in touch with reality and so the more you doubt. Ironically, in going into OCD land, you sometimes feel you are getting deeper into reality, but it's exactly the opposite: the more you go into OCD, the further away you go from reality. The sequences are as follows:

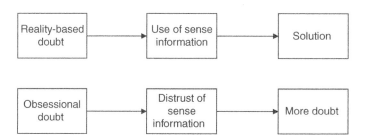

You might argue that it is exactly because you are unsure of your senses that you doubt. But our research shows it is exactly the opposite. It is only when you are certain according to your senses that the obsessional doubt then takes over and tells you *not* to be sure of your sense information. It trumps the senses and creates doubt on the basis of a good story, not on the basis of sense information.

How it seems to a person with OCD:

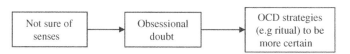

How it actually is:

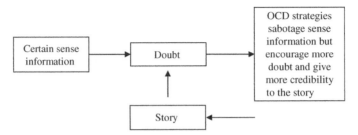

Going into the OCD Bubble Makes You Less Secure

OCD sabotages the very action it is supposed to make secure. First of all, people with OCD are often so caught up in the OCD Bubble that they are not aware of what is going on around them. They may not hear their baby cry. They may not notice a car looming up. They may not realize they are being pickpocketed. But OCD actions can also directly sabotage the aim of being secure. For example, testing a door several times per day will make it loose. Asking people if you said the right thing because you are afraid to upset them will eventually make them upset. Staring at a locker to make sure it is closed properly so you won't be robbed will draw the attention of thieves. Scrubbing hands to remove invisible infections will eventually destroy protective skin.

Remember that you go into the OCD spiral on the basis of a subjective doubt which is generated by a story. The more you go into OCD, the more you generate doubt, since this is the only outcome. OCD reinforces doubt so it cannot give you anything else. You think you will find a solution in continuing the questioning, but mostly you just doubt more. Sometimes a rule will let you out of the spiral. Example: 'I've done this five times' or 'I've put in a lot of effort so it must be done'. But you are *never* more certain of real information than when you started the doubt; you are always *less* certain. The reason is because you were certain before the obsessional doubt came along, but the OCD made you doubt your sense of certainty with its story. So now you are not focused on reality at all but on a story. So actually OCD is exposing you to more potential danger whilst you are absorbed in its story. We have met people who have ignored real dangers and been hurt because they were too absorbed in their OCD spiral.

Entering the OCD Bubble Makes You More Stressed Out

Going into the OCD Bubble is often difficult to resist for people with OCD. This is because the OCD tempts you with the illusion of providing a solution to the obsessional doubt. Everything would be so much better if only you could do the ritual and solve the problem. But that feeling is going to be very short-lived. You will get in fact the opposite of what the OCD is promising, because giving in to the OCD is like giving in to someone shouting orders at you. Initially you feel less stressed. But one thing should be clear: performing the compulsive action does not make you less stressed, *it makes you more stressed out.*

OCD makes you more stressed because you are constantly putting in more effort than necessary and doing irrelevant actions to make yourself feel secure. But effectively, you are working overtime for nothing, and worse, all your effort is sabotaging your security. At the end of all this, you are more anxious than when you started. That's why people often end up avoiding OCD situations. It all seems so stressful. Anticipating, preparing, all that extra attention, muscle tension: you're worn out, and yet you think OCD makes you less stressed! OCD is some con artist! You only feel better because you have given in to a screaming bully, and if you do as the bully says he or she stops screaming for a short while, but of course in the long run you reinforce the bully. It is for this reason that staying out of the OCD Bubble and recognising the cross-over point will help you go a long way towards your recovery from OCD.

Client Exercise Sheet 7
The OCD Bubble

The exercise for this 7th step of therapy is the same as the one you will find on your training card. You will go through this exercise at least a couple of times each day every time an obsession occurs with the purpose to stop you from automatically falling into the OCD Bubble. You will not be asked to completely resist the OCD. But you are asked to *see* that there is a moment of choice before the compulsive urge arrives and that you are not completely at the mercy of the OCD.

The exercise consists of a number of different steps, which will slow the entire obsessional process down. The first step is to identify the first thought that carries you from the real world into the imagination. The second step is to slow down the process of crossing over from reality into the imagination. The third step is to hold still between the worlds of the imagination and of reality without reacting to the doubt. The final fourth step is that you will reflect on how obsessional doubt is resolved.

Step 1

You already have some practice in identifying obsessional doubts and the particular story behind them, and determining whether or not there is any direct evidence in the here and now for the doubt. Ask yourself the following questions whenever a doubt occurs:

1. What was the first thought that came to mind that took me beyond the senses?
2. How does this thought make my senses *seem* irrelevant?

Step 2

As soon as you have identified the particular thought that makes you cross from reality into the imagination, do not immediately react with rituals, avoidance or anything else. Hold off everything for at least one minute and try the following visualization. Imagine yourself standing in the middle of a bridge. This bridge is the thought that carries you from the world of the senses into the world of the imagination– the cross-over point. Standing on the bridge makes you feel you need to act upon the doubt. You cannot help but feel that the doubt will be resolved somehow at the other end of the bridge through carrying out a ritual, avoidance or some other way of trying to solve the problem. However, look back for a moment into the world of the senses where you came from. Out there, the doubt was irrelevant. There was nothing that supported the doubt to begin with. You can choose to move into the world of OCD, think more about the doubt, try to solve it somehow and likely get more upset, *or* you can move back to the world of the senses where the doubt is 100% arbitrary and irrelevant. Try to hold your balance like this for at least one minute, and longer if possible.

Step 3

Now again you can choose what to do. You can move further into the doubt with the hope that you will find some kind of resolution in the world of OCD, or you can decide that the doubt is arbitrary to begin with, and move back to the world of the senses. If you went into the OCD, ask yourself this: did you eventually stop the rituals as dictated by the whims of the OCD? Do you think the doubt is resolved permanently? Will it come back in similar situations? If you decided to move back to the world of the senses, ask yourself on what basis you decided the doubt was imaginary and not something that needed your attention. Did you use your senses in deciding whether it was imaginary? How permanent is this resolution?

Step 4

Write down the most important thoughts that took you beyond the senses (or your 'inner senses'), and add them to the obsessional story using the entries. Hand them over to your therapist in the next session so that he or she can help you adapt the obsessional story.

Thoughts that took me beyond reality:

_____
_____
_____
_____
_____

Client Training Card 7
The OCD Bubble

Learning Points (Front)

- OCD takes you beyond the senses into more doubt – the OCD Bubble.
- There already is certainty before the obsessional doubt.
- OCD does not keep you safe and secure. It makes you insecure and sometimes unsafe.

Daily Exercise (Back)

Step 1: Identify the thoughts that you have during the day that try to take you beyond the senses. Ask yourself how this thought makes your senses *seem* irrelevant.

Step 2: Hold off every ritual and feeling associated with this thought for at least one minute. You are now at the cross-over point in between the world of the senses and that of the imagination. Look in both directions, and realize you can make a choice.

Step 3: Make your choice. If you went into the OCD Bubble, ask yourself later whether anything was resolved. If you move back into the world of the senses, ask yourself what was there to help you stay there.

Step 4: Write down the most important thoughts that took you beyond your senses. Add them to your OCD story.

Cartoon 10. The O'Seedys' doubt depot.

Client Quiz 7
The OCD Bubble

(Please check all answers which apply)

1. OCD makes itself believable by ...
   - ○ making you confuse imagination with reality.
   - ○ going beyond the senses.
   - ○ disconnecting you from reality.
   - ○ all of the above.
2. Allowing yourself to go into the OCD Bubble makes you ...
   - ○ less secure and more unsafe.
   - ○ feel better.
   - ○ doubt less.
   - ○ none of the above.
3. Reality-based doubt differs from obsessional doubt in that ...
   - ○ there is a solution to it.
   - ○ it uses sense information.
   - ○ it will never lead to compulsive rituals.
   - ○ all of the above.
4. Being inside the OCD Bubble ...
   - ○ makes it very difficult to resist compulsions.
   - ○ will increase the likelihood you will end up there again.
   - ○ is best dealt with by not going there in the first place.
   - ○ all of the above.
5. In the OCD Bubble, you are ...
   - ○ more likely to contact reality.
   - ○ more likely to be unaware of surroundings.
   - ○ better able to cope.
   - ○ least exposed to risk.

Please check your answers by referring to the Quiz Answers Sheet provided by your therapist.

Chapter Ten

Reality Sensing

The Cross-Over

The previous step in treatment has helped the client to learn to identity the cross-over point from reality into the imagination. The next step - step 8 of the therapy - is aimed to help the client to further reduce in the pull towards the OCD Bubble by exposing not only the unreal nature but the falsehood of the obsessional inference. The unreal nature of the doubt follows directly from the imaginary and irrelevant nature of the doubt, which guarantees that the OCD doubt is always against reality. The client is shown that there already exists a certainty prior to the doubt and given through the proper use of the senses, which if trusted can dispel the doubt. In fact, to regain their certainty about reality the client needs only to return to trusting and using their senses and common sense in the normal way before the doubt took over.

Away from Reality

The idea that OCD doubt is always false can be introduced to the client through establishing that the obsession actually goes *against* reality. So even though the obsessional doubt may be possible in the abstract, it is not really possible in the here and now. It is not an actual probability. This can be formulated by the therapist to the client as follows:

'I would like to introduce another idea to you that directly follows from what you have learned so far, which is that obsessional doubt is always false. Now, we

Clinician's Handbook for Obsessive-Compulsive Disorder: Inference-Based Therapy, First Edition.
K. O'Connor and F. Aardema.
© 2012 John Wiley & Sons, Ltd. Published 2012 by John Wiley & Sons, Ltd.

already have established that OCD occurs without direct information from the here and now, which makes it entirely imaginary. We have also established that is it irrelevant to the here and now, because there is no evidence in reality for the doubt. But it goes even further than that. Your doubt actually goes against reality, and this is exactly what makes the doubt wrong and false. Can you see how your doubt goes *against* reality?'

Falsehood of Obsessions

The therapist should keep in mind that while the falsehood of the obsessions may be self-evident to him or her, clients with OCD have an inferential confusion between reality and possibility. To them, there is nothing quite as clear-cut to say that the obsession is false, since they started out with the idea that the obsession is a valid possibility (no matter how improbable). Such common sense with respect to the unreality of the obsession could be lacking in people with OCD. Hence the importance of the previous therapy steps, where the client has learnt the following:

1. Obsessions occur without any direct link to reality. They originate from the imagination.
2. Obsessions are irrelevant to reality since there is no evidence to support them in the here and now. They are not valid possibilities.
3. The client crosses over from reality into the imagination when having an obsession by going beyond reality.
      These three steps should lead the client to be able to now fully comprehend and accept the final step:
4. Obsessions go *against* reality. They are *always* irrelevant to the here and now.

This logical progression of the therapy in step 8 is explained in detail below.

Going Against Reality

Once the the client has grasped the general principle that the obsession is always false since it contradicts reality, the therapist then proceeds to discuss the client's specific case to show him or her how the obsession goes against reality. The therapist only needs imagine having the same obsession as the client, and ask him or herself how it goes against reality, especially given the presence of compulsive behaviours. Washing the hands and seeing they are clean is incompatible with the obsession 'I might be contaminated'. Seeing and feeling the door is locked are incompatible with the obsession 'The door might be unlocked'. Not having actual undesired sexual urges is incompatible with the obsession 'I might be a sexual undesirable'. In all of these cases, the obsession goes against what is sensed out there or sensed inwardly.

When Reality Gets in the Way

Even though a reality check should quickly disconfirm any anxiety, it generally fails to do so in clients with OCD due to the obsessional story that renders reality irrelevant. The client therefore needs to create an alternative story that does take into account reality-based information. This alternative story will lead to a conclusion opposite to that of the obsessional inference. Such an alternative story can initially be proposed by the therapist. For example, the following dialogue constructing an alternative story is with a client who is worried about contamination:

T: So can you pick the paper out of the waste paper bin?
C: No, I can't touch it. . . . I told you, it's been in the bin, that means it's dirty
T: So if you touch it, what?
C: I can't touch it, I'd have to wash my hands, you've no idea. . . . I wash and wash 'cos I know it'd be dirty.
T: Yeh, but why is it dirty? I mean, do you see dirt?
C: No, but it's where it's been . . . in there, I mean you know it's a waste bin, it's dirty, it's full of I don't know, like muck and stuff and people they throw things in, it's dirty, they might spit, it's disgusting, you know . . . I mean forget it.
T: So, what would convince you it wasn't dirty?
C: Nothing.
T: So, if we did a load of tests on the paper. I mean high-tech tests, with experts and microscopes and they found no dirt, would that convince you?
C: I don't know if I'd be convinced. . . . I mean there's error in those tests.
T: Well, maybe several independent experts.
C: I don't know, I don't know.
T: Would you be more prepared to touch it if you knew about the tests?
C: [Hesitates] No. Would I. . . . I don't think so. No. No.
T: OK, now I'm going to tell you a story about the waste paper bin. Actually it's largely ornamental. Nobody uses it except me and I only put very clean pieces of paper in it. Nobody else is allowed near it, no dirty people come in here anyway and there is no muck or spit anywhere about here. It's cleaned thoroughly every night, and everyone who goes near the bin wears gloves before they touch it.
C: You're telling me that? Well if I believed that . . . are you serious?
T: Yeah, it's perfectly clean. Look for yourself, for all the reasons I said.
C: You're sure?
T: Can you touch it now?
C: OK I'll touch it, but only because of what you said. [Client touches paper bin.]
T: Do you feel the need to wash?
C: No, not right now, because I believe what you said. . . . But maybe later if I think about it . . .

Alternative Stories

Therapists should in mind that subjective elements can be included in alternative stories. Subjectivity is an inherent part of how we normally reason and stories add to the reality value of our conclusions. The key difference is that non-obsessional stories include direct links to reality and would therefore never lead to an obsessional conclusion. In step 9 in the next chapter, we cover in more detail how to construct a more enduring alternative story. The aim here is more immediate and to knock the OCD story off its pedestal and at least temporarily make the person doubt the doubt. This can be a playful and fun exercise that well illustrates both the impact of reality and the power of the imagination to the client, especially when both act in unison.

The key question always to be posed after constructing an alternative story and modifying the clients reaction to obsessional target is:

'But what's changed? The target object or the story?'

The idea is not that the client believes the alternative story or tries obsessionally to replace one with the other but that the alternative story knocks the OCD story off its pedestal and makes the client doubt the doubt. In other words, there is part insight, part rote practice, part immersion in the story. It is essential the client understands the rationale and what we are after, otherwise the exercise may lack purpose.

There is no point in practising blind or machine-like. It is important that the client understands the importance of time and rehearsal and that their OCD story will not change overnight. Otherwise they may expect instant results and become discouraged.

Doubt Distrust Versus Reality Sensing

The relationship between OCD doubt and reality is like the children's game 'paper, stone, scissors'. In the same way that paper always beats stone, so reality will always beat the imaginary doubt . . . if the client lets it. OCD's trick is to con the client into staying in the imagination where, of course, doubt reigns.

Finally, the client should be encouraged to act upon on the knowledge that the obsession is false by not engaging in any compulsive behaviours. After all, if the obsession is false then it makes no sense to engage in compulsive behaviours. It is important that the therapist and client do know and feel that the obsession is incorrect. Difficulties in this area should be identified and resolved.

Learning to Trust What the Senses do not Say

Some clients with OCD assume that if their senses do not sound the alarm that is not because the senses are doing their job and see no cause for alarm. Rather they think the senses were asleep on duty or not sensitive enough to detect any error. So the doubt becomes maybe there was a problem but my senses didn't detect it properly. This omission fear is itself part of distrusting the senses. This can be put to the client as follows:

'Part of trusting your senses is also trusting what and when they do not say there is a problem, then that means also that for the senses all is OK. If you are in the habit of closing your door or showering in a certain routine, then your senses are in 'default' option. In other words, as long as all runs smoothly, the senses sound no alarm. But when something out of the ordinary occurs, *then* your senses may jolt your awareness and say wow . . . something is amiss here.'

Reality Sensing

Now that the client has realized that they use their senses and reasoning differently in everyday life from how they do in OCD, it is time to capitalize on this point and look exactly at what they do differently. Of course, we are up against habit which says it's normal to be different at different times or which accords the OCD situation more importance or more danger. Obviously then in targeting a non-OCD situation, it's a good idea to consider that it's an important and potentially risky one (e.g crossing the road, driving, cutting vegetables, using an ATM at night). The important point to draw out is that the senses are used, without any extra effort, that they are trusted and that the decisions are made on the basis of sense data in the here and now. It's important to note exactly what is not present in the everyday OCD examples.

A problem encountered in losing OCD is the client's fear of what will fill it up. We have found that a frequent obstacle to recovery is that the client fears that something else will fill up the void left by the OCD which will be as bad or worse. These exercises at the end of the chapter help the person to understand that it will be filled up naturally, by normal reasoning and awareness as in existing non-OCD situations.

Overuse of the Senses

The client may feel they are already using their senses within the OCD. But overuse is not proper use. Clients with OCD often seem to have the tendency to put in too much effort and do more than is necessary. For example, the difference between 'staring' and 'looking' should be discussed when the client begins to use the senses in the proper way again in obsessional situations. It may help again to compare the proper use of the senses to a non-obsessional situation for the client to get a feel for the naturalistic proper use of the sense. A client reports:

'Well, I overuse my senses. I stare for a good 15 minutes at my door before I leave it in the morning. In fact, my eyes feel strained. So I know I've used them.' But this is not using the senses in a sensible way; quite the opposite. It is an obsessionally driven use of the senses. Since normally in taking in information we rely on our senses to tell us naturally what is there, we don't need to force them to focus. An opposite complaint is 'I genuinely don't know what I should normally see or check for. You need to help me.' In this case, the therapist might ask the client to explain to a little child how they should carry out the job using their senses. Inevitably they can easily do so.

Helping the Client to Let Go of the Doubt and Trust the Senses

Example 1

C: So I can't help it, the idea jumps into my head and then I can't get rid of it.

T: You were walking down the aisle.

C: And then I saw this red stuff dripping down.

T: And what did your senses say?

C: Well, that it was sauce or jam ... but then like I said ... here comes the OCD with well it could be blood.

T: But you knew it was sauce.

C: Well, it could have been ... but how could I know for sure?

T: So what did you do?

C: Well, I was going to ask the manager ... but in the end I just left and never went back. But it's still there, that it was blood and it could have got on to me.

T: But you *know* it wasn't.

C: How can I know for sure? I mean, I didn't do tests or anything.

T: Supposing the liquid dropping had been green.

C: Well, I guess it wouldn't have been so bad.

T: Would you have wanted tests or anything?

C: No, I would probably have just moved on.

T: So you would have been happy not to have known any more than what your senses told you was there.

C: Yes, but in the case of the red, I really didn't know.

T: Supposing your little nephew had been with you. And supposing he had asked about the red stuff. What would you have said?

C: Well, I would have said it was a broken jar and the sauce had run out.

T: So you did know what you saw.

C: Well, it was most probably sauce ... but I couldn't be sure.

T: But in the case of the green sauce, you didn't feel you needed further information.

C: No, it didn't upset me.

T: So in most areas of life your senses tell you what you need to know to function properly. Obviously there is always more information we can gather about anything. I look out the window and see it's snowing; I don't know the exact shape of the snow flakes, their exact distribution over the area. Information I could seek. But since I'm just going out shopping, I don't *need* this information. I just need to know if it's snowing or not. Are you agreed?

C: OK.

T: So when you say you need more information to be sure and you can't rely just on senses, this is not a question you ask elsewhere in your life.

C: No, I don't feel the need.

T: So just asking that question is part of the obsession. Because asking it means already you've doubted all you really need to know.

C: So I should just accept what the senses say and not question it ... move on.

Helping the Client Let Go of Extra Effort

C: Yes, I am extra-vigilant when I'm walking along. I'm looking out for people that look like they're contaminated.

T: How do you know?

C: Well, I don't but I'm checking on complexion, anything odd, obviously scruffy or dirty people.

T: So the vigilance keeps you in a high state of alert.

C: Yes, sure. I'm nervy but it keeps me safe. I mean I don't want to inadvertently get infected.

T: Do you check for bricks falling off of buildings? Or banana skins aon the pavement?

C: No, why would I?

T: Well, it can happen and what if you were hit by a roof tile or slipped on a skin or even both at the same time?

C: [Laughs] Well, I think I'd spot a banana skin, and there'd been signs in the street about falling tiles.

T: OK, but you're not able to detect a really contaminated person or a potentially contaminating situation with the senses.

C: Well no, because there are no visible signs. Exactly, that's just it, they could look normal.

T: If they look normal in appearance, how are you able to detect them in the normal way?

C: Well, I'm hoping to see some small sign. That is, you wouldn't see just normally.

T: Like what?

C: Like I saw a guy in the bar with a rash on his face ... well, it could have been an infection.

T: What did your senses say?

C: That it was a rash from shaving but...

T: So really, you're not being extra-vigilant to reality. You're putting a lot of effort into creating doubt and imaginary stories about what your senses say is normal.

C: Well, that's one view.

T: I mean, anything you actually see becomes a sign that what you see is not as it appears.

C: So ...

T: So you're dismissing your senses in favour of your imagination.

C: Sort of.

T: You might be better to save all that energy and either imagine the world completely or let the senses do the work in a non-effortful way.

Decision Chart

Proceeding to the Next Step in Therapy

- The client accepts that there is no need to do anything 'extra' when sensing reality.
- The client realizes that any extra effort takes the client away from, not nearer, reality.
- The client understands that Obsessional doubt goes against reality.

Client Worksheet 8
Reality Sensing

Imaginary Story

So far, you have learned that OCD is supported by an imaginary story. You also knows that the OCD is not really relevant to reality because there is no sense information in the here and now to support your doubts. Now you will move on to understand that the OCD doubt is *always* false because it goes against your senses.

OCD Deconstructed

Now that sounds a brazen claim; after all, you might say, OK it may be imaginary, OK it may be irrelevant, but even irrelevant imaginary ideas can come true, or just be true by coincidence. However, in the case of OCD, research shows that it is always false because of the way the OCD story is *constructed*. The doubting takes you away from the here and now by making you believe a story that has nothing to do with the current context. It tells you to ignore your senses. So it is *against* reality from the word 'go', that's why it's false.

Sensing the Certain

Think of hourself in your kitchen. Your senses have already told you that all is correct, that there is no dust. In fact, your senses have given you *certain* information as they always do on the current state of affairs. The OCD then goes against this certainty by creating an imaginary story. But since the original sense information was correct, it came from your senses and is real, then the OCD must always be unreal.

The Proof

The proof that the OCD doubt and story is false is that never once, in our research experience, has an OCD 'maybe' turned out true. Ask yourself, how often has your OCD doubt been correct? Did you ever find any real proof that your doubt was correct?

Sense information I've locked the door. Everything is fine.	**OCD story land** But maybe the lock isn't quite closed because maybe some dust got into it and maybe … maybe … and maybe. …

The doubt of course jumps in so quickly you don't realize that you were certain before it arrived. This is why you have been working hard in the previous step on learning how to identify the cross-over point that leads you into the imagination. This combined with the knowledge that there already is certainty before the doubt will give you a fighting chance to recover from OCD.

Feeling Certain Today?

Finding certainty about reality is not a difficult thing to do. For example, if you have frequent obsessions about maybe having forgotten to lock the door, or 'perhaps' the cheque you put in the envelope was not signed, do you actually take into account what your senses have told you just a moment before? After all, you have *felt* the door lock. You may even have tried to open it after locking it. This is exactly the sense information you have to start taking into account. And you should start taking it into account as soon as you find yourself crossing over into the imagination, because it clearly shows up the obsessional doubt as false and unreal.

Get Real

You may feel this situation does not apply to you. Perhaps because you feel there is not always sense information around to tell you whether all is OK. It is true that the here and now it is not always about physical sense information alone. But it is about *reality* which we know is derived directly from outer and inner sense information.

For example, if you have the obsessional doubt that you might suddenly hurt someone, then you have to ask yourself what reality tells you about this idea. When do you have this idea that you might hurt someone? Does it make any sense to have this idea when you are not angry at anyone? Does it make sense when such a thought occurs when you are standing somewhere minding your own business? In the case of obsessional doubt, your *actual* state of mind will always completely conflict with the doubt. So it's not always just the physical senses that make the OCD wrong. It includes your inner reality as well – your 'inner senses'.

Reality Sensing

Reality sensing is about staying with information from the here and now. This means, that you will actually take notice of what is there instead of making assumptions of what is there solely on the basis of an imaginary OCD story. Instead of avoiding a situation or adding doubt to it by going off in the imagination, you will define reality by relying on information from the five senses and common sense. And as you have learned in the therapy so far, relying on the senses will leave no room whatsoever for obsessional doubt. For example, do you look at your hands after you feel an urge to wash? Do your senses play any role at all right now? When you check whether you left something unlocked, does it matter whether you heard and felt it lock? Often, for people with OCD, this type of sense information is not given any attention, since the OCD story has found a way around it. But, it is the only reality that gives a resolution to your obsessional doubt, and that means learning to trust the senses again – and knowing that this is enough.

Easy Does It

Can it be so easy that all it takes is to trust the senses? Yes and no. It's easy, because if you really trust your senses and common sense, then there will be no obsessional doubt. It's not so easy, because trusting the senses will give you the feeling you are not doing enough. The OCD has told you for a long time to do more and more, and even then it may still not be enough. So doing less will leave a void and a feeling that you are not doing enough. That may produce anxiety, discomfort, or fear. Yet, you *are* doing enough, and in fact all that you can do, if you trust the senses. In short, it is time to trust the senses once again. And if you do so, you will end up at an entirely different conclusion from that of the obsessional doubt. There would be no doubt. There would only be certainty.

Realizing that there is certainty about reality before the doubt is exactly the goal of the exercises before the next step in therapy.

"I'm giving him a wide berth. I don't want his germs jumping on me."

Cartoon 11. Safety first.

Client Exercise Sheet 8
Reality Sensing

The exercise on this worksheet will help you practise everything you have learned to far. You will begin to use and trust your senses in obsessional situations. And if you trust your senses, you will have all the certainty that you need to dismiss the obsessional doubt. Do not worry that you have to be successful each time. The more you do the exercise, the more your confidence will go up, and the easier it will get over time. Again, the exercise here is the same as the one on your training card, just described in more detail. Try to do the exercise at least several times a day when an obsession occurs.

1. When an obsessions or thought occurs that takes you beyond the senses, hold still and imagine yourself between worlds – a bridge between reality and the imagination.
2. Focus your attention back to reality, and look what is there. Only look once and take in the information of what your senses tell you. Don't put any effort into this.
3. Realize for a moment that this is all the information you need and that trying to obtain more information from elsewhere means you have already crossed into OCD land.
4. Look down from the bridge you see yourself standing on. Take note of any feeling that makes you feel you are not doing enough. It is the void that is left behind by not engaging in any rituals. It represents all the anxiety and discomfort you feel by not going into OCD land and only trusting your senses.
5. Take a moment to realize that this void is merely imaginary, and that there is certainty by remaining in the world of the senses. Try to feel that sense of certainty. It is common sense. There is absolutely no need to cross the bridge into OCD land.
6. Next, act upon the information from your senses by dismissing the obsession and not engaging in any compulsive rituals.

There are a number of things you need to keep in mind while you are doing the exercise, which is to use the senses in a natural and effortless way. Trusting the senses means you use the senses normally, as you would do in any other situation where you have no obsessions. Anything else means you have already passed into OCD land. Of course, you can still get back, but try to avoid any of the following:

1. Staring: if you are staring, you are putting in too much effort to overcome your OCD. You are in your OCD Bubble the moment you stare.

2. Fast looking: creating ambiguity by quick looking will reinforce your imagination. Just look naturally as you would do in any other situation where you have no obsessions.

3. Imposing your imagination on reality: if you can't see something clearly (for example: something in the distance that you may feel justifies the obsessional doubt), be aware that this is not 'real looking'.

Doing this exercise often will make it progressively easier to stay out of the OCD Bubble and not act on your obsessions. You will even find that your obsessions will begin to disappear, occurring far less often and becoming less intense. And the best part is that the imaginary void will slowly disappear, as it fills up with more normal reasoning and awareness which is real. So go out there and get to know your real self!

Basic Steps to Reality Sensing

1. You intend using your senses exactly as you do in everyday non-OCD situations.

2. You will tune into the world in a natural non-effortful mindful way, open to whatever happens.

3. If you are performing an act, you decide on what criteria you will observe with your senses to know the task is accomplished.

4. If an OCD doubt appears on the horizon and tries to muscle in on the action, you dismiss it and appeal to your senses to know what is actually there or is really happening.

5. You stop the task when your senses and common sense say what needs to be done and when all is done.

Examples

You shower yourself . . . your senses say you are clean . . . You do not wait and reflect on whether maybe you are clean. You leave the shower.

You lock your front door. Your senses say it's locked. You go about your business and dismiss any subsequent doubt as irrelevant.

Client Training Card 8
Reality Sensing

Learning Points (Front)

- Obsessional doubts are wrong and false.
- Obsessional doubts conflict with reality.
- Reality sensing is staying with the information from the here and now.
- Trusting your senses will add to your confidence each and every time.

Daily Exercise (Back)

Follow this sequence:

Step 1: When a doubt or obsession occurs that takes you beyond the senses, hold still and imagine yourself between worlds – a bridge between reality and the imagination.

Step 2: Focus your attention back on reality, and look at what is there without effort.

Step 3: Look down the bridge between worlds and take note of any feeling that you might not be doing enough. It is the void left behind by not engaging in any rituals.

Step 4: Realize this void is imaginary, and that there is certainty in the world of the senses. Try to feel that ground under your feet. It is common sense.

Step 5: Act on the knowledge from your senses by dismissing the obsession and not engaging in any compulsive rituals.

Client Quiz 8
Reality Sensing

(Please check all answers which apply)

1. Obsessional doubts are wrong and false because...
    - ○ they make you feel terrible.
    - ○ they are totally impossible.
    - ○ they go against reality.
    - ○ none of the above.
2. Reality sensing is about...
    - ○ trusting your senses without effort.
    - ○ something you already know how to do.
    - ○ keeping the OCD at bay.
    - ○ all of the above.
3. Overusing the senses occurs when you are...
    - ○ 'staring' instead of 'looking'.
    - ○ in the OCD Bubble rather than in reality.
    - ○ not really trusting your senses.
    - ○ all of the above.
4. If I feel I haven't done enough to see...
    - ○ this means I'm incompetent.
    - ○ I will endanger myself.
    - ○ it is OCD making me doubt.
    - ○ my seeing is deficient.
5. Reality sensing includes trusting...
    - ○ my five senses and my common sense.
    - ○ questioning what I really feel.
    - ○ seeking reassurance.
    - ○ keeping a written note of all I see.

Please check your answers by referring to the Quiz Answers Sheet provided by your therapist.

Part III
Consolidation

Chapter Eleven

A Different Story

A Different Story

In this step 9 of the therapy we return the client to the art of storytelling. The client is now familiar with the way in which an OCD story has convinced them to doubt. Clients will have learnt how to be aware of the reason and rhetoric of the story and how the detail and flow of the story convince and immerse them in the story and carry them along to the inference of doubt. The task of the therapist now is to help the client to construct a different story and, in the process:

1. Master the trick of constructing narratives.
2. Grasp that beliefs about reality are powerfully affected by stories we tell ourselves.
3. Be wary of filling in too many sense gaps in reasoning about the world with imaginary scenarios.

The aim is *not* to replace the OCD story with another story but rather to dislodge the status of the OCD story as the *only* story. In a sense, this part of the therapy complements returning the person to the world of the senses and reality sensing.

The Doubting Story Revisited

The OCD story has previously been elicited by establishing that the doubt does not arise from the here and now. The story can be revisited by the therapist as a

Clinician's Handbook for Obsessive-Compulsive Disorder: Inference-Based Therapy, First Edition.
K. O'Connor and F. Aardema.
© 2012 John Wiley & Sons, Ltd. Published 2012 by John Wiley & Sons, Ltd.

way of presenting the client with the contradiction between the sense information and the doubting inference as in:

'Your senses say the door is locked or your hands are clean, but you claim you need to go beyond your senses because you can't trust them. Why? Well our bridging game which we describe below, provides us with some of the answers.'

The Alternative or Counter Story

The client is familiar with how a counter story can temporarily resolve the OCD doubt through changing the OCD story to eliminate the justification for doubt (see Chapter 10). Example:

OCD story: Well, there could be something wrong with the lock. I read about locks not working, and I'm not too mechanical so it could be something is not clicking and I don't know what. I once broke a watch trying to wind it up. If I was burgled, I'd be very upset and ashamed.

Counter-story: I've locked the door many times; there has never been a problem. I locked doors, cars and ladders all the time; I never made a mistake. I know exactly how to use a lock, and my senses give me feedback. What happens to others or what I did with a watch is irrelevant to a lock.

Here the alternative story is built up with the client so that all aspects of the OCD story which could induce doubt are countered by more reality-based alternatives. Usually the person will agree that doubt has reduced or even disappeared . . . at least temporarily. The success of the story may be qualified with 'But how do I know it's true?' or 'Well, in spite of all that, I still believe the OCD story'. This is fine because at this stage you are showing (1) they are both equal stories; (2) very importantly, when asked the person will agree that the OCD story is the less realistic; and (3) you're demonstrating rapid, if very temporary, resolution of the doubt simply by changing a story.

Now we create an alternative story more systematically through a series of narrative exercises. The first way to prompt alternative reasoning stories is to play bridge with the client.

Let's Play 'Bridge'

In this game, you need to connect two statements by a bridging statement to make them seem logically linked.

Example 1

The cat jumped out of the window.
Tom ordered a third beer.

One bridging story could be:

The cat jumped out of the window and ran along the street into the pub. He jumped up on the table and knocked over Tom's second beer, so Tom reordered a third beer.

Obviously what makes the link between the apparently unrelated sentences is the story, which literally fills up, or bridges the gap, between them. The richer and more detailed the bridge, the stronger the link seems.

Example 2   Let's take another pair:

The snowman only had half a nose.
Johnny caught a cold.

One bridging story could be:

The snowman only had half a nose because the carrot had been broken in half, and Johnny felt so sorry that he ran all the way to the grocer's to buy another carrot without his coat on. It was a bitter cold day, and Johnny caught a cold.

The bridging can apply to any unconnected statements, no matter how seemingly far apart. The processes which make bridging work are that the first statement becomes a launch pad for a series of credible connecting events ending exactly at the last statement. In the end the two statements form the beginning and end of a seemingly indivisible narrative unit. The story has detail, connectivity, transition and flow to carry us along convincingly for the ride over the bridge.

Bridging in OCD

A bridging process occurs in OCD reasoning and it works on the same lines, using the same processes as in the bridging game. However, in the case of OCD the link is between a certain perception and a doubt. Furthermore, the two statements contradict each other. However the OCD story links them together.

My door locked fine.
But it could be open.

OCD bridging story:
My door locked fine but there could be a fault in the lock. Doors do get left open, I can't see the lock mechanism, so it could still be open.

The client can begin the alternative story by using the bridging technique noted earlier but changing the two statements.

My hands look clean.
So I'm perfectly safe not to wash.

The alternative bridging story could go like 'Because my senses tell me they are clean and I have no proof otherwise, I'll accept they are clean just like in other walks of life, so ...' The client may be anxious initially that she or he is expected to construct a complex and convincing story straight away. In fact, the best way to construct the story is phrase by phrase, whereby the client adds elements daily which gradually take the form of a narrative.

As an example, here is the case of a client developing an alternative story about locking the door. The first element connecting the statements:

I locked the door with my key.
I have no need to check it further.

might be

... and I heard or saw nothing wrong.

Later the client may add:

Everything was as usual and nothing strange occurred.

Later the client may embellish details:

... the lock is sturdy and has never failed to function.

Building Up the Alternative Story

The alternative story is all about bringing home the imaginary nature of the OCD story by creating alternative possibilities.

Once the client has mastered the reasoning and rhetorical devices in the construction of the OCD story, these same devices can be knowingly employed to construct an alternative story. The end result is for the person to experience a small change in conviction and anxiety regarding the OCD story as a result of constructing and rehearsing the alternative story.

The important criteria are that the alternative story incorporates elements antagonistic to the OCD story to arrive evidently at a non-OCD nondoubting conclusion. The easiest way is for the elements to be based on realistic perceived events and experiences, since by definition these are likely to go against the OCD possibility. However, the client can also use imagination in a positive sense bringing in imagined possibilities which are more aligned with reality if not yet completely real.

Example: My hands look clean. So there's no need to wash them later. I imagine them staying clean since I'm not touching anything dirty. I imagine feeling how clean they are.

Dos and Don'ts of Alternative Narratives

1. The story needs to be built up organically, bit by bit by the client, in following the structure, detail and flow of the OCD story.
2. Content should be drawn from the client's experience and observation to improve credibility.
3. It should not be repeated as an automatism, nor abbreviated for speed.
4. The degree of client absorption should be monitored to ensure credibility.
5. The impact of the client's alternative story on credibility of the OCD story should be monitored.

The impact of the alternative story on the OCD story can be improved by the build up of more and more details. With increased immersion in the alternative story, the absorption in the OCD story will weaken.

The therapist then explores how the client can make a start with practising some of these alternative stories in his or her own environment. In particular, the client should be encouraged to practise alternative stories in situations where the OCD is normally triggered. This should be done *before* the client has crossed over into the imagination. The certainty that is available through the (inner) senses needs to be identified in each of these situations.

The importance of incorporating reality-based information into these alternative stories should be discussed as well, including the appropriate use of the senses during alternative exercises.

Rehearsal

It is essential for the client that the alternative story is built up and rehearsed, but the aim is not to replace the OCD story, rather to dislodge the OCD story as the client's default option, so it is not there in the back of the mind the whole time, just waiting to spring up. However we do not want a rote repetition but rather a reflective recounting of the alternative story until it becomes almost well rehearsed. At that point the OCD story will become less accessible. This will take a little time (perhaps a few days).

The important mission for the therapist is to help the person develop the ability of creating stories and in particular building up a rich alternative story. The client, through this exercise, should then understand that the OCD story is just a story and that it gains its power as a good story. The grip the OCD has over the client is due to the rhetorical power of the story. The client understands that their conviction and commitment to OCD were literally just due to a story.

This insight is important since it dispels the notion that the client has a deep seated, intransigent OCD belief. Rather the client realizes it is only by repeating, even by default, the OCD story that the person maintains the obsession. The point then is for the client to compare the created alternative story with the OCD story and see the similarities. The alternative story is just a way of understanding the OCD story. It is not intended as a foil or as a counter to the OCD story. The idea is not that the client starts repeating the story every time the OCD story comes along, but that the person uses the experience of the alternative story and his or her understanding of the narrative process to dismiss the OCD story as just another story.

Decision Chart

Proceeding to the Next Step in Therapy

- The client is able to create alternative story.
- The client accepts that OCD is just a story.
- Immersion and anxiety about the OCD story begin to decrease.

Dialogue

The following transcript illustrates realization of the OCD story as a story:

T: We've seen that the OCD, even if it can be very invasive, is very selective. What do you think this means?

C: That it focuses on very specific problems. Me, for example, I'm afraid of contamination but not by just anything, very specifically through chemical products linked to insecticides.

T: Exactly. You reason one way concerning insecticides and another way concerning other potential contaminants. Why's that?

C: It's a story. There's an obsessional story for the insecticide but not for the other contaminants.

T: Right. For the other contaminants, as in the rest of daily life, there is no OCD story so you use your senses. It's easy for you to trust your senses: there's no competition. But for the insecticides, it's cut-throat competition. Your senses are giving you information as always, but the OCD comes in with its ever-ready false story in a very loud voice.

C: Yes, I certainly try to ignore it but sometimes it's really convincing.

T: Absolutely. OCD is very skilled at turning direct information around and leading you into the world of possibilities. But you can be equally creative. Remember how you convincingly made up a story about a substance which initially you didn't fear.

C: Yes I remember the bacteria *E. coli* and how you can catch it from tap water.

T: But in reality you're not at all preoccupied by *E. coli*.

C: No, not at all.

T: But you made up a very believable story which supported the possibility that the water from your tap was contaminated.

C: Yes but I knew I made it up.

T: OK, but OCD invents stories in the same vein. Compare the OCD story with the one you invented. Do you see similarities in the arguments?

C: Yes. In both cases there is the use of common knowledge that substances or bacteria exist. There are also what you termed logical calculation, arguments from authority and 'received wisdom'.

T: So the two stories are composed of the same type of arguments. We can in both cases also identify the reasoning devices used to make the doubt seem real. The processes are the same. OCD always functions in the same way to make a possibility seems credible. That said, what conclusion can be drawn about the validity of your OCD story?

C: Well, it's not 'truer' or more believable than the one I invented.

T: Exactly. You have no more reason to fear being contaminated by insecticides than by *E. coli* bacteria. In both cases you can trust your senses. There is no need to rely on a story, no matter how convincing.

Client Worksheet 9
A Different Story

You saw earlier how the OCD convinces you to doubt by creating a story. The story is made up of a sequence of reasons or justifications as to why you should doubt. The strength of the argument lies largely in the fact that it is a story, not a sequence of events. The importance of viewing the argument as a story is that as a story it has considerable power because it does more than just state facts. It is dynamic, it moves us along from a starting point to an end point and it's like a journey where we pass all manner of images and events on the way.

The Candid Camera

Suppose I pick up a pen and try to convince you the pen is really a secret camera. I could just state this pen is a camera and discuss the make and type of camera. This statement on its own might not be too convincing. But suppose I relate a story about it being built in the same factory as James Bond's special car. How the developer won a prize for his work. It was tested in field trials in different situations. Finally it was patented and is now in general use as a spy pen.

Now all I have done here is to connect up a series of statements and observations in a sequence to make them more believable. One piece of the story 'piggybacks' onto the next piece and so on, until there is an accumulation of experiences supporting the idea. Also one begins to live in the story. The lived-in feeling comes from a number of devices. Firstly there is the dynamic aspect of 'moving along' in the story. Secondly there is the detail of the scenery as you go past it. The richer the scenery and the descriptive detail, the more it is lived in. also there is feeling of being immersed in the story and the detachment from everyday life, which allows the imagination free rein. You not only conjure up images and transitions as the story moves you along, but also build the scenes in your imagination and make the events seem even more vivid, personal and meaningful. So you become immersed or absorbed in the reality of your story. As you go off into the imagination, what at the outset might have appeared completely impossible now appears almost logical.

For example, let's take a ludicrous example, a flying pig with you between its trotters. It could never happen . . . but let's build up a story. . . .

The Flying Pig

Your friend is working for an experimental genetic laboratory where the scientists have been working some time on mating birds and mammals.

They've succeeded with rats and doves, and they are moving up the evolutionary scale. There have been several popular films exploring the idea of mutant humans and of course there was Dolly the cloned sheep, so who know what is possible. Right! So when you arrive at the laboratory, your friend tells you his team have mated an eagle with a pig. One of the testing criteria is assessing the load the mutant animal can take, and your friend asks if you would take turns as a volunteer to be transported by the flying pig over the local town. See how absorbing it is!

I'm No Good at Stories

You may say, 'But I'm not too good at creating stories' or 'I have no imagination'. But as we have seen, you have built up and lived in an OCD story which was essentially imaginary. Now it's time to use that same imagination creatively to your advantage. In following the steps in the exercises, you will find the resources to build up the story and feel the effects of immersion in the story. This exercise will allow you to understand exactly how the OCD works its bad magic on you!

Client Exercise Sheet 9
A Different Story

John's story about why he doubts his door is locked

Well, I always worry about the door being properly locked. I close it very carefully, paying attention to every action. The click of the latch, the resistance of the door when I push it shut. But I still doubt if it's really closed. I think of a door I once saw swing open after the person thought they'd locked it, and well I'm not an expert on locks and some can spring open automatically. My friend had a garage door once which just opened in the middle of the night. Mind you that was an electric lock. When I test the door, it seems shut but I don't know how shut is shut. I mean how much movement is allowed. Of course, if I was robbed because I left it open, I'd feel terrible.

John's story is a good example of an OCD story justifying the doubt. Now the first point to note is that all of the reasons given by John relate to other times and other places. None relates to what he is observing in the here and now. Obviously the story can't be relating to the here and now because his senses say all is OK in the 'here and now'. But he feels justified in drawing on events he has heard about second-hand, connecting up completely different events and imagining sequences. However, these all make him 'doubt' what he is actually seeing in the here and now.

Do you think John is justified in doubting because of these reasons? You might say yes because sometimes we need to rely on our 'intelligence', 'know how', or 'memory' despite the fact that these came from us, not from the outside. For example, if I've read somewhere that one area of a town I'm visiting is dangerous, I might be wise to avoid it even though I have no evidence in the 'here and now' that it is dangerous. If I know from experience that every time I leave the house with more than three accessories, I'm likely to lose one of them, it may be a good idea to take precautions even though there is nothing lost in the here and now. If I know I'm prone to slip on ice, then it might be sensible to watch out when I walk on ice even if I've not already fallen. All these 'reasons' for caution are valid. This is because either they are based on real information from outside sources applicable to the here and now, or *I* myself have had direct *experience* of them in *identical* situations. The reasons do not come from second-hand information, hearsay and invented stories.

Now let's return to John and then to the justification for your own OCD doubt. Is John's story based on facts *related* to the here and now or on justifications *remote* from the here and now? Don't forget, *relevant* means that your intelligence about what could be there is drawn from evidence, authority or experience based directly and immediately on the current case.

Try this exercise. Say which of the following statements is based on the *direct evidence*. 'Maybe the door is locked because . . .'

1. 'This lock is old and sometimes jams and fails (in reality) to lock the door'.
2. 'I read about someone who left the door open'.
3. 'It could be a statistical probability that I leave the door open'.

Which one justifies the doubt in the here and now?

'Maybe the door knob is contaminated because . . .'

4. 'Microbes exist, so my hands could be contaminated'.
5. 'I touched a knob which I saw had mud on it'.
6. 'It's common knowledge you can catch germs from other people'.

Again, which one justifies the doubt in the here and now?

The correct answers are 1 and 5 only. Were your answers correct?

So let's try building up your alternative story along the bridging game lines. First we start with your sense observation. I see the car door locked. I know it's locked because my senses say so, and whenever I lock it I always do so correctly. It's a good door lock, it's never been faulty and there's no reason to think it's faulty now. So I'm going to shop, and when I come back it will be locked. How do you feel now about your doubt?

_____

_____

_____

OK. Now return to the story and fill in even more detail. For example: I remember how the door stayed locked even in cold weather, and when I had a bump I can't remember the lock ever jumping open. For it to not to be locked after I locked it, there would need to be some major unheard-of problem. How do you feel now about the initial doubt?

_____

_____

_____

Just to be sure, go back one more time and try to add in any other details you may remember which could enrich and add density to the story. Remember that the elements can be from experience, common sense or realistic conclusions.

So now note down your own final detailed alternative story:

_____

_____

_____

_____

_____

It's the Way You Tell 'Em

Other devices which can help you tell a good story include:

- *Richness in detail*: Part of the immersion comes from absorption in details of the story. The richer and more nuanced the details, the more credible.
- *Smooth transport*: The second is the transporting nature of stories which seem to take you along with them on a journey. All stories travel from A to B on a seemingly credible route.
- *You are along for the ride*: The third element is that you are in the stories. It's not just a third person narration like listening to a audio-book read by a famous actor.
- *It's personal*: A fourth element is the personalization of the happenings around you and that the key transition points are dramatic and meaningful and touch you emotionally. You can use the first person.."I"
- *Imagination*: A fifth point is the use of the imagination where, of course, anything can happen and very powerfully.

Client Training Card 9
A Different Story

Learning Points

- We all create stories about our lives and ourselves.
- These stories are convincing and rich in detail, the more they are lived in.
- Stories can transport our feelings and beliefs.
- Stories define who we are and where we are going.
- Changing our stories changes how we live in our world.

Practice Card

- Be aware more and more during the day when you are telling and relying on stories.
- In particular, it's important to be aware of stories about the self some of which may not be factual and therefore not true.
- If the OCD story comes along, catch it as it leaves reality, wind it back to the start and change its detail, point by point, by replacing the OCD argument with an opposite counter-point. Reinforce your alternative arguments with a fact or observation derived from reality. If necessary expand on the alternative story by adding bits which lead to an alternative conclusion. Finally, rehearse out loud the alternative story . . . as a story. Measure the effect the story has on the credibility of the OCD story and how much you believe it is a story, not a fact.

After you've rehearsed your alternative story, indicate your responses to the following statements on the scale of 0 to 10.

- I believe my OCD story is a fact.

Not at all   Definitely
0_____ 10

- I believe in spite of all these exercices that my OCD story is the most credible story.

Not at all   Definitely
0_____ 10

- I realize my OCD story is just a story like any other.

Not at all   Definitely
0_____ 10

Client Quiz 9
A Different Story

(Please check all answers which apply)

1. The alternative story is . . .
   - ○ to replace the OCD story.
   - ○ to highlight the storied nature of the OCD.
   - ○ to create another obsession.
   - ○ to go off into the imagination for no reason.

2. The story needs to be . . .
   - ○ made up straight away.
   - ○ built up bit by bit.
   - ○ taken from somewhere else.
   - ○ be mechanical.

3. The story needs to be . . .
   - ○ rehearsed reflectively.
   - ○ learnt by rote.
   - ○ read to me by someone else.
   - ○ left in a drawer.

4. The story makes me aware that . . .
   - ○ the OCD story is just a story.
   - ○ the OCD story is telling me the truth.
   - ○ you can't believe anything.
   - ○ I'm a good politician.

5. The story is repeated as . . .
   - ○ a simple phrase.
   - ○ a series of statements.
   - ○ a tape recording.
   - ○ a narrative.

6. In order to be convincing, the alternative story . . .
   - ○ includes many realistic details.
   - ○ relates to strange experiences or observations.
   - ○ avoids all speculation.
   - ○ is written or heard in the third person.

Please check your answers by referring to the Quiz Answers Sheet provided by your therapist.

"Just **double** checking the lamp is switched off, dear."

Cartoon 12. Where's the sense?

Chapter Twelve

Tricks and Cheats of the OCD Con Artist

Tricks and Cheats of the OCD Con Artist

In one of the final steps-step 10 in the therapy-the therapist helps the client reinforce and consolidate the primary message of IBT that obsessional doubt has nothing to with reality in the here and now. The client's failure to recognize the subjective and imaginary nature of the obsession is almost always due to the obsessional story, which makes it appear that the obsession does have something to do with reality. Specifically, the OCD uses several rhetorical reasoning devices to make an imaginary possibility seem like a realistic probability. These reasoning devices are part of the OCD story in the form of various reasoning and imaginative *processes* which add credibility to the obsession.

The Implication of the Reasoning Devices

In this chapter, we review the various reasoning devices feeding inferential confusion. The devices are illustrated in the Figure 12.1. Each of these inputs has already been addressed in previous steps. The aim here is to highlight devices to which the client may be susceptible in order to increase awareness of their role in OCD reasoning. Category errors, irrelevant associations and apparently comparable events are about mismatching objects, events, activities. Conceptual blending similarly blends obsessional thinking and behaviour with an innocuous or virtuous concept which in reality is totally distinct. Distrust of the senses and reliance on possibility are the core

Clinician's Handbook for Obsessive-Compulsive Disorder: Inference-Based Therapy, First Edition.
K. O'Connor and F. Aardema.
© 2012 John Wiley & Sons, Ltd. Published 2012 by John Wiley & Sons, Ltd.

Figure 12.1 Radial diagram of reasoning and imaginative processes giving rise to inferential confusion.

components of inferential confusion. These inputs include ideas about going deeper into reality, selective use of the facts and of the senses (e.g stories). Absorption in the imaginary sequence creates a reality value to the obsession, leading the client to feel and live the consequences, dispute with obsessions as thought it was credible, and use testing and neutralization behaviours. The reasoning devices may represent discrete operations in formal logic and heurisitics but it is unnecessary for the therapist and client to finely differentiate between them and they can be grouped under common headings. The important thing to keep in mind here is that reasoning devices of whatever kind, always make it *appear* the obsession is relevant to reality when it is not. This is best presented in a client-friendly format as 'The Tricks and Cheats of the OCD Con Artist'. It should be conveyed to the client that the OCD has many tricks and cheats up its sleeve tempting the client to go unknowingly beyond reality. Often, the reasoning devices accomplish this in a manner that disallows the client from realizing that she or he has in fact left reality behind. In fact, the OCD will often present going into the imagination as having gone *deeper* into reality, while the opposite is the case. The identification of the reasoning devices only serves to further invalidate the obsession. There is no need for the client or therapist to clearly separate all of the reasoning devices of the OCD except to assist the client in seeing exactly how any one specific reasoning device relevant to the client invalidates the obsession.

The reasoning devices that lead up to obsessional doubt should also be understood as particular process characteristics operating in OCD that are challenged on the basis of irrelevancy to the OCD situation rather than on the basis of their content. In other words, the therapist does not challenge the specific content of the beliefs or thoughts that are contained in the narrative leading up to the obsessional doubt. It is emphasized to the client that all these reasoning devices are subjective and occur either in contradiction or in the absence of sense information and so are not relevant to the 'here and now'. In this chapter, we review the various reasoning devices feeding inferential confusion. The devices are illustrated in the Figure 12.1. Each of these input6s has been addressed during the program. The aim here is to recap on devices where the client may be susceptible to increase awareness of their role in OCD reasoning.

Category errors, irrelevant associations and apparently comparable events are about mismatching objects, events, activities, conceptual blending, similarly blends, obsessional thinking and behaviour with an innocuous or virtuous concept which in reality is totally distinct.

Distrust of the senses and reliance on possibility are the core components of inferential confusion. These inputs include ideas about going deeper into reality, selective use of out of context facts and of the senses.

Absorption in the imaginary sequence creates a reality value to the obsession through feeling the consequences, living the fear. It leads to disputing with the obsession as though it was credible, and to testing and neutralization.

In this step, the therapist explains the most common reasoning errors with specific examples of how they lead to inferential confusion. Generally, it is advisable to first use an OCD story that is neutral to the client since it is less likely to provoke any objections from the client. Afterwards, the therapist can show how at least some of these reasoning devices also apply to the client's OCD narrative story.

If the client has objections to the subjective nature of a particular 'trick' or 'cheat' of the OCD, it is important to view these objections as an opportunity rather than label them as argumentative, controlling or otherwise on the part of the client. These objections originate from the OCD and not the client, and as such, they provide an opportunity to understand the grasp of the OCD rather than challenge a client's resistance.

Inverse Inference

One of the earliest devices we identified in an inference-based approach to OCD was the concept of 'inverse inference' based on clinical observations that people with OCD often employed a reverse kind of reasoning when reaching a conclusion about reality. For example, in the case of contamination, the client with OCD may employ a reasoning such as 'I see the table is clean, but there have been many people sitting here so there may still be dirt on it'. So instead of starting with actual observation based in the senses, and then coming to a conclusion as to the cleanliness of the table, the client with OCD prioritizes their obsessional belief in their own reasoning, and dismisses any sense information that goes against that idea. In turn, this primacy of the obsessional belief in reasoning gives rise to inferential confusion, where the client confuses an imagined possibility with a probability based in the senses. It makes it appear to the client that the obsession or doubt has something to do with reality, although it does not.

Since the identification of inverse inference, we have identified a number of other reasoning and imaginative processes in OCD giving credibility to the obsession. For example, 'category errors' and 'irrelevant associations' often form part of the narrative unit, where the client mixes up two unrelated categories to justify the reality of a particular obsession (i.e. 'My friend once forgot to lock his garage, therefore my garage could be unlocked'). Another related reasoning device would be the use of 'out-of-context facts, where the client wheels in facts into out-of-body story to justify the obsessions even though these facts have nothing to do with the here and now (i.e. 'germs exist, therefore I could be contaminated'). A more complete list is provided in Figure 12.1, which could be given to some clients, although more client-friendly labels and descriptions of most of these devices are available in the accompanying worksheet.

Reinforcement in the Last Steps of Therapy

The identification of the tricks and cheats of the OCD in situations that still pose problems to the client is also one of the last steps of IBT. The resolution of OCD will always lie in explaining to the client that the reasoning devices of the OCD render the obsessional unreal. It should also be clear to the client that *doing* always follows from *knowing*. So each time the client is unable to act in a non-obsessional manner, there is a thought or reasoning device that needs to be identified and resolved. If the client still experiences difficulty, or if progress is slow, it may be necessary to reinforce or repeat certain exercises and worksheets in this process, particularly those relating to reality sensing. There may also be other obsessions that have not yet been addressed. Depending on the degree of generalization across obsessions in the course of treatment so far, it may be necessary to repeat the entire cycle of therapy, or parts thereof.

Client Worksheet 10
Tricks and Cheats of the OCD Con Artist

OCD is a con artist, and a very good one and much better than a standard sales person repeating the same old pattern. OCD is far more dynamic, easily adapting to new situations, using every trick and cheat in the book to make you doubt reality. Just think about it for a moment. The OCD has not benefited you in any way. You feel the consequences of having OCD all the time, and yet, you are still buying its wares. OCD is a con artist and a brilliant one at that.

To stand a chance against the OCD, you will have to begin start seeing through the tricks and cheats of the OCD con artist, identifying them and seeing what's wrong with them and how they strengthen/reinforce your OCD. To do this, the first point to remember is where the tricks and cheats of the OCD are located. They are part of your own OCD story and your inner dialogue in the form of thoughts, beliefs, associations and anything else that makes you doubt. They are those ideas and thoughts that somehow give credibility to your obsessional doubt. The second point to remember is that the *content* of these beliefs, thoughts and facts is not in question. It is about how you apply these thoughts in a situation that is not really relevant, and often in contradiction to reality that matters.

Both these two points are something you have already learned in the previous sessions. The new point, however, is to see how the OCD is often able to get around these other two points by using all manner of tricks and cheats, which nonetheless always come down to the same routine. And seeing how it always comes down to the same routine will help you see through the OCD con artist in a way that would be difficult to do if you were to debate with every little thought association and idea the OCD comes up with. So first point: never argue with the OCD. Better to simply see why what it tells you is unreal and then move on to spend your time on to more interesting things.

The one thing that all of the tricks and cheats of the OCD have in common is that *they make you believe its arguments have something to do with reality but they do not.* Each time you get into the OCD Bubble, the OCD will have accomplished just that. For example, one of the tricks of the OCD is make you believe that you are actually going *deeper* into reality when listening to the OCD. It may tell you for example that you are contaminated, because if you would just look with a microscope, it would be obvious that germs are present. Likewise, it may tell you that the door may not be locked, because the hidden mechanism behind the lock might be broken. Alternatively, if you suffer from pure obsessions, the OCD may tell you, even though there is no evidence, that you have violent impulses. They might be there if only you would go deeper into your mind, into some hypothetical unconscious. In all these instances, the OCD makes it seem you are going deeper into reality, while the opposite is actually the case. Can you see how OCD is one slippery eel?

There are many tricks the OCD uses, but do not let yourself be confused by that. Whatever the trick, the OCD will always try to convince you that your doubt has something to do with reality while it does not. Below we have described some of the many tricks and cheats the OCD uses. See if you are familiar with any of them.

Mismatching

'Mismatching' is a very common trick of the OCD to confuse you. The OCD will often propose all sorts of events that have happened elsewhere, and that happened to someone else in order to make your doubt somehow more credible in the here and now. For example, if you have obsessions about locking the door, the OCD might say something like 'My friend often drives off and forgets to lock his garage door, so mine might also be unlocked'. Or if you were concerned about being poisoned, it might something like 'I heard of a poisoned medicine one time, so my food could be poisoned'. The trick of the OCD is here that it uses all manner of apparently comparable events and irrelevant associations to justify the doubt. It makes it appear as if your doubt is relevant to reality. Yet, none of these are relevant at all to the here and now. There is a *mismatch* between your own actual circumstances and these events. It is like saying you must get rid of your old car, because your friend had a car of the same model and it broke down. Such arguments make no sense when your car is functioning fine. Another aspect of mismatching we have covered in the therapy is blending where OCD blends OCD thinking and behaviour with a sometime 'noble' or 'desired' but unrelated attribute such as 'being perfect', 'ecological', or 'safe'.

Out-of-Context Facts

The OCD is often very selective in how it applies information to your situation. It often comes up with facts, to give credibility to the doubt. For example, the OCD might say something like 'Microbes do exist, so therefore there might be microbes infecting my hand' or 'People die unexpectedly all the time, so I might die now'. Such facts are often not incorrect, which is why they are so powerful in making you take the doubt seriously. However, they still do not have anything to do with reality in the here and now. The facts themselves may be true, but as applied in your situation they are false. These facts are used by the OCD entirely out of context. They have nothing to do with here and now. When the OCD uses out-of-context facts, it actually uses two tricks at once. Not only does it use 'mismatching', but at the same time it uses facts that seem so very true. It's one of the more powerful cheats in the arsenal of the OCD, because it combines two tricks at once. Example: it's a fact that drivers sometimes knock down children, so since I drive a car I could be such a driver.

Living the Fear

One of the nasty tricks of OCD is that it can *simulate* reality, as if there actually was sense information in the here and now that justifies the doubt. This is because the story of the OCD can be so convincing that you actually begin to experience the story 'as if' it was real with all the physical feelings. But just because you are able to feel something does not make it real. For example, if the OCD convinces you that you are ill, then you might actually start feeling nauseous and weak. Or, alternatively, if the OCD convinces you that you might be sexual deviant, then you might imagine being like a sexual deviant so vividly that it makes you feel like you are one. Under these circumstances, it can be difficult to tell what is real and what is not. The key to remember here is that these feelings come *after* you started to doubt and worry. They are the result of your doubt, not the cause of it. They are not real even if it seems like they are.

Going Deep

The OCD is not deep even though it may present itself this way. Often, the OCD tries to go beyond reality by making it seem it is going deeper into reality, while in fact the opposite is the case. It always takes you away from reality. For example, as we mentioned earlier, the OCD might try to justify that your hands are contaminated and that there are germs on your hands by suggesting that if you would look with a microscope, it would be obvious that you are contaminated. But such arguments do not go deeper into reality but deeper into your imagination. So when the OCD presents you with something that seems deep, realize that the opposite is the case. OCD is actually quite superficial.

Reverse Reasoning

Upside-down reasoning is a key trick of the OCD, which is also often part of the many of the other cheats it uses. Normally, when we reason, we start with an observation in reality, and then come to a conclusion about what is there. So for example, if you see a door hinge coming loose, you might justifiably doubt whether or not the door is locked properly. The OCD often turns this reasoning completely upside down. It starts with an idea, or fact, and then comes to a conclusion about what is there. It is a bit of a bullying approach where reality does not come into the picture at all. For example, it might say, 'People must have walked on this floor, therefore it is dirty'. This is similar to saying, 'Cars break down all the time, therefore mine is probably broken as well'.

Distrust of the Senses or Self

The most frequently used trick of the OCD is that it makes you distrust your senses or your own self. It is the lifeblood of the OCD. If you trust in your senses or your own self, the OCD cannot exist. The obsession simply makes no sense if you were to take reality into account. Yet, the OCD will always try to convince you that you need to leave the world of the senses behind, and find resolution to a problem that is not really there.

Double Jeopardy

This is a nasty trick whereby the OCD gets you not because you tried to ignore it but exactly because you obeyed it. The principle here is that the OCD gets you if you do and if you don't. So for example you might go back and check that the light was switched off because OCD said it might not be. Now you're feeling reassured because it was off (as your senses and common sense told you all the time) but not for long. OCD now comes in with 'Ah, it was OK before you checked it, but now after you've checked it you may have made it unsafe'. Cheeky eh!

Again, We Come Back to Testing it Out

A con trick that we brought to your attention before is for the OCD to provoke a testing behaviour. For example, Matthew fears he may secretly enjoy pornography which he finds morally objectionable. So he seeks out photos to test himself. Then OCD says ... aha, you must be perverted just to look at the photos. Sneaky O'Seedy, eh!

Let's Discuss It

Another trick is for the OCD to invite you to discuss and consider your doubt or questioning as a way of resolving it. You start to doubt your competence in the face of knowledge of your competence. But just as you are about to dismiss it, OCD jumps in with 'Well, we really should consider this doubt, what does it mean, how it can be resolved. Let's consider it together and turn it over ... and over ... and over ... etc.'

We alert you to all of these tricks above so that you can spot the OCD con not by trying to argue with it, but by simply seeing how its tricks make your doubts irrelevant and false.

But maybe this time...

Another OCD argument to be avoided is the 'yes, but maybe this time the doubt is founded'. Whatever the OCD has predicted in the past has never materialized. Normally this fact would be sufficient for you to have no more dealings with OCD. Afterall, if every appliance you bought from a shop was broken, you would probably not buy anymore. However, OCD with its trademark 'maybe' gets to you with 'well maybe this time'. But since this 'maybe' resembles all the other false 'maybe' in the past, there is no reason to treat it differently.

But maybe later...

In a similar vein OCD may threaten consequences not immediately but later. This distant threat poses a particular problem with superstitious obsessions where the client may be convinced that a catastrophe could befall them not now but weeks, months or years ahead. Clearly the threat cannot be disproved by reality testing since it is in the future. However this 'maybe later' is an obsessional doubt construed in exactly the same way as other obsessional doubts and hence is equally irrelevant.

"The Gazette 1989..Travel Section..pg. 56? Yes, I have it. I knew it would be useful one day...but, er...where is it?"

Cartoon 13. The useful hoard.

Decision Chart

Proceeding to the Next Step in Therapy...

- The client understands the reasoning devices that can trick them into believing OCD.
- The client can identify these device in the client's own obsessional reasoning.
- The client is aware how to detect the tricks and treats as they occur.

Client Exercise Sheet 10
Tricks and Cheats of the OCD Con Artist

The goal of this exercise is for you to learn how to better identify and counter the tricks and cheats of the OCD. Remember, you never argue with the OCD. Rather than analyzing the relative merits of an OCD argument it is better to see how the argument is flawed right from the start. Remember, there is not even a small likelihood that the arguments for the doubt may be correct, due to the particular way this doubt comes about. The obsessional story takes you away from reality, which makes the OCD always irrelevant and false *even if* it is possible in a very abstract sense. If you still have problems with this idea, then you will need to address this issue with your therapist.

Now, take your OCD story, and note each sentence or partial sentence in your story. Each of those sentences contain a specific trick or cheat the OCD uses to convince you it is real. Next, using the accompanying worksheet, write down which of the tricks or cheats apply to each sentence in your story. First write down the trick or cheat that best applies. Often, other tricks and cheats will apply as well, which you can write down as second or third.

To make this a bit easier, first look at the following example, given previously, of someone who thinks her hands could be dirty and so she must wash her hands:

Example 1

So, I say to myself: Well, my kids were playing outside and like I know it's dirty outside. I've seen the dirt on pavements and I think they may have touched something dirty.

Selective out-of-context facts (over-reliance on possibility)

They picked up something from the street, dirty paper or dog shit, and then I say well if they're dirty then I'm going to be dirty.

Mismatching (category error)

And I'm going to make the house dirty, and I imagine the house dirty and me with my dirty hands, so I start to feel dirty.

Absorption in the imagination (living the fearful consequences)

So I go in and wash and I can't stop, you know, it's like a voice in my head, saying over and over again, you're dirty, even though you're washing and you see nothing you could still be dirty.

Distrust of senses (living the fear)

How quickly were you able to dismiss the different elements in this contamination story? Were you able to see how each of the tricks and cheats of the OCD applied here? If the story was different from your own, then you should have been fairly easily able to dismiss it as irrelevant and wrong. And this is of course what you are also striving for with your own OCD story. So try to do the same thing and write down each of the tricks and cheats that apply to the separate elements in your own story.

In addition, the exercise on your training card focuses on real-life situations where you find yourself having a doubt. Each time an obsession or doubt occurs, you will be asked to (1) uncover the trick and cheat of the OCD underlying the doubt, (2) see how this trick makes the doubt irrelevant and wrong, (3) remember your alternative non-OCD story to replace the obsessional doubt, and (4) dismiss the doubt. The whole exercise should last no longer than 1–2 minutes each time. Don't forget, the OCD would want you to think it over, one more time, two more times . . . three . . . and it will never be enough. If you find yourself doing that, then the OCD has already lured you into OCD land with yet another trick. Eventually however, you will be able to see them all, at which point the OCD will give up all together.

Client Training Card 10
Tricks and Cheats of the OCD Con Artist

Learning Points (Front)

- OCD uses tricks and cheats to make it *appear* that your obsession has something do with reality while it only takes you further away from reality.
- The tricks and cheats of the OCD include *mismatching, living the fear, out of context facts, reverse reasoning, double jeopardy, testing it out, going deep and a distrust of the senses (or self)*.
- Your non-obsessional story brings you closer to what is really there since it is in accord with reality.
- Seeing through the tricks and cheats of the OCD con artist will make the OCD disappear.

Daily Exercise (Back)

- Each time an obsessional doubt occurs, identify the specific trick and cheat that gave rise to the doubt.
- Realize how this trick makes the doubt false and irrelevant.
- Imagine vividly how the situation would feel like if the non-OCD story applies.
- Let go of the obsessional doubt after you recounted the non-OCD story. It is the only thing that is real.

Client Quiz 10
Tricks and Cheats of the OCD Con Artist

(Please check all answers which apply)

1. The tricks and cheats of the OCD are . . .
   - o unconvincing.
   - o part of your OCD story.
   - o too difficult to catch.
   - o none of the above.

2. Mismatching can consist of . . .
   - o matching up two different unrelated categories.
   - o an irrelevant association.
   - o using out-of-context facts in your OCD story.
   - o all of the above.

3. Living the fear . . .
   - o can overwhelm you emotionally.
   - o makes it difficult to tell the difference between reality and imagination.
   - o occurs after you have already begun to doubt.
   - o all of the above.

4. Going deeper into reality . . .
   - o reveals the true nature of reality.
   - o is just another OCD trick to remove you further from reality.
   - o makes your OCD more profound.
   - o all of the above.

5. Blending occurs when . . .
   - o a positive term is mixed up with an OCD behaviour.
   - o you agree with the OCD.
   - o you perform a series of rituals.
   - o you disguise your OCD.

6. To counter the OCD con artist . . .
   - o you look at its arguments from every angle.
   - o you see how the arguments do not relate to reality in here and now.
   - o you argue as best as you can with it.
   - o none of the above.

Please check your answers by referring to the Quiz Answers Sheet provided by your therapist.

Chapter Thirteen

The Real Self

The Real Self

In this step -step 11 in therapy-the therapist show how OCD does a good job of hiding or denying the client's real self. In particular following inferential confusion, OCD may define the self by who the client could be rather than who the client is. The key points for the clients in this step 11 of the therapy are:

1) building up authentic self-attributes
2) constructing a positive self-theme
3) basing future plans and actions on the authentic self
4) comparing the real and OCD constructed self

The real self is the person the client is in reality, and is revealed by exercises designed to describe real attributes in the everyday world.

The client has already learned about the OCD self and how OCD has tricked him or her into believing they could be someone they are not or fear to be. The complement of this knowledge is to know the authentic self and begin to plan actions and thoughts in line with the authentic self, not the OCD self.

This part of the therapy can be introduced as 'Now we will find out who you really are'. Sometimes when asked to describe themselves, people with OCD will be stuck, often repeating superficial descriptions or describing themselves in terms of their OCD. Sometimes the client will identify strongly with the OCD or be under the impression they have no self and need to lose the OCD and start from scratch in

Clinician's Handbook for Obsessive-Compulsive Disorder: Inference-Based Therapy, First Edition.
K. O'Connor and F. Aardema.
© 2012 John Wiley & Sons, Ltd. Published 2012 by John Wiley & Sons, Ltd.

constructing a self. It is important to put the person at ease and insist that actually who they are is just a question of observing what they think or do in everyday life. The notion of repositioning the self can be introduced through a metaphor of changing seats or positions to change the observation point in order to better observe a spectacle.

Most clients will have a hard time coming up with positive self-attributes. A lot of self-perception will be based around the fact that they have OCD. It's well worth emphasizing to the clients that they have many other traits besides OCD and helping them to identify all the activities and accomplishments they can do and have done despite the OCD.

Who You Really are ... and Who You are Not

The OCD possible self is a negative empty self, and it is important to start by filling up the client's empty self. Most clients with OCD have difficulty describing positive traits; they are more in tune with who they are not. They tend to report the narrative behind why they could be this disordered unhappy person whom they fear.

It is important to reposition the clients towards who they really are by linking everyday actions to what sort of person this means they are. Clients often feel they have to reveal heroic traits, but all we want are everyday building blocks.

The clients authentic self can be contrasted with the OCD constructed negative self to pinpoint exactly why they can never be or become the self whom they fear, since this self goes against the real self.

The authentic self is essentially revealed through mundane prompts about everyday life such as:

o   Do you wait in line?
o   Have you opened the door for someone?
o   Do you offer to help?
o   Do you keep your word?
o   Do you have friends and are you kind to them?
o   Do you appreciate good food and the like?

These questions concerning everyday life allow the client to build up through their actions a picture of the client who they are in reality. This then becomes a self-narrative. So the therapist might elicit an action from the client and then turn it around to reflect the type of person who would do this action. The therapist can help the client to begin to construct the real self as follows.

'Now let's look at who you really are. No heroic traits or feats are required. No noble Shakespearian qualities, just a repertoire of who you are which we build up from ... well ... who you really are and how you think and behave. We're not interested in perfect or ideal selves. Just the type of person you really show yourself to be in the real world. So, do you constantly make mistakes? Do you buy people gifts? Do you open doors or give up your seat for older people? Do you constantly forget dates or jobs? Are you a completely indifferent to all around you?

If you wait in line, then we can infer you are a patient person.
If you open doors, you are a polite person.
If you sometimes forget dates or jobs, then you are just like anyone else.
... And so on.'

The therapist can practise with the client building up self-attributes until the client is able to recognize their attributes and translate them into personhood.

In order to acheive this it can be helpful for the client to write an autobiography, recounting in particular how their positive attributes helped them in life.

It is also useful to start planning future actions with the client on the basis of their newly (re)-found authentic self.

The therapist will also be helping the client to reconnect with authentic feelings and recognize desires, needs and emotional reactions without denying them.

To remember recent moments when the client received compliments from others and to try to relive the moments briefly and experience again the pleasant sensation associated with the compliment.

It may be important for the therapist to point out to the client that acceptance of the positives is key. The client should be discouraged from dismissing the positive by saying:

- Everybody has qualities so that doesn't count.
- So what? What use is it?
- Or qualifying the positive with: 'Maybe, but ...'

Self-Components

In the same way that OCD has led the client to distrust the senses, it also leads the client to distrust the self. In both cases what could be trumps sense of self as shown in the complementary diagrams below.

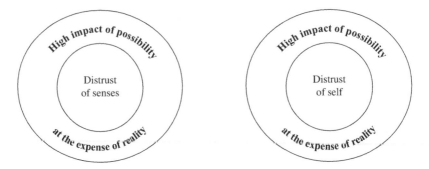

There are two related main components to inferential confusion applied to self.

1. Distrust of self (cognitive component).
2. High impact of possible self over the real self (imaginative component).

Inferential confusion of the self leads to an over-reliance in OCD of who the client could be, or more precisely who the client fears she or he could become if the person does not take OCD precautions (safety behaviours, compulsive rituals and other neutralizations). The central self focus in OCD then is not on the self as is but on the self as could be. This is illustrated in the diagrams below.

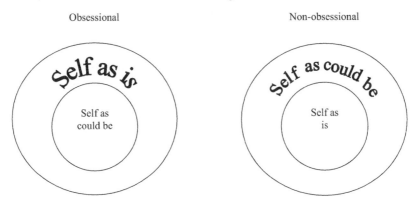

Self-Feelings

Reconnecting with authentic self-feelings is a key part of reconstructing the real self. The client will likely have ignored or suppressed real feelings or desires due to the persistent doubt created by the OCD self. The client may complain of having no experience of feelings. Assuming the client does not suffer from alexithymia, the therapist can coach the client in noticing feelings with reference to bodily sensations. Starting with feelings of hunger and warmth, the therapist can progress to detection of more complex feelings and sensations.

Obstacle

The therapist may meet with the following obstacle. The client protests that he or she really is not in touch with feelings.

C: I don't know what my real feelings are.
T: Do you know when you are hungry or when you
   want to go to the toilet?
C: Yes.
T: Well, you are also able to detect finer emotions such as affection and desire
   to please. The OCD has simply led you, in certain areas of your life, to distrust
   these feelings and even deny them.

Now recall how you felt when you really desired something, when you really intended to act. Try to connect with the spontaneous thoughts and feelings which arise.

Decision Chart

The Client Is ready to proceed to the Next Step When . . .

- The client has listed and recognized authentic positive attributes of self and identified authentic self feelings.
- The client has realized that the authentic self is different from the attributes of the self that OCD was saying he or she would become.
- The client has at least accepted the need to reposition themselves towards the world based on seeing and planning projects in the light of the authentic self.

Client Worksheet 11
The Real Self

You have become familiar with the idea that OCD created an illusionary self which it said you might become: The feared self. The real self is marginalized by a focus on this feared self you think you could become. This feared self led you to take all sorts of precautions and to doubt your ability because you genuinely believed the OCD. But the OCD self was just another story and the possibility can be pushed aside. Now you need to establish your real self so it can move to the centre of your being. On the basis of your vulnerable self-theme, identified at step 4 in Chapter 6, write here the self whom OCD made you fear you could become.

e.g. I feared being negligent
     I feared being a moleste
     I feared being inferior

The OCD Feared Self

The OCD self was really centred on who you were not, and with that perception goes many negative ways of viewing the self. These include things like: always comparing yourself to others to your disadvantage, never accepting positive comments and refusing to accept you possess any worth-while qualities. Here in this worksheet, you can practise changing these ideas which will help you to build up an authentic self (an authentic, not idealist or egoist, self).

When comparing ourselves with others, it's important to learn to compare in many dimensions and to focus on the positives.

o   I'm not as good as him.
o   I'm not as strong as him.

One-Dimensional World

We usually judge others as better on only one dimension: she is better than I; he is sharper than me. But in fact everyone is multidimensional. We are all defined by our work, our roles and our values. Everyone is unique and not limited to just one dimension. Another obstacle is to be continuously comparing yourself on abilities you do not possess. No one ever got a job based on a CV full of attributes the person does not possess: 'I'm not good at X', 'I've no talent for Y', so when you start to think negatively about yourself, e.g 'I'm no good at X, I've no talent for Y', counter-balance with a number of positive qualities that you really possess. Possessing a real sense of self not only grounds you in who you really are but also brings other benefits. You are much less likely to worry over small incidents where things went wrong. You feel able to take your place in the world, feel pride about yourself, and weather criticism and bad moments.

Real Desires

Recognizing your real self and attributes also puts you more in touch with your real desires. You may have been living a life of shame and self-denigration because of your OCD. You may often have felt your own wishes and needs are not important or can be sacrificed because you don't deserve otherwise. Now you can follow your real heart and desires in your life-projects.

Client Exercise Sheet 11
The Real Self

Note a series of everyday actions you performed today:

_____

_____

_____

Now focus on the positive qualities each of these actions requires:

_____

_____

_____

So putting all these qualities together . . . *who are you?*

_____

_____

_____

Feeling who you are

There are a number of sources we refer to in order to know who we are. Obviously our observations of our performance in activities are important. But as we noted previously, knowing and recognizing our real feelings are other sources. OCD is very good at convincing you to not trust your senses. You can end up doubting if you really feel an urge to do something or not. This is because the doubt intercedes and disrupts the line of communication. An important part of knowing who you are is accepting your feelings and desires. This means you need to recognize when you have a real intention, inclination and desire for something. Avoid reflecting on what you might or could have felt. Your real desires are the authentic you, not OCD, in the same way you now know that your real activities and accomplishments are you, not OCD.

Exercise

Whenever you are doing an action, slow down and identify your real feeling and desire in that situation.

_____

_____

_____

How does this real desire, intention or feeling, correspond with what OCD says you might be?

_____

_____

_____

Write an autobiography of yourself emphasizing your accomplishments and positive achievements in life. (Try 500 words to start with)

_____

_____

_____

Think what you would need to have done to become your OCD feared self.

_____

_____

_____

Is there any chance of you really being your OCD feared self?

_____

_____

_____

The Self and Others

Another source of reference as to who you are is other people. But here you must be specific in your questions. Ask your partner or your best friends what are your qualities. You can prompt them if you wish with suggestions. But usually they will volunteer traits on their own. After all, if they are friends, they must see something in you that they like. There will probably be a tendency for them to be on the kind side, so you must ask several sources and ask for examples to back up the qualities they identify.

_____

_____

_____

How do these observed traits match up with the OCD self?

_____

_____

_____

Finally, it is important to list your own dearly held values and principles in life. It's true that we don't always live up to our ideals. But they constitute a part of ourselves and our understanding of who we really are.

My values are (e.g. honesty):

_____

_____

_____

My goals in life are (e.g. to be a good friend):

_____

_____

_____

My principles I try to live by are (e.g. respect people):

_____

_____

_____

Now again compare how these qualities relate to what the OCD would say you are capable of:

_____

_____

_____

Viewing yourself in a nondistorted mirror
What are my strong points?

_____

_____

_____

What do others say about my particular unique qualities?

_____

_____

_____

For what situations, activities or tasks do others thank or congratulate me?

In the home: _____

_____

_____

At work: _____

_____

_____

In personal relations: _____

_____

_____

At leisure: _____

_____

_____

All together, I can say I possess the following positive qualities: _____

_____

_____

A Varied Life

I fulfil a number of roles in life:

_____

_____

_____

Fulfilling these roles makes me proud of myself:

_____

_____

_____

In the past, I have overcome a number of challenges due to my strengths and abilities:

_____

_____

_____

In the future, I can see myself continuing to cope and accomplish what I wish:

_____

_____

_____

This is my self and I'm proud: I have the right to be seen, treated and respected as the person I really am.

_____

_____

_____

It is important you receive feedback from friends and from yourself reinforcing your newfound real self. This means literally going out and being yourself and observing and accepting the benefits. It is important you make time to do activities you enjoy and carry out activities which interest you and stimulate you. Not only do these activities give you pleasure, but also they will reward you and increase your self-confidence. Automatically, if your self-confidence is high, this brings down the hold of the OCD self and helps to ensure your complete recovery.

Client Practice Card 11
The Real Self

Learning Points

Your OCD self is the opposite of your real self.

- Focusing your actions and projects around your real self grounds you in your real resources.
- The OCD self hid who you really are behind a mask that scared you into believing you might be something different.

Practice Card

- Whenever you carry out an activity or receive a compliment, ask yourself, 'What does this say about me, my real authentic self?'
- It may say you are competent or resourceful or at least capable. By contrast, the OCD said you were the opposite.
- So now compare your true attributes as you and others visibly recognize them with your old OCD theme.
- Note here the contradictions.

"oh no! Three 3's in a row..that's bad luck.. I'm not answering it!"

Shane, you didn't answer that call, I picked it up and it was the radio station giving away a free holiday! Bad luck for you, eh?

Cartoon 15. Bad luck.

Client Quiz 11
The Real Self

(Please check all answers which apply)

1. My real self . . .
   - is similar to my OCD self.
   - is often the complete opposite of myself.
   - is an unknown quantity.
   - fluctuates.
2. My knowledge of my real self . . .
   - is built up by observing what I am in real life.
   - is discovered by personality test.
   - is too difficult to find out.
   - is who I assume I am.
3. Sources for discovering my self include . . .
   - knowing my feelings and recognising my abilities.
   - slips in Chinese cookies.
   - the latest brain machine.
   - what I imagine people think of me.
4. When I ask people who I am . . .
   - they will lie to please me.
   - each will see a different person and I'll be confused.
   - they will all be wrong.
   - they may all mention authentic traits which are all different.
5. My authentic self is shown by . . .
   - trusting the OCD.
   - my real goals and values in life.
   - pretending to play another person.
   - reflecting and meditating about the meaning of life.
6. The OCD self . . .
   - is partly true.
   - goes against my real self and camouflages reality.
   - is the person deep down I might be.
   - is a person I might become in the future.

Please check your answers by referring to the Quiz Answers Sheet provided by your therapist.

Chapter Fourteen

Knowing and Doing: Moving On and Preventing Relapse

Letting Go

This chapter the final step - step 12 in therapy -where the client is helped to:

1) move on to a life without OCD
2) identify and deal with lingering OCD-related emotions, and assess the need for acquiring other coping skills
3) prepare a procedure to permit maintaining gains and prevent relapse

The therapist may notice that for some clients it can be difficult to let go completely of certain obsessions. Usually this indicates that the person still gives some, at least minimal, credibility to the OCD story or to the power of the story. In other words, the person has not bought in completely to the IBT model and is trying to have it both ways. If so, then the therapist and client will need to revisit aspects of the therapy to be rediscuss and to uncover the blockage.

The client may subscribe to the 'just in case' idea of keeping the doubt in mind since you never know . . . just that small possibility . . . and so on. The client may also be giving into the doubt simply out of fear of persisting emotion accompanying the obsession. The person has perhaps spent years experiencing days of turmoil if they didn't give into a then credible doubt, leading to intense anguish and avoidance. In this case the therapist and client need to make a distinction between then and now. The client will be able to move quickly past the repercussions in the here and now

---

Clinician's Handbook for Obsessive-Compulsive Disorder: Inference-Based Therapy, First Edition.
K. O'Connor and F. Aardema.
© 2012 John Wiley & Sons, Ltd. Published 2012 by John Wiley & Sons, Ltd.

and, then quickly dismiss the doubt. The fear now is anticipation but an anticipation which is created from past, not actual, experience and the client will find it relatively easy to let it go.

Mastery

In the final steps of therapy the client is developing a sense of mastery to protect gains and give a sense of control over subsequent events. This is based on:

1. Confidence in knowing the IBT model
2. Confidence in current successful control over OCD and in progress towards recovery
3. Experience of change in OCD intensity and associated feelings
4. Experiencing the diminished importance of OCD and its impact on life

In this final step the therapist is also helping the client explore positive aspects of their authentic self, so that he or she can reposition towards goals and aims of life where the client moves forward rather than escapes insecurity. The person is no longer trying to avoid becoming a feared self but rather is embracing their strengths, attributes and virtues in planning actions and activities. Necessarily, OCD vigilance plays less and less part in their life.

Combining IBT with Exposure

Combining IBT with an exposure *in vivo* approach may be indicated for some clients who find themselves able and willing to do the exposure exercises after IBT and where some anxiety may remain even though the obsessional conviction is weak. The client's understanding of the basic principles of exposure and response prevention can help in overcoming unreasonable feelings and anticipations. Exposure, where there is continued emotional or cognitive avoidance, can be useful at the end of therapy. Typically, here, the person may be caught up in how they remember they used to feel when they suffered from the obsession and how they anticipate feeling now.

Example

The example below shows a client who is managing her anticipatory fear. This dialogue is from Mary (see Chapter 2) towards the end of her therapy when her doubts about red being blood were zero and her confidence in not performing compulsive rituals was near 100%, except when anticipating stress or under pressure.

C: So it's when I'm in a hurry or suddenly the doubt's in my face like out of the blue.

T: OK.

C: Yeah and then I'm like . . . oh no . . . I can't let the OCD ruin this meeting or whatever and I know if I just do the ritual . . . and in several seconds I'll be better.

T: But . . .

C: But well I know in the medium term I'm encouraging the OCD, I'm giving it oxygen. But . . .

T: But . . .

C. Well, look, if I don't give it I'm scared. I'm scared I'll get emotional. I won't be able to cope and the doubt's going to be there . . . I dunno how long, maybe days, haunting me.

T: OK, I understand. But on the bright side you've dealt with a lot of the OCD. I mean, like seeing red at the supermarket. What happens there now?

C: Well, I can just go past it. It's true. My husband often remarks that I just carry on in places where, before, I would have had a problem big time.

T: Great. That's real progress. So if we see what's happening really, now you're not experiencing the anxiety and preoccupation you were experiencing beforehand.

C: That's true, but I'm afraid mostly of the emotion. You know how I can get emotional. I mean it sweeps over me. I really hate it.

T: OK. Well firstly as you know the obsession and all the doubt and fear start when you leave reality. That first cast-off point where you go further in your mind from reality.

C: Yeah, I know and I try to always get myself back to ground.

T: Good. So if the doubt is unfounded, the consequences and emotions are also false.

C: Yeah, but they're still there.

T: OK, I see. But emotions can only hang around so long if they're not serving any purpose and you know they're not serving any purpose, don't you?

C: Yeah, it's just a leftover from how I used to be.

T: Well good news, there is a law . . . the law of habituation, which shows that as long as you do nothing to feed it, the emotion will decrease and go away by itself. The more times you don't feed it, the quicker it will disappear.

C: Oh . . . well, that's good news.

T: So we will systematically apply this procedure to instances where you anticipate emotion that you think you might not be able to manage.

But I Still Lack Coping Skills . . .

Generally speaking, the abilities and skills of people with OCD are masked by OCD, and it's important for the therapist to discuss this point with the client. The client notion of a deficit may be OCD driven and part of OCD sales talk. Once clients have mastered reality sensing and repositioned towards the real self, their activities could well function normally. Such a potential outcome should be explored to the client prior to considering whether there is a need for extra training in any skills. The therapist might say:

'We covered in some detail in the last few steps of therapy how the obsessional doubt goes against reality since it is based on imaginary reasoning. So now how do you replace the OCD reasoning? Well, the good news is you already possesses solid resources, notably the senses and common sense. Now you can trust the senses over the OCD and if you catch your imaginary doubt before you cross the bridge, all you have *is* your senses. The trick is to get used to trusting your senses and not doing anything else'. It's a bit like the children's game 'paper, scissors, stone'. Stone always beats scissors, and likewise reality always beats the imagination, if you let it in. So the trick is to wheel back as fast and far as you can to reality . . . where you left your senses . . . and let your real senses take over. You've no need for extra OCD effort.'

The therapist might also explore other non-OCD situations where the client's self and skills work well. It may be that after living in the shadow of doubting the client feels out of practice, and it is appropriate to ask the question, 'Is it deficit or OCD?' In In the same way that the client's real self was always there already and always had been, but was muted by OCD, so the client's coping skills may also be intact.

Continuing to Reposition the Self

A principal aim of IBT is to reposition the self towards the authentic self. This is unlikely to be completely achieved within the 15 to 20 therapy sessions, but is an achievable work in progress in a matter of months.

The repositioning therapy work involves helping the client to:

- Act in accordance with real identity based on real attributes.
- Accord the self positive feedback for all accomplishments (including overcoming OCD).
- Explore activities which promote authentic self view and rely on authentic talents.
- In particular, expose being yourself and relating to with friends, family and colleagues, without fearing negative OCD-driven consequences.

Clearly, once the self is completely repositioned away from the OCD feared identity, the OCD theme is no longer relevant or acted upon. The source of the doubt is resolved.

Keeping Thoughts in Mind

If the client reports that the obsession is still appearing, the client may be subtly maintaining the obsessional thought and it may be important for therapist and client to recap how thoughts can inadvertently be kept alive. The reality is that our thoughts, even the ones we don't want, are really always part of our ongoing consciousness. Thoughts come about in the context of our current being and doing, and they persist since we are maintaining them in our mind because we think they are or might be useful. The person's initial conception of the obsession is usually of an intrusion or what we term a 'fly in the head model', where it seems as though the thought has been injected into them and they can't get it loose. Clients may even literally tap their heads saying, 'How can I get rid of this thought?' or 'If only I could get it out of my head'.

The term intrusion is unhelpful because it gives the false impression of a fly in the head which we need to ignore for it to disappear or be chased out of our minds. If we keep thoughts around, it is because we see a utility to keeping them there. The utility may be obvious or subtle.

Reasons for keeping thoughts alive:

- They're telling me something.
- I better keep an eye on them.
- I want to see if they are still there.
- I need to know if they come back.
- Should I be doing something about them?
- Maybe I need to think them through once and for all.

Recent research has clarified the role of metacognitive motivations to keep thoughts around. Some of these metacognitive motivations are obvious and have been equally applied to worry. A person may feel it is correct to worry, to show seriousness.

The therapy approach here is in line with a model which views thoughts as maintained actively by the person. In OCD, the person creates the doubt and actively nourishes its persistence through thinking and other behaviour. Once the person understands this basic model of thought maintenance, reasons for keeping the thought around come out more clearly. The most frequent reasons seem to be related to importance, security, utility and protection. A second level relates more to 'telling me about my self', 'alerting me to my problem' and 'keeping me from danger'. A third level relates more to 'helping solve the problem', 'keeping it around to go into it' and 'finding out what's at the base of it'. A fourth level seems to be more elusive and often automatic and includes 'checking to see if it's there', 'keeping vigilant in case it appears' and 'keeping an eye on it in the back of my head'. Included here may be counter-productive thought suppression strategies such as deliberately trying not to think of the obsession, or maintaining a blank mind or finding a mental distraction. In sum, if the thought is staying around in the mind, it is being actively maintained either by a persisting credibility or by metacognitive strategy.

A much clearer way of thinking about our thoughts is that they are a form of behaviour and come about as part of our acting in the world. There are all sorts of ways to prime ourselves to have certain thoughts. If we view obsessional doubts as inferences instead of intrusions, then they are arrived at on the basis of reasoning. In other words, the thoughts are effectively conclusions putting into question previously held knowledge.

The person may initially respond in generalities such as 'Well it could happen . . . how do I know?' But again some insistence on why this particular story is possible will bring out more elaborate reasoning. Obviously, one major problem will be how we know the story is not just a post hoc rationalization produced impromptu to cover tracks. The answer to this is that the stories are the context or ground from which the inference arises. We know this since they are consistent, they follow a characteristic reasoning path and changing the story changes the obsessional inference.

Reinforcement in the Last Steps of Therapy

The identification of the tricks and cheats of the OCD in situations that still pose problems to the client is important. The resolution of OCD will always lies in conveying to the client that the reasoning devices of the OCD render the obsession wrong. It should also be clear to the client that *doing* always follows from *knowing*. So each time the client is unable to act in a non-obsessional manner, there is a thought or reasoning device that needs to be identified and resolved. If the client still experiences difficulty, or if progress is slow, it may be necessary to reinforce or repeat certain exercises and worksheets on their therapy, particularly those relating to reality sensing. There may also be other obsessions that have not yet been addressed. Depending on the degree of generalization across obsessions in the course of treatment so far, it may be necessary to repeat the entire cycle of therapy, or some parts of it, while going through the different stages of treatment for these other sobsessions.

Relapse Prevention

The client needs to be aware that relapse prevention is basically assured by continuing to implement the steps of programme. In other words, continue trusting the senses and keep on the reality side of the bridge.

The client should be vigilant for any OCD theme situations which may take them by surprise, in particular when they are unexpected. For example, if the client's theme is to be contaminated unknowingly and the client sits on the train next to someone who seems to have a strange skin disease. The client can apply the exact same steps as always. Where did the doubt come from? Is the client spiralling into imagination? The therapist can cover with the client the procedure for preventing relapse on excercise sheet 12.

Will the client ever be completely free of OCD?

The evaluations we receive from clients generally indicate that the obsession vanishes in different stages. Firstly, the obsessions come along and disappear quicker. Secondly, there is far less emotional reaction. Thirdly, there is increasing recognition of the lack of utility in going into the obsession and of having a firmer grasp on reality.

I've got to take precautions not to hit someone. I'll hunch my shoulders, stuff my hands in my pockets, stare straight ahead, walk stiffly...

Wow! See that weird looking guy? Do you think he could be dangerous?

Cartoon 16. Uptight out-a-sight.

This is the report of a client's experience of dealing with her obsessions 6 months on from successfully completing IBT for ruminative obsessions.

"OK, so the OCD still grabs me . . . but less, much less than before. The anxiety only goes so far . . . it's not right up there like before. It doesn't hang around even days now like it did . . . maybe now a few minutes or at most an hour. The quicker I dismiss it, the less it hangs around. I know full well it's bullshit and I stay calm about it and just move ahead. I don't even start questioning or reflecting on it since I know then I'll be in it. Life is too short . . . I say to myself . . . why do I need to waste my time considering these doubts, nothing ever happened . . . nothing ever will happen . . . so I just let it go".

Decision Chart

The Client Is Ready to Move On If . . .

1. The person has prepared for relapse prevention in the face of future challenges. This will mean the client
    (a) Identified situations or events most likely to provoke difficulties.
    (b) Formulated a plan of action to deal with existing beliefs or emotions.
    (c) Listed concrete ways to improve and receive feedback from friends family and colleagues about the repositioned self.

Cartoon 17. In control.

Client Worksheet 12
Knowing and Doing: Moving On and Preventing Relapse

If you have followed the therapy steps carefully, then you will have made significant inroads into the OCD and you will have noted changes. Now you need to maintain them. Maintaining is a question of continuing to put what you have learned into practice. Effectively, you become your own therapist. If you have already reduced your obsessions and compulsions to a significant level, then there is little chance that you will slide back to where you were at the beginning. You will no longer have OCD. However, depending on where you are in your progress, you could be vulnerable to slips.

The main causes of slips are the following:

1. *Lack of focus or attention*: You are not adequately focused on applying the IBT strategies in all their details. For example, you slip back into giving a doubt a certain credibility. Or you place it on the back burner for later.
2. *A state such as fatigue or excitement*: In fatigue, you simply become too tired . . . or believe you are too tired to deal with the OCD. However, if this is the case, remember when the OCD had you working overtime, not just for nothing but also to sabotage yourself. Of course, at that point it all seemed natural and you expanded the effort without thinking. Now you don't need to. It's best here to prepare yourself by priming or prompting yourself to deal swiftly with any obsession by dismissing it immediately. As you now know, it will then just disappear quickly.
3. Unexpected high risk situations touching off insecurity and evoking your OCD self theme.

A note also about states of excitement. You may be caught up in a preoccupying positive state and so not accord enough attention to dealing with obsessional thoughts. Holidays are a good example here. You are enjoying yourself and really don't want to be bothered to deal with obsessional thoughts. However, OCD can easily ruin a holiday. You get the idea in your head that you are contaminated. Next day, after a night of obsessing, you're on the plane home, forfeiting your luxury holiday.

The more usual reasons for slippage are stress. In the OCD context, the most common stress may be any event which triggers your insecure OCD self-theme. For example, if your theme is 'I could be a person who makes small errors', pressure to perform an important job could well trigger the insecurity which will trigger the OCD.

In other words, a number of stressors could fit the bill of eliciting the insecurity. Now obviously you may have dealt with some of these trigger situations in your therapy. The problem is that some situations are not foreseeable. In other words, they may jump out at you unannounced. Hence the benefit of repositioning your self-theme. Obviously the more you are convinced that you are not the self that OCD says you are, the more you will identify with your real self. Don't forget that OCD makes you over-vigilant and nervy looking out for situations when you are most vulnerable.

Remember that your doubt is created. It does not suddenly appear out of nowhere. So providing you don't create it, it won't appear.

Inadvertent Slippage

Another caution concerns the potential problem of inadvertently slipping into the OCD by default. It may be a memory of the OCD which gets you thinking of it. Or it may be the OCD trickster's tricks. Saying something like 'OK, now is all right, but how can I be really sure I didn't expose myself to danger in 1996?'

Another point to work on is eliminating all the little safety behaviours you may have maintained. None of these safety behaviours are helpful. These can be very subtle and include:

1. Keeping a look out.
2. Checking to see if OCD is there.
3. Keeping it on the back burner.
4. Avoiding certain information, thoughts or topics.
5. Subtle cognitive avoidance such as deliberately not thinking of a certain subject.
6. Seeking reassurance or guidance 'to be sure'.
7. Repeating the ritual very quickly or just once or twice.
8. Condensing the ritual into a word. For example, a client who needed to repeat a religious phrase several times when he saw 'bad coincidences' (e.g. 2–3 ambulances going by) condensed the phrase to 'mmm'. Another client may condense a ritual into a rapid movement.
9. Subtle 'testing behaviour'.

Exercise Sheet 12
Knowing and Doing: Moving On and Preventing Relapse

- The best way to maintain the gains you have made in your therapy is to continue to put into practice the coping strategies you have learnt.
- It is important first of all that you recognize the progress you have made. Please go back and refill in the forms you filled in at the start of your therapy.
- How much improvement have you shown?
- If you have reached this stage, you will have gained a lot of insight and will have changed quite a bit of your way of thinking and behaving.
- What points specifically have you learnt, and which particularly help you?

_____

_____

_____

_____

Preventing Relapse

1. Identify future possible high risk situations, events, activities from your original self-efficacy scale.
2. Run through the sequence of how these could occur: trigger - doubt - emotion - ritual.
3. Rehearse stopping for a minute or two before you cross the bridge.
4. Be sure to label the doubt as obsessional doubt and hence invalid.
5. In general, it is helpful to label characteristics of the situations likely to trigger the doubt as ones that touch the insecurity related to your theme. If your vulnerable self-theme turns around ideas that 'you could be a bad worthless person', then you may be more susceptible to events which seem to elicit this theme.
6. Three questions to ask to help identify OCD doubt: (a) Is it a <u>DO</u>ubt? (b) Do I experience that old <u>N</u>egative OCD feeling? (c) Does it touch my <u>T</u>heme? If the answer to all three is 'yes', then it's OCD doubt to be dismissed. DONT go there.

If You do Slip Up

1. If you find you've slipped into an OCD doubt, do not panic. This slip does not mean you have relapsed. . . or lost out. On the contrary, you cannot unlearn your gains so easily. The slip may simply be part of the up and down of the learning curve and it will be helpful in the long run if we turn it into a learning experience.

2. So first of all retrace your steps. See where you went into the OCD. That is where you crossed over into OCD land.
3. What was particular about your state or activity at that point? Were you stressed, preoccupied, insecure, tired, etc. . .?
4. Identify precisely the reasons you think OCD was able to grab you at this point. Please record the reasons for future reference:

    _____

    _____

    _____

    Depending on the reason you may wish to recharge your knowledge by reading the worksheets and excercises.
5. Now how can you prevent OCD grabbing you here again: (a) Be aware of the trigger; (b) Rehearse resisting OCD at this point; (c) See your self moving on past the trigger in a non-OCD fashion.

Rehearse the solution until you feel you have mastered this OCD slip up. Ask yourself:

- Are there any other similar situations you need to consider?
- How confident do you feel now in dealing with this slip? Please note 0-100%
- If the confidence is less than 80%, repeat the steps above.

Dealing with Remaining OCD Elements

- You may still be experiencing past emotional reactions. You anticipate becoming anxious or worry that the thought will hang around because it used to do so. Remember this is no longer the case.
- The quicker you catch the OCD, the faster it disappears.
- We noted the importance of filling up the void left by the OCD with you and your goals and activities at the forefront.
- Think of activities which will give you more strength and recognition as a person.
- You might like to begin new activities, or make changes to your lifestyles which will allow you to explore more of your potential.

Complete Resolution of OCD

- You give zero credibility to the doubt.
- You have no reactions, emotional and behavioural, to the doubt.
- None of your behaviour, thinking or anticipating is driven by the doubt.
- You now react and use your senses in your old OCD situations as you do in any other situation.
- You plan ahead on the basis of the person you know you are, your authentic self.

Client Quiz 12
Knowing and Doing: Moving On and Preventing Relapse

(Please check all answers which apply)

1. Knowing and doing . . .
   - are two completely different operations.
   - can never easily go together.
   - are related, since doing is a natural consequence of knowing in the right way.
   - take a lot of courage.
2. Keeping what I have learnt is . . .
   - very fragile and could disappear tomorrow.
   - is learnt and will never completely go away.
   - depends on how I feel.
   - depends on how stressed I am.
3. The way to keep progressing is to . . .
   - keep practising and rehearsing what I have learnt.
   - read as many books on OCD as I can.
   - try to repeat in my head the key points of my therapy programme.
   - stay calm.
4. Integrating the therapy implies . . .
   - I automatically apply what I've learnt without effort.
   - I need to constantly repeat what I should know.
   - I carry prompt cards around with me.
   - I tell other people about IBT.
5. If I continue to rehearse the steps of IBT . . .
   - the OCD will get worse.
   - the OCD will be resolved.
   - I'll still have bad emotions.
   - I'll still believe a little in obsessions.
6. Relapse prevention involves . . .
   - identifying future high-risk situations touching my OCD self-doubt.
   - analysing any slips to better cope next time.
   - keeping confident about my progress.
   - all the above.

Please check your answers by referring to the Quiz Answers Sheet provided by your therapist.

Client Practice Card 12
Knowing and Doing: Moving On and Preventing Relapse

Learning Points

- Becoming non-OCD is a question of continuing to put the IBT steps into practice.
- Usually if you succeed in overcoming OCD for 6 months, you will not relapse.
- If you slip up, identify where you slipped up and retrace your steps to the appropriate worksheets and exercises.
- If you managed to deal with OCD throughout your therapy, you are capable of dealing with it for good.
- The insights of the programme should bring you eventually to complete resolution of your OCD.

Practice Card

- Foresee stresses which might affect your insecurity.
- Plan ahead for any life events or occurrences likely to touch your sensitive theme.
- Carry on with the exercises which give you a sense of who you really are.
- Try to initiate non-OCD activities which give you feedback on your real self.
- Consider yourself non-OCD, and build your life and activities around your real self.

How much of you is non-OCD? ☐%

If it is less than 80%, you may profit from repeating the programme steps to see where you are still caught up in OCD.

Cartoon 18. The untouchable.

Chapter Fifteen

Trouble-Shooting

General Clinical Points

This chapter covers clinical issues and queries arising in the course of IBT for OCD and explains how to respond to them.

Cognitive ritualizing

A general risk of cognitive interventions in the treatment of OCD is that they may become a neutralization tactic. For example, in cognitive therapy an instruction such as asking the person to ignore the obsessions or intrusions may lead to obsessive attempts to ignore the thought. In IBT, the client may start to contrast non-obsessional narratives with obsessional narratives 'to think' one's way out of the OCD. Similarly, the client may obsessively attempt to use the senses to counter obsessional doubt. The safeguard against this is that the client understands the model prior to cognitive interventions and hence the rationale behind contributing an alternative story and and using the senses. The client needs to use their senses naturally without extra effort and learn to not give the OCD situation any special status as compared to other situations.

See-sawing comprehension

Clients may show comprehension in the therapy sessions, but show slippage in between sessions. This is a natural consequence of learning and should not be

Clinician's Handbook for Obsessive-Compulsive Disorder: Inference-Based Therapy, First Edition.
K. O'Connor and F. Aardema.
© 2012 John Wiley & Sons, Ltd. Published 2012 by John Wiley & Sons, Ltd.

alarming to either the client or therapist. Equally the client will experience good and bad weeks in applying IBT strategies. It is helpful for the therapist to clarify to the client that this is a normal process as we overcome habits, and that even with ups and downs, the client will eventually be on an upward slope.

Combining IBT with other cognitive therapy

In principle, IBT can be combined with other cognitive therapy as long as the models do not collide. For example, there is no reason to not address reactions and beliefs about the obsessions along with doubt in IBT. This may be useful with clients caught up emotionally in reactions to and the consequences of the OCD. However, IBT would locate the origin of obsessions within primary doubt, not within appraisals. Thus, care should be taken when combining approaches to distinguish reactions to and beliefs about obsessions from reasoning processes leading up to the obsessional doubt.

Combining IBT with exposure and response prevention therapy

Similarly, IBT may be combined with some techniques and interventions that are shared with *in vivo* exposure and response prevention. However, not doing the ritual in IBT involves a distinct rationale. IBT does not request clients to do anything out of the ordinary such as inhibiting or preventing actions. IBT would expect the client to align behaviour with reality sensing and where the client is able to keep the OCD story at bay, the compulsive behaviour should cease. IBT is highly cognitively oriented where a general preference is given to changing cognitions before engaging in behaviour rather than the other way around. Some clients may experience difficulty letting go of compulsive rituals, either due to habit or emotional invest-ment. In those cases, ceasing the compulsive ritual may be helped by the addition of response prevention strategies by the client, particularly in the reality sensing stage.

One could argue that any therapy, once it arrives at the point of applying new thinking to everyday action, is practising exposure. So no matter if this phase is termed experiential learning, reality testing, behavioural experimentation or reality sensing, effectively it remains exposure and hence should follow the guidelines of exposure.

This is a very strong argument if all these behaviours are identical. However, this is not the case. Even though the act of facing reality is here a common element, an act is defined effectively by its intention and its context. Picking up a telephone to convey bad news is not the same act as phoning a friend for a light chat even though both involve picking up a phone. Indeed, the way the phone is touched and handled will differ in each case. Similarly, the act of facing reality with the intention of acting normally and using the senses is not the same act as facing reality and preventing an action, knowing that anxiety will increase and follow an habituation trajectory.

Exposure and response prevention are a sophisticated procedures. Complex parameters are involved in understanding and effectively implementing the approach. One important aspect is the choice of targets which, as several authorities have noted, need to be chosen realistically. A particularly useful form of exposure which can be readily combined with IBT is eliminating cognitive or behavioural avoidance or escape behaviour.

Possible conflicts between IBT and behaviour therapy

There is an important distinction between IBT and other CBT. The emphasis in IBT is on creating awareness of the difference between the possible and the real. In other words, the target of IBT is the inferential confusion process, not exposure to feared objects. One client we saw was troubled by images of naked women, which he claimed kept popping into his head. He was very religious and felt this was sinful. He had already consulted with a psychologist who had decided on exposure, and had exposed him to nude photos of women, explaining that it was quite normal to suffer intrusive images about sex and nudity and indeed the majority of the population experienced them. The client was appalled and said even if the majority did experience them, he didn't care since it was not admissible for him, and he terminated therapy.

One could argue that *had* he continued with exposure excercises he would by the law of habituation, have dampened his adverse moral reactions to nudity. However, for IBT several problematic issues spring from this exposure. Firstly, the client clearly was not willing. The exposure went contrary to his values about viewing nudity. Secondly, experiencing images of naked women was not his problem. It was rather the possibility that he might experience them.

The client's preoccupation with nudity was maintained by the doubt that he could have an interest in nudity and where he did directly imagine nudity, it was in an effort to test himself and see if his fears were grounded. His inferential confusion was generated by a story that he'd read of religious people falling foul of sexual codes. He knew that he was human with sexual feelings, that sometimes you could be tempted by the devil, and so on. The key here to treatment was to understand the nature of thought-thought fusion, confusing thoughts about the possibility of a thought with experiencing the thought itself. In fact, exposing the person to real nudity could be said to have potentially reinforced his doubt that he could really look at nude images. Indeed, it constituted a form of 'testing behaviour'.

To give another example, a female client was obsessionally preoccupied that she might not always behave correctly and, for example, would often go to great lengths to ensure that her rubbish was discarded in the correct recycling bin. This obsession led to repeated checking rituals and constant distress that she might have infringed a code or a regulation by inadvertently placing an item in the incorrect recycling bin. The exposure exercise planned with her behaviour therapist had been to place objects willy-nilly in the bins without regard to their nature and to tolerate the discomfort.

Again for IBT this exercise raises several problems. Firstly, the treatment challenges the values of the person. One could argue that respect for codes and regulations, even minor ones, is the foundation of civil society. Indeed, some authorities impose fines for wrongly sorting items for recycling. The therapist would no doubt argue that it was the excessive nature of the client's values which led to the OCD interference in life and necessitated the intervention. But were her values really the cause of the excessive nature of her rituals? According to IBT, it was the doubt generated by inferential confusion that *maybe* she hadn't sorted properly. In other words, the problem was that the client was convinced she might not have carried out the task correctly when in fact the doubt was unjustified.

Other examples where IBT conflicts with the use of exposure excercises would be basically any exercises which the therapist would be unwilling to carry out themselves. Examples include placing and keeping the hand in a bucket of muck, crossing the road against the lights or replaying scripts or scenes of extreme mutilation or death. The IBT rationale is that these exercises do not locate the real targets; they often violate common sense and common codes of behaviour in both therapist and client. Few would choose ordinarily to leave their hand in a bucket of muck or to mentally expose themselves to scenes of mutilation.

Since the aim of IBT is to help the person regain confidence in acting on their common sense, such exercises are counter-productive and may even reinforce the notion that the doubt is real. The exercises could constitute a form of 'testing' behaviour. On the other hand, as noted, exposure and response prevention exercises aimed at overcoming cognitive or behavioural avoidance (e.g. of ideas, information, people and situations) can be extremely helpful.

The riposte to this questioning of some exposure exercises may be that they work. But since the early days, we know that exposure is inadequate to reduce obsessional conviction without response prevention. Response prevention *in vivo* requires exposure not only to the trigger situation, but it will also require exposure to and toleration of the obsessional doubt. So it may be RP which is the key element in ERP, and the careful therapist-contrived adversive stimulus scenarios may be irrelevant or even counter-productive to progress. Prevention of the rituals will impact on the doubt producing them, even if this doubt is not directly addressed in therapy. There is evidence that inferential confusion reduces after behaviour therapy.

Generalizing IBT over different obsessions

In most cases, successful IBT will generalize to other types of OCD situations and obsessions than those specifically addressed in therapy since overcoming inferential confusion is the key to resolving any type of OCD. However, the therapist may need to repeat some worksheets and excercises and go through the various steps in therapy tailored to other obsessions that have not been addressed previously in treatment. The doubting sequence, for example, may need to be separately developed.

Jumping ahead too fast

The major problem likely to arise in the early therapy steps is the tendency for both client and therapist to jump ahead too quickly to confronting the validity or verity of the doubt. The first few steps simply seek to establish a logical fact. *Either* the source of the doubt is from the senses in the here and now, *or* it comes from within (i.e. from the client). There are logically only two options for the source of conviction. It will usually be immediately obvious to the client that the source of the obsessions is not in the senses – since of course a key aspect of inferential confusion is that the client cannot trust their senses. The client may immediately start to contest the distinction between real versus nonreal on the basis of the senses by producing one of the inferential confusion reasoning errors such as 'Yes, but just because you can't see it doesn't mean it is not real' (also called 'out-of-context facts'). During the first steps of therapy, the client can be reassured that for the moment we are not contesting the validity of the argument. We are not asking them to disbelieve the reasoning, but simply to recognize that the 'proof' for the doubt nonetheless comes from the client – not from the senses.

Criteria for each step

It is important the client meets criteria before deciding to progress to the next step of IBT. Each of the different steps in therapy builds upon previous steps. Therefore, it is important before moving on that the therapist ensures the client meets all criteria for progressing to the next step. Partial understanding of one step in therapy will lead to problems in later steps. It is better to err on the side of caution and proceed through each successive stage slowly while taking care that its main points have been understood.

OCD controlling the therapy

A problem may arise where OCD controls the therapy. Most obviously, OCD may have set an implicit barrier which says 'You can't go any further than so far'. Hence, the client with OCD will only improve so far. Maybe the OCD will impose a metacognitive belief such as 'If I [the client] improve, I will actually get worse'. Another form of OCD controlling the therapy is the client engaging in preparation 'to not do the OCD'. In fact, the client uses the OCD to *not* do the OCD in an OCD way.

The therapist should identify the point where the client gets stuck and be sensitive to factors that impede further progress towards successful treatment outcome.

The power of metaphor: language in therapy

Metaphors tend to be very powerful in organizing the client's experiences. It is important to use metaphors that explain progress rather than use any self-defeating metaphors clients already use. Terms such as 'fighting the OCD' need to be avoided since it sets the person up for treating the OCD situations differently from other situations. Flowing metaphors are encouraged where the person moves past the OCD, turns back over the bridge and carries on towards resolution.

Competing messages from outside authorities

Competing messages from outside authorities may include adverts or scary news stories. For example, the client may have seen on announcements that they need to wash their hands several times a day. Similarly, news stories such as those on severe acute respiratory syndrome (SARS) may be mentioned by the client as proof for his or her obsessional doubts. It should be clarified to the client that this information is not the cause of OCD, but rather it is wheeled in by the client to selectively support the OCD story. As such, this reference to authorities can be treated as any other reasoning device of the OCD that makes the OCD seem plausible.

Competing therapy models

Other competing messages may originate from mental health professionals in different models. In these cases, the client needs to be reassured and told that if he or she feels comfortable with the IBT model, it probably applies to him or her and not to be discouraged. The clients may have previously received psychotherapy for OCD which locates the origin of OCD in processes other than obsessional doubt. In the initial psycho-education session, the IBT model will have been explained, and as the different CBT models are in practice not incompatible so this point can be emphasized. However, in all likelihood, if the person is still seeking help, the other approach was not 100% successful. The reasons for the failure can be addressed since frequently they relate to the importance of addressing and response prevention the primary doubt.

Challenging beliefs and values

The use of exercises is always in collaboration with the client is at all times. It is important to avoid any confrontation. In IBT the team is the client and the therapist working against the OCD, and the therapy progresses by the client identifying the nature of the OCD and how it detracts from functioning and self-confidence. It is especially important that the client's values not be inadvertently challenged in the guise of confronting the OCD. As we have seen earlier in blending, clients with OCD tend to confuse perfectly acceptable expectations with OCD, and may use these terms to explain the OCD. The client may wish to have things 'well done' or even 'perfectly done'. Normal values of perfectionism or even rigid codes are unlikely to be the cause of OCD, or even related to it. Hence, they should not be challenged in therapy. There is a temptation – more in other models than in IBT – for the therapist to locate harsh moral codes in the client, or rigid thinking as a factor in the appraisal of events to be challenged in therapy. Clients may be told to be more flexible in their thinking, to tolerate uncertainty, to be less perfectionistic or to abandon feeling responsible for others. In IBT, where there is a semantic confusion or blending between these normal terms and OCD, it is simply a case of realizing the confusion – since it is not beliefs that cause OCD, but inferential confusion.

Another related mistake is challenging directly or inadvertently the client's values. This is sometimes seemingly encouraged by the client who believes he or she is too perfect, too religious, too hard working, too honest or too responsible (see blending). In all cases, even though the client may adhere to these values, it is never the values which cause the problem. It is the idiosyncratic application of inferential confusion which the client then labels as part of his or her values.

The therapy is not then to change moral values or beliefs, but to overcome inferential confusion and this reasoning process is distinct from any value. In the same way as the therapist cannot end up arguing facts so the therapist does not end up arguing values.

Contraindications for therapy

Contraindications for therapy are when the client is strongly opposed to the IBT model. Secondary gains or interpersonal dynamics maintaining the OCD that render the client unable to dedicate time and energy to the programme are further contraindications for therapy. Comorbidity can pose obstacles and slow therapy but is not in itself a contreindication.

It is important to distinguish OCD from other anxiety disorders, and in particular tic disorders. Certain repetitive thoughts (e.g. replaying a song in one's head) are often better conceptualized as mental tics with a distinct aetiology. Personality disorders may interfere with treatment, but differ in terms of treatment compliance. In our experience, narcissistic personality disorder is particularly problematic. However, mild personality disorders do not merit exclusion from IBT.

Problems identifying primary inferences

A problem sometimes encountered is the unravelling of the primary inference or doubt in OCD. Frequently, the primary doubt is self-evident – 'Well, maybe I left the stove on', 'I thought my hands could still be dirty' or 'Maybe I'd need it one day'. But sometimes the client will be at a loss or draw a blank when asked to identify the doubt.

It might be tempting here to say simply, 'well, there's no primary doubt and that's that', and feel understandably that to persist in trying to find a primary inference is only going to put words in the client's mouth. But the logic of OCD is that there always must be a primary inference if the action is a compulsive ritual, since the aim of the ritual is to neutralize obsessional anxiety and the anxiety must spring from a doubt of some kind. Of course, it is possible that the action is a stereotypical gesture or a tic in which case it is not OCD. But one way to establish the presence of the primary inference is just to pursue logic. Why this action – tidying the room or smoothing the cover – and not something else? All that is required is a logical premise – for example, 'I'm cleaning the table, because maybe it needs cleaning'. The type and style of this action will mostly be due to the primary inference of doubt.

Therapist effects

One problem that may arise in therapy is inferential confusion on the part of the therapist. As noted earlier, inferential confusion probably exists on a continuum in the population, So we all react in a small way to some aspect of inferential confusion as heuristic devices. The degree of absorption of course is distinct, but this can still lead to inferential confusion. As a result, the therapist may be inclined to agree with some of the client's arguments as valid reasons behind the obsessional doubt, while forgetting that these reasons arise in inappropriate situational contexts and without sense information that would justify the doubts they lead up to.

There is also the problem of unfamiliarity with the technique. Therapists trained in other techniques may feel uncomfortable if they are not challenging the content of the reasoning directly or not immediately carrying out behavioural exercises with the client. IBT of course does involve doing; it is a cognitive therapy and the doing follows from the thinking. The method and approach are client-friendly – clients click well with the initial exercises – but the therapist may need to master the model completely before using it.

The symbolic nature of OCD

Is all OCD symbolic? The role of the imagination emphasizes the essentially nonphysical source of the obsession. Imagination is representing what could occur, symbolic of what is feared. However, in a sense, since all OCD is selective, this implies there are other qualifications, not just physical, to the contamination, checking, hoarding and so on. There has recently been interesting work on mental contamination whereas a person can feel contaminated just by thinking or imagining immoral thoughts. Why is somebody bound to wash after touching a handrail but not a pot of glue? A Client does not obsess about all dirt. Clearly it is what the dirt represents and the symbolic implications for self. This symbolic selective nature is brought home in IBT partly by revealing the client's self-theme and also by demonstrating the selectivity of the obsessions . . . persuasive though they may be.

Case Illustrations

The following extracts from cases who received IBT illustrate important issues in the use of IBT with different forms of OCD. Accompanying data where available, are presented respectively for each of the individual cases 1-8 in the 'Case illustration: clinical data' section.

The case material and data were provided by one of three therapists trained in IBT: Robert Safion, Natalia Koszegi and Geneviève Goulet.

The first two cases illustrate therapy for obsessional conerns about harming. These obssions are sometimes referred to as 'impulsion phobias'; that is the fear of committing impulsive acts. These obsessions are considered as largely ruminative or 'pure' obsessions since the neutralizations are mainly mental acts e.g analysing or suppressing thoughts. Although there is often accompanying behavioural avoidance (e.g of sharp objects) and visible safety behaviours (e.g keeping hands in control. In IBT the particular inferential confusion process targetted here is a confusion between the possibility of experiencing an impulsive thought and the actual experience of the thought, or what we term thought-thought fusion.

We preface these cases with a brief discussion of clinical and conceptual points in the IBT approach to such pure obsessions.

Inferential Confusion in Pure Obsessions

The inferential confusion process in pure obsessions is primarily characterized by confusion between *possible*: thoughts, urges and motivations, with those that are actually there. The possible are not actual thoughts with a motivational component or thoughts that come about in a normal way. Instead, the thoughts in obsessional ruminations are metacognitive thoughts but, because clients with ruminations act *as if* the thoughts are actually experienced like any other thought, they cannot do anything else other than take these thoughts seriously whether or not they appear senseless and absurd.

For example, take the following doubt of an client concerned with aggression: 'I might think of hitting someone . . .' or 'I might go crazy and hit someone. . . .' The person imagined having a thought about aggression instead of actually having it. An actual thought would take a form such as 'I *will* hit that person in the face. . . .' or 'I *feel* like hitting that person in the face. . . .' both of which contain a motivational component as opposed to being solely based in the imagination. In other words, the unwanted thoughts are almost always *imagined.*

Essentially, the client with pure obsessions is caught in a perpetual cycle of metacognitive processing, which disallows the normal stream of consciousness to take its course, due to confusion between metacognitive thoughts about thoughts that have not occurred and the experience of the actual thoughts. Trying not to have the thought always implies its possibility, while thinking of the possibility of the thought is experienced as having the thought. We refer to this process as 'thought–thought fusion', since it confuses thinking about having a thought with the experiencing of the thought.

Of course, the metacognitive thought itself does occur and by no means is the metacognitive thought imaginary. However, if this metacognitive thought refers to a state of affairs that is non-existent (the assumed occurrence of a thought that has, in fact, not occurred), then this metacognitive thought *reflects* an imaginary state of affairs. So, to the extent that imaginary things refer to things that are not there, the thought about a possible thought is an *imagined* thought.

Thought–thought fusion forms part of the wider problem of inferential confusion in which the person confuses an imaginary state of affairs with an actual state of affairs based in the senses. However, thought–thought fusion specifically refers to an imagined *cognitive* state of affairs within the person (e.g., the erroneous metacognitive thought about blasphemy, sexuality, impulses, etc.) and elicits largely *covert* compulsions, while the wider definition of inferential confusion applies to both covert and overt compulsions.

Conceptualizing a pure obsession as an imagined thought (the thought of thoughts one could have or might have, but did not have) is able to significantly enhance our understanding of the phenomenology of obsessions. First of all, it explains parsimoniously why obsessions are often experienced as ego-dystonic. After all, if obsessions are thoughts about thoughts that are not really there, then they are unbounded in their absurdity and senselessness.

Second, because they do not actually have the thoughts, people with OCD usually accurately perceive the thoughts as alien and absurd. Yet, at the same time, the person with inferential confusion will never be sure whether such thoughts are part of himself or herself or whether they actually signify something else, exactly because their nature and occurrence are imagined.

Finally, as these feared thoughts are imaginary in the first place and have not actually occurred, the 'obsessions' cannot readily be removed from consciousness by reality testing or thought control. Trying not to have a thought that is not there obviously will be a fruitless endeavour unless the person with obsessional ruminations comes to recognize the imaginary quality of these thoughts, which is the goal in treatment.

The lived-in reality of pure obsession

Understanding an obsession as a metacognitive thought does not mean that the client with may not experience very vivid images and scenarios accompanying the initial thought. However, such scenarios are the result of confusing a metacognitive with an actual thought or impulse. The result of this confusion might trigger a whole scenario of harm with all the accompanying emotions and images *as if* a particular thought or impulse were actually present. The obsession becomes 'lived in' as if really there.

The 'lived-in' character of the obsession or inference may be further exacerbated by confirmatory strategies. Clients may put themselves into situations that may provoke the thought in order to confirm that they still have (or do not have) the (imagined) thought. For example, after some improvement, clients may become preoccupied and worried that the obsessions may return, which easily becomes a self-fulfilling prophecy. Clients may engage in frequent self-confirmatory tests, such as one client who imagined that he could have sexual thoughts towards a relative. So when in the presence of the relative the client continually focused on the possibility of the thoughts, hence confirming the fear that the thoughts could occur.

Clearly, the development of new obsessions can take the form of thoughts such as 'What other terrible things can I think of?' One of our clients put it quite clearly: 'When my obsessions get very severe I imagine what could be worse than this obsession and then something worse always comes along'.

Metacognitive confusion

Thought–thought fusion, or metacognitive confusion, does not occur in a vacuum. The context triggering the thoughts about thoughts may be a word, a feeling, a memory or an idea. Initial thoughts of 'God', 'sex' or 'violence' frequently form triggers. For example, a client had once imagined that a woman could read his sexual thoughts and be shocked by this and reject him. The fear was based on a particular abstract conversation about women's reactions to men. So every time he was with a woman, the obsession was triggered by the idea that he might have sexual thoughts which could be read by the woman.

The following is a paraphrased narrative of a client explaining the origin of one of her obsessions:

I dreamt of stabbing someone and enjoying it, which means I have the hidden desire to actually stab someone. The dream felt so real that I might be able to do this in real life also. I know I never really hurt anyone in real life since these obsessions have started, but there always might be the possibility that I could. Even though I read about similar obsessions of other people and I know that people with OCD are not dangerous, their obsessions were never totally the same, which means I still might be dangerous.

In other words, the thought that the clients could have a thought is still an inference grounded in personal narrative, which lead up logically to the obsessional doubt about 'maybe' experiencing a thought. The narratives produce 'believed-in imaginings', and the concern is to unravel the idiosyncratic story and refer to this story in order to understand the obsessional conviction.

Exaggerated reactions to the (possible) occurrence of thoughts may very well be relevant in the sense that cognitive elaboration on thoughts that could possibly occur may further detract the person from the normal stream of consciousness and strengthen the reality value of the obsession. However, an inference-based model would claim that these reactions only exist by virtue of the metacognitive confusion that the thought has occurred. Thus, the inference-based model would in the case of pure obsessions still identify peculiarities in the reasoning process that gives rise to the initial obsessional inference.

CASE 1

The following is an extract from a session recorded with client, David, who completed the therapy successfully in 20 sessions. The transcript demonstrates well the identification with the client of the difference between thinking about the possibility of a thought and experiencing the thought.

The client, David (38) was married with 3 children and worked successfully in information technology. His obsessions had begun in his 20s but were recently worsened following insecurites due to work and an accident.

The client was in his living room watching TV. Alone. Everyone else had gone to bed. Out of the blue he had a thought including the words 'go do it' meaning go harm or kill one of my family members. At the same time, David experienced a 'sensation' like a tension, feeling and urge to act on the thought.

Transcript

C: I first experienced an intrusion that was something like 'go do it'.
T: What did 'go do it' mean?
C: Go hurt them . . . kill them (his family). Then there was a kind of feeling, like an urge to say an impulse.
T: Then you kind of scanned yourself to see if it was an impulse?
C: Yes, do I feel like I have an urge, type questioning?
T: The feeling came first or what you are calling the thought came first?

C: The intrusion came first then there was this uneasy feeling.

T: Then you wondered about the feeling? And then in your wondering you started to ask yourself questions.

C: Yes, why am I having this feeling? It seems more real. Why does it seem so real?

T: Can you describe the feeling?

C: It's hard, I use the word 'urge', I use the word 'feeling', I am not sure.

T: What is we are talking about here?

C: It is the intrusion and then the feeling.

T: But you were wondering if this feeling was an urge. Would you say that you had some feeling in response to the intrusion and then you started to wonder if that was an urge?

C: Yes. Started to wonder if what I was feeling was a real lack of control I guess. I am asking myself, why do I feel this way?

T: Feeling what way?

C: That I could have this urge to act on the intrusions.

T: That you *could* have this urge, you were wondering.

C: Then I started to feel like I did have the urge.

T: So the sequence is you had an intrusion, then had a feeling and then wondered if the feeling represented an urge. But were you having a pure urge or a feeling of tension from the intrusion that elicited doubt as to whether you were having an urge to harm?

C: That is where I guess I get confused.

T: Well, let's look at what an urge is. Can you think of a situation where you say that you had an urge for sure?

C: Well, eating a hamburger. Something fatty and unhealthy that I know I enjoy eating, that I get a craving for.

T: How did you know you were having an urge?

C: (long pause). Well, because I know that I like that food and I really wanted it.

T: Did you have any doubts about having that urge? Or do you doubt now that you had that urge?

C: No, I know I did.

T: So you never say to yourself: 'What if I really want a hamburger?'

C: Because I don't feel the need to question it.

T: Why?

C: Because the urge is harmless.

T: But you don't feel the need to question that you are having an urge or not?

C: Right.

T: Let me ask you. What if an adult pushed your daughter to the ground waiting for ice cream and then wanted to push her again? What would you feel and what would you do?

C: I would be angry and I would push him away.

T: You would want to push him away?

C: Yes, definitely.

T: Do you see a difference between that feeling, that impulse, maybe that you want to push him and what you experienced that night?

C: Yes, they were very different.

T: Would you say that in one, you wondered whether you wanted to hurt someone (your family) and in the other, you wanted to do something aggressive physically?

C: Yes, that is true. They are very different. But that night I felt that I was having an urge.

T: When you say urge, do you mean it in the way that you usually mean when you say you are having an urge? Like the urge in the ice cream scenario?

C: That is what I am confused about.

T: Well, that confusion is at the heart of your OCD.

In the subsequent session, the therapist and client are grasping the core of his inferential confusion.

C: Well, that night, I kept thinking that I think 'this feels like an urge'. But then I realized that I was off into the world of imagination and I caught myself and said: 'back to reality'. Then I felt a huge gap between what I thought I was feeling and what was actual. Then I said: 'This is OCD and tomorrow is a new day'. But it didn't take away from the scariness of it completely because I wasn't 100% convinced it was not real.

T: But you were able to go that far, pushing back OCD that night?

C: Yes, but I didn't go into panic mode whereas in the past I would have tried to not go upstairs and completely isolate myself.

In a subsequent session, David reports awareness that the doubt about harming his family is not accompanied by authentic feelings.

T: So David, what was your reaction to what we worked on last week?

C: Well, it had a big impact. It helped me understand it more . . . made me more of a believer that it is OCD . . . this gave me proof that I am really not having urges. Because when you look at it that way, I can see that the intrusion is totally absent of the want and the emotional side of that type of an urge. Bringing me into a situation where I really would be angry like the example you used if someone pushed my daughter down, you feel angry like you want to punch that person . . . and then contrasting that with my OCD helped me see the difference between the two. For me, the exercise highlighted the absence of intent. When you have the intrusions, you wonder if there is some sort of thing that is causing you to have unconscious emotions and something is causing you to have some sort of feeling that you are not right and that maybe you are angry about something that you have not processed or something. But when you are having them totally absent of any anger, it doesn't make sense.

T: So projecting yourself into a situation where you know you really would feel anger and urges to be aggressive helped you see the difference between the two?

C: Yeah. That is completely different than the obsessional thoughts when *there is nothing there*. If I can feel angry about someone pushing down my daughter, why can't I recognize if I were feeling the type of anger that would make me want to harm my family? I can see that makes *no sense*. The exercise helped me see that I am not feeling that type of anger or that an urge to hurt them. . . . It still doesn't answer the question 'Is there something subconscious there?', but highlights the fact that there probably isn't anything there.

T: So the example helped you see the difference between what you actually would feel if intending harm and the OCD narrative, where intrusion and doubt are happening. But what isn't happening is a real urge to harm. What do you think makes you still wonder if there is something there?

C: Part of it is the 'what if . . .' What if there is something deep down in me that I am angry about, that I am not consciously recognizing, or what if I flake out . . . what if I lose self-control . . . If I can have a thought, who knows what will happen?

T: So that would be an OCD way of looking at it. What would be a non-OCD way of looking at it?

C: If I have a thought, it doesn't matter because I know that it is not something I want . . . those other scenarios that I am thinking of is not what is actually happening. I think you mentioned something similar early on in our sessions. At the time I think it was good to hear but it didn't . . . it wasn't as easy as it is for me to see it now . . . it didn't penetrate or make as much of a dent in the doubt as it does now.

T: Because back then the doubt was?

C: Overwhelming.

T: Yes, you were too absorbed into the doubt to see. I think it is a transitional process away from the doubt. But once you 'get it', it is like popping a bubble: the doubt is gone.

C: It is definitely a process. I think you are changing the way your brain works. I still need to build up more trust in myself. I still find myself neutralizing. I see a knife on the counter and I get nervous. I just want to get to the point where I just see a knife on the counter and that's it. But I still get an uncomfortable thought or nervousness, but it is not nervousness. . . . I guess I am expecting an intrusion . . . that still happens; so I just put it in the sink . . . so I definitely won't get an intrusion. . . . But at the same time I know this is just adding to the intrusion.

T: In what way does it add weight to the intrusion?

C: I don't have to avoid it because so what, it is not real.

T: Whereas when you put the knife in the sink. . . .

C: I am thinking it is going to bother me.

T: What is the 'it' here?

C: The intrusions.

T: Well, I also think that when you put the knife in the sink, you behaving as if the intrusion were valid. This is where the 'it' turns into something it isn't. . . . When you put the knives into the sink, the obsession becomes *a lived in experience*. It is what we call absorption in IBA.

C: That is the part is the toughest to grasp. I am the type of person that just wants to solve something. I just want the problem to end. I just want the intrusions to go away. But the process to get there isn't just to make it go away. I am starting to realize this more and more. To be able to just understand that what I am thinking is not real, then it is easier to dismiss. But there are moments when it can make me feel like a bad person.

T: But one thing you still see is that, as you continue to see the difference between what is real and where you get absorbed and tricked, then you will see that the intrusion doesn't need to go away because it has no meaning, it is just an annoyance, nothing more. But what about these 'unconscious feelings or emotions' I think you said? You are still having doubt here, I see.

C: Yeah, I start to think 'What if there is a reason . . . what if there is some . . . what if I am unhappy being married with kids and that deep down it is manifesting itself this way?' Not that I am having any feelings like that, but I keep searching for other reasons that I could be having these intrusions.

T: I'm sorry. Did you say you are *not having these feelings?*

C: No.

T: So *there are no feelings?*

C: No.

T: You know this?

C: Yes.

T: But you are looking for them even though they are not there?

C: Yeah. This is where I get stuck?

T: Confused maybe? Are there positive feelings about your family?

C: Absolutely.

T: And you know this? They are not 'what if' positive feelings?

C: No, they are real.

T: But you are doubting these based on what?

C: Based on nothing but my worry or doubt that they are there.

T: Well, again we are back to the confusion between what is and what you imagine could be. You know you are not really having these feelings, that you are really not angry toward your family. You can see the doubt is supported only by doubt. After seeing that you are really not having urges, your OCD is backed into a corner and grasping for straws. But what is it reaching for? What your senses and common sense tell you? Or for the next imagined possibility? The next Alice in Wonderland?

C: The next what if, I guess. But you know, thinking about this, even if the 'what if I didn't want to have kids' were true, I still wouldn't want to hurt my family. That wouldn't make any sense either.

T: I agree. Even if the imagined 'what if I didn't want to be a father' were true, and I say 'what if' because you say you DON'T FEEL that way. But even if that imagined possibility were true, there is nothing in sense that tells you you would want to hurt your children. The real story is that you love your family and you are a great dad and husband. Very nice work!

CASE 2

This next case highlights resolution of the inferential confusion between a possible thought of harming and a real intention to harm. The therapy in this case was completed in 12 sessions.

A young male (18 years) Graham, studied at college. His obsessions developed in adolescence. He was currently studying and was functioning well and living autonomously. Graham also suffered generalized anxiety and attention deficit disorder. His obsession was that he could aggress someone. The part of therapy which helped the most was to question himself about what is happening in the here and now when he had the idea that he could attack. For example, Graham was convinced he wanted to kill his cat because he sometimes held his cat tightly in his arms and so this meant he could smother the cat. But paying attention to the emotions he experienced, he realized he suffered from neither hate nor a desire to do harm. In fact, his feelings were the contrary: he was full of affection for the cat. Below are extracts from Graham's OCD and alternative stories.

OCD story: 'perhap I could be aggressive'

Perhaps I could aggress others because I feel I sometimes hurt my cat, so therefore I could hurt a human being. I feel guilty when I hold my cat which means I must have bad intentions. I also identify sometimes with violent characters in films and comics. Also I sometimes sympathize more with the criminals than victims, and I get upset when a criminal receives a long sentence.

Alternative story: 'I have no intentions to hurt anyone'

I know I don't have any real intentions to do harm to others, and I know I really love my cat. When I do wrong, I always feel guilty and I don't enjoy it. I'm sad about animal cruelty and revolted by torture. I take good care of my cat. I feed him and give him drink. I stroke and brush him. On the rare occasions where I hurt him, it was unintentional and I felt bad. I know this is a real feeling of guilt, not pretence, since I feel my lungs retract and my abdomen descend. I have no intention to harm anyone. When I play with my little cousin, we have fun. I do not hurt him.

Discussion concerning the irrelevance of obsessional doubt to the 'here and now'

T: So, Graham, as we saw last time, the OCD arguments contain a certain logic and are very convincing.

C: Yes. I found it somewhat reassuring to know why I perform the rituals, that there are logical reasons which push me.

T: We observed last week how OCD convinces you that you could be violent.

C: Yes indeed. Actually what happened this week really scared me in a convincing way.

T: Very good. Keep this in mind, and we will use it later to test out the idea that the OCD arguments, as logical as they appear, are in fact irrelevant and false at the time they enter your head.

C: What? They're false, irrelevant . . . I don't think so.

T: Obsessional doubts, unlike normal doubts, don't draw on evidence in the here and now. Rather they depend on subjective reality. Now let's look at your example you mentioned from this last week.

C: Yes, well I was convinced I was an aggressive person since I hurt my cat and I know antisocial people are cruel to animals. I heard it in my psychology course.

T: What happened?

C: Well, I took my cat in my arms but he wanted to jump down, so I forced him to stay in my arms and I squeezed him. After a while he began to scratch and meow because I squeezed too hard. Later I reflected on this and concluded I could be an antisocial person cruel to animals.

T: OK, but how did you feel at the moment the cat was resting in your arms?

C: Well, when I was holding him, I felt good. It's when I rethought about it later that I felt guilty.

T: You felt good when you held your cat?

C: Yes, but that's all the more disturbing that I should feel good when I'm hurting the cat.

T: Did you have the intention of hurting your cat?

C: No, no. I didn't intend to hurt him, just play with him. I'm like that. I play with my sister also. Sometimes I pinch her . . . it's part of the game. We fight a little, but it's affectionate and if I hurt her, I'm really sorry.

T: So you fight with people you love.

C: Yes, that's it.

T: . . . And sometimes you're a bit maladroit.

C: Yes, you could say that.

T: OK, so for the next week I'd like you to focus on your feelings and ideas at the moment you are playing with your sister or your cat – in the 'here and now', not after.

C: OK.

Next session:

T: So Graham, what did you observe?

C: Yes, I had a good chance because the feeling arrived strong with my cat.

T: What happened?

C: I experienced a great wave of affection for my cat. As if I loved him too much. I wanted so much to put him in my arms that I had trouble holding back.

T: Do you think your affection is similar to the feelings an antisocial person feels when he or she harms an animal?

C: No, no (laughing). I really understood when I observed myself this time that it's not at all the same feeling. I know I do not want to harm my cat. I've too much affection. I love him. My reaction to my cat is really just a gust of affection which renders me a bit abrupt. He just finds my grip too tight, but I don't want to harm him.

T: So now, do you see how the OCD arguments are irrelevant?

C: Yes. It's crazy but the OCD had me believing... but it's unfounded. I notice sometimes I convince myself that I could be someone or other and I convince myself with all sorts of ideas, but I'm seeing it differently now.

CASE 3

This case reports and details the steps in the successful treatment delivery of IBT after 12 sessions for a client with multiple obsessions.

Mike, divorced, aged 48, had experienced OCD symptoms since the age of 10. Despite chronic persistence of symptoms, he had managed so far to function, but recently, he felt his OCD had become worse and he was reaching the end of his tether. Mike's principal compulsions was checking the stove before leaving the house and feeling the need to trace groups of four lines when he felt he might experience intolerable emotion.

Global functioning indicating severe difficulties at work, social life and leisure and daily activities. Mike mentioned being unable to take on employment with any responsibility. In fact, he was working as a dish washer despite a university degree. The obsessions lasted 5 hours a day, and the compulsions 2 hours a day. Mike was not taking medication and suffered no other Axis I or II disorders, although he reported past depressive episodes.

The doubt 'Maybe I could experience intolerable emotions' was more difficult to elicit since Mike had always taken it for granted that he would not be able to tolerate an unusual intense emotion. He rated this doubt as 100% probable. The percentage scores here indicate the level of conviction in the doubt as a real possibility.

Mike's concern was that he could explode or break down if he didn't trace lines, and this would happen *if* he really did experience intolerable emotions. Mike felt most rituals were 100% necessary when he was in the OCD trigger situation but often considered them much less when outside the situation.

The therapist verified the scores on the clinical scales on a second occasion and then decided with Mike the order in which the obsessions could be addressed in therapy. Mike and the therapist targeted two principal primary inferences: 'Maybe I did not turn the stove off' and 'Maybe I could experience intolerable emotions'. Mike also kept a diary throughout therapy measuring daily degree of anxiety and interference associated with OCD, duration of obsessions and compulsions and degree of beliefs in his two obsessional doubts.

The first part of the treatment program entailed identifying the characteristics of obsessional doubt and understanding the distinction between obsessional doubt and normal or authentic doubt. The therapist elicited from Mike several instances of reality-based questioning in everyday life, such as smelling a burnt odour, shivering in a draught from an open window or the sound of a tap dripping. The authentic doubts were justified by sense-based information in the here and now and were resolved through reality-based decisions in the here and now. Conversely, Mike's obsessional doubts were created subjectively by him and were not resolved by seeking further information. For example, he checked his stove in the absence of any reality-based valid reason to check, and this checking elicited no new information since he was only rehearsing his doubt.

Mike agreed that the obsessional doubts were subjectively created, but he still gave them credibility. He mentioned spontaneously that his doubts could well be the 'fruits of his imagination'.

The doubt was not grounded in current reality, how did it come about? To answer this question, the therapist asked Mike to 'let the OCD talk': that is, expound the arguments by which the OCD convinced him to invest in the doubt and perform his rituals. How did he justify doubting when his senses said otherwise? Mike came up with the following arguments:

- I'm a bit scatterbrained. I'm easily distracted. I'm prone to forget things. I've made mistakes in the past. I have left apparatus turned on in the past.
- You read about people causing fires by leaving stoves on.
- I heard about a fire in a fire station caused by a casserole left burning on the stove.
- If it could happen to a fireman, it could happen to me.

The doubts were mainly justified by appeal to generalized hearsay, conventional wisdom and subjective logic, but were not based on realistic information in the here and now.

The therapist illustrated from Mike's non-OCD areas what is meant by 'relevant to the here and now'. The therapist considered events where Mike had reacted appropriately in the here and now, such as seeing mud on a handle and wiping it off, or crossing the road and getting out of the way of a car. Mike was encouraged to contrast the subjective source of the OCD story remote from the 'here and now' with the reality-based source of his non-OCD reactions.

The exercise at home was to examine the justification for doubting each time it occurred. Mike noted at the end of the week that in reality when he checked, he knew the stove was turned off. So he began to question both the relevance of the doubt and his compulsive checking. He also reported that he found it easier to question his doubt when it applied to physical events like leaving the stove on. However, he felt he was less able to apply the technique to his doubts about experiencing intolerable emotions.

In a creative excercice the therapist recounted two stories, one about her office belonging to an eminent scientist now departed and how fixtures were installed precisely and carefully for his benefit. The second story related how the room was previously used to store dust bags, and that it was the worst office in the building and the therapist was only installed here because she was new and there was no other office. Mike agreed that his perception of the room modified according to the story. The point of the exercise being that although the room (i.e. reality) has not changed his perception had been influenced by the story. Mike reported understanding how the OCD story gave his doubt an 'existence' and made it seem alive. He also noted that his tendency to create images about the consequences gave more credibility. For example, a strong image of a fire made the possibility of his house burning seem more real. With the power of the OCD narrative in mind, Mike went back with the therapist to see what aspects of his OCD story made him 'live' in the doubt as though it was real. This time the separate OCD arguments were joined up into a more flowing narrative.

OCD story: 'Maybe I left the stove on'

I need to check my stove each time I leave my apartment because I know I am an absent-minded person and so I can forget things. It did happen once that I left a pot boiling on my stove; it could have set fire to my apartment. Also, I heard that a fireman forgot to remove a pot from the stove right at the fire station and it set fire to the station. It is reasonable to think that if firemen forget pots on stoves, it could happen to anybody and especially to those like me who tend to be absent-minded.

Alternative story: 'The stove is off'

I don't need to check my stove when I leave my apartment because I know that once I turn it off, it stays off. Therefore, I don't have to go back and check it once more. Even if I am sometimes absent-minded, I can make the distinction between my stove being on and it being turned off. My eyes still see well. Once I see that the stove is off, I don't have to check it until next time I use it. So, for instance, if I don't use my stove one morning and then leave for work, there are no reasons why I should check my stove. If I use it and shut the stove off, I can leave without checking it again.

The therapist reinforced the power of the OCD story by looking at how the OCD story generated characteristic OCD feelings.

The therapist covered the formal reasoning devices (see earlier) in Mike's OCD narrative that invalidly convinced him to believe in the doubt. In Mike's case the principal devices were inferring, on the basis of imaginary sequences, out-of-context facts and irrelevant associations. Although Mike found these formal reasoning devices interesting, the knowledge had less impact than the earlier insight in previous sessions about the subjective, irrelevant, remote nature of his OCD story.

The therapist contrasted the way Mike reasoned and inferred elsewhere in everyday life. Again this highlighted the difference between common sense, real-life coping, and OCD coping, where he essentially rehearsed a doubt and never arrived at resolution. For example, when crossing the road, did he stop and stare, imagining cars could be there that he might not have seen? These exercises also led to questions about why he reasoned like this in some situations but not others.

Mike was able to generalize the IBT strategies to the other obsessions, such as 'Perhaps the door is not properly closed', 'Maybe the tap is not properly closed' and 'Maybe I don't have the right information'. He had more trouble with 'Maybe I will experience intolerable emotions' and the therapist helped to elicit the following narrative justifying this obsessional doubt.

'I heard of a group of people who needed therapy because they couldn't deal with strong emotions. Some had cracked up or became depressed. If you experience too many bad emotions the system cannot tolerate it. It sounded like me because I'm closed up and don't show my emotions since I have painful memories of being ill at ease in the past'.

The therapy he had heard about involved talking and expressing emotions. Since Mike lived alone, he had started writing down his emotions, and after a while he just drew series of lines. He chose to draw specifically four lines because in school, corrections had to be repeated four times; thus, he believed four to be a complete number.

In the case of Mike's self-theme centred on the possibility that he could be someone who could fail to function adequately at any time. The story justifying the doubt included arguments that he had always been told he wasn't capable and that he lacked the right resources. Mike felt he hadn't accomplished much in his life, and that each time he faced a challenge, he didn't succeed well enough. Therefore he needed to be extra vigilant to make sure he had the right information and to consider all angles and eventualities to ensure he functioned normally.

The therapist reoriented him towards his real self by following IBT principles and constructing and rehearsing a self-narrative based on his actual characteristics in the here and now.

> I have good capacity to succeed. When I actually face challenges without doubting or avoiding, I cope well. In reality, I've attained several life objectives which I set for myself and which not everyone can achieve (e.g. education). When I plunge myself into a task without first analysing my capacity, the more I feel confident in myself, which shows that doubt gets in the way of who I really am.

This re-positioning towards the real self was an on-going project at the end of therapy at the 12th therapy session, Mike showed substantial improvement and had also succeeded in generalising IBT well to his other obsessions, so that the therapist did not need to redo IBT for each obsession separately. At post-treatment evaluation, Mike scored in the non-clinical OCD range.

The following dialogue illustrates the client's experiece of letting go the doubt "Maybe I could experience intolerable emotion".

T: So, how was your week?

C: Well, I experienced something really strong this week. . . and I am glad that I could get out of it. If I had come here yesterday, you wouldn't have recognized me because I was so completely absorbed into my OCD. . . like it used to be a few months ago. At least, I got out of it after 3 or 4 days, not like before when I could stay up to 2 months in that state, completely absorbed by my compulsions and afraid I might just be unable to tolerate my emotions.

T: What was different this week compared to how it used to be?

C: Hum. . .this week, after a few days stuck into my OCD, I recognized that state, that OCD state in which I feel numb, like "not there" at all. . . and I could see reality last night in the evening and then I came back gradually in reality and this morning. . .OCD did knock, knock, and (laugh) I didn't answer. I felt like there is no way I am going back there, into that bubble, in my imagination. I could finally see this morning how OCD was completely false! But, let me tell you, that OCD is strong. . .so strong, I could not see anything else for these few day.

T: Can you tell me what triggered your OCD and how you got absorbed into it?

C: Well, I felt this time like I was spontaneously absorbed by my OCD unlike other times we discussed about, where I could feel OCD getting me gradually to cross the bridge more and more. But no, this time was different, like. . .you know when something happens and an 'emotional memory' is suddenly awakened, we learn that in theatre lessons, it is like when you drink a coffee ,for instance, like your grand-mother use to make. . . and all of a sudden, you have all sorts of memories that comes with the smell and the taste, you have all these feelings . . .

T: Yes, I understand, these emotions arise spontaneously as if you where there, at that time, feeling the exact emotions you had at that time. They felt as if they were part of your reality in the here and now, didn't they?

C: Oh, yes! As if I had lived that exact experience!. . .that's what happened but it was a painful feeling, like when your heart break because your first love rejects you abruptly, it is a shock. Well. . . without going too much into detail, I got involved in an emotional situation with a friend. And then my OCD told me: 'you know that feeling and you must not go there because it will hurt you like before, remember how it was painful and my OCD said, you won't be able to tolerate that feeling again, you have to do something about that feeling, you've got to do something or else, you won't go be able to take it'

T: I see, it didn't feel like a doubt but rather like a certainty about having to evacuate these feelings.

C: Oh ya! It was going 'Do something about it because you won't survive'!

T: Were you able to recognize that you were in the OCD bubble? . . .and stop and see reality?

C: No, not for the first two or three days. . .I didn't realize. But then, a friend called me because he needed someone to talk to. . .he is going through a rough time right now so I invited him over to my place. . .and for the time he was with me, I had to go back to reality and put aside temporarily my OCD thoughts because he really needed someone to listen and to give him some advice. Then, after he left, I was alone again and was quickly absorbed into my OCD bubble, but, because my friend and I were talking about his problems in <u>real life</u>, I sort of got the feeling that I could see. . . or sense my reality. . .I could compare his situation to mine. I just knew that I was living in my imagination and not in reality. . .yes. . .and, I had the feeling that all along, I knew that reality was there in a way but that I ignored it. So, I told myself, "Do you really need to go there? Is it helpful? Are you really evacuating your emotions?" and I answered: "It is funny but I felt like two parts of my personality were talking to each other, could it be?"

T: I would rather say that OCD is not part of your personality but it is strong because it is supposing something that frightens you and catches your attention strongly. You react to OCD because you feel it is telling you something very important and can protect you from a lot of pain. Then, the more you get involved with OCD thoughts, the more you feel OCD is part of you but it's not. At this moment, do you think that OCD is part of you?

C: Well. . .you're right. . .if it was a part of me it would be here this morning and it is not. I don't feel pain, I feel good. . .and I don't need to do anything special with my feelings. I don't believe my OCD right now. . .feelings take care of themselves. . .I mean, you don't have to intervene or anything. It is much worse when you start to listen to that OCD who keeps you wondering about what to do with your emotions and getting you into imagination and then, it never stops! This morning as I said earlier, OCD was there, but it was weaker and telling me to do something with my feelings and I saw it from the reality side of the bridge . . . and it had no power.

This case illustrates two key points in successful treatment with IBT: firstly, the ease of generalization of IBT techniques to other obsessional doubts once the principles of IBT are understood; and, secondly, that targeting the source doubt gets round the need to address the range of catastrophic secondary consequences, since if the initial premise is invalid, so, by definition, are all the consequences, however horrific and frightening.

CASE 4

This next extract highlights the role of OCD logic in justifying an unusual compulsive behaviour. The therapy in this case was completed in 20 sessions.

Sharon (32 years), a mother of two young children, remembers very clearly the moment the OCD began. She was 27 years, and a short while after the birth of her first child, a friend had joked that if the baby cried too much she should put it in the oven and cook it like a small chicken. The Sharon had seriously posed the question 'Could I be capable of such a thing?' From that point on she had begun to fear she could really harm her children. So to protect herself through 'magical thinking', she had begun to perform diverse compulsive rituals such as memorizing or writing down certain series of numbers. The compulsions had developed with time. At the beginning of therapy her dominant compulsions consisted of collecting objects which she had seen for the first time (that is, they were unusual to her). Sharon had developed the habit of lifting out electoral signs of candidates, orange cones on the highway and price tags on groceries. She had even been warned or expelled from shops where such behaviour was not tolerated. She took considerable physical risk in leaving her car on the highway to collect objects such as cones, bits of wood. She didn't hoard them but afterwards threw them into waste bins.

Her understanding of the diverse steps of the program was very good, and Sharon showed herself open and motivated from the start. She experienced some difficulty in identifying OCD supporting arguments. From the moment she was able to break the automatic nature of the compulsion and realized how and why the OCD story was convincing her to perform the compulsion, the compulsion decreased. Sharon still noted unusual objects but had no desire to take them up, and she stopped making detours and returning especially to pick up objects. She had developed a security behaviour of restricting her vision to avoid seeing disturbing objects which she ceased. Sharon's vulnerable self theme, 'I could be a bad mother who could harm her children', she deemed rapidly inappropriate and she was able to reposition herself towards her real self. Post therapy, after 20 sessions, Sharon had zero compulsions and zero belief in her doubt. She had no avoidance or safety behaviour and reported a higher self-esteem. At 6 months follow-up, the score at the YBOCS showed Sharon was in complete remission and the following dialogue illustrates her recovery.

T: So the OCD convinced you to pick up pieces of wood from the ground to prevent bad luck from affecting your children.

C: That's right.

T: Now we have already identified the OCD arguments which support this idea.

C: Yes, the objects which lie around on the ground are 'threats', 'oddities'. If I leave them there, that means I accept them! Good people don't do that, they make sure threats are eliminated. If I don't behave as a good person would, this will be turned against me and bad luck could touch the people most important for me: my children.

T: OK. So that's the OCD logic. Now do you believe it's possible to provoke good as well as bad luck, like winning the lotto?

C: No . . . unfortunately.

T: But why not? If OCD logic is correct and your behaviour can provoke bad luck, then in the same way you should reason, it can provoke good luck? But you don't follow the same logic with good luck, that say tapping three times on the head can increase your chance of winning.

C: It's true, there is no logic in reasoning one way for happy events and another way for bad events.

T: Exactly! The OCD applies its rules completely arbitrarily. Because the rules are not related to reality, they can change on whim tomorrow morning.

C: Yes and that's what has happened to me. For several years, to prevent bad luck I needed to memorize a series of numbers. Now it's as if the OCD has changed its ideas along the way. Before I needed to count numbers, now it's pick up objects.

T: So you no longer believe memorizing numbers can prevent bad luck?

C: No. I know very well it's completely irrelevant.

T: How do you know?

C: Well . . . it's just common sense. All I was doing in memorizing numbers was . . . well . . . to memorize numbers. I kept my brain busy and occupied my memory with the task. But that's all. Nothing changed concerning what happened in real life.

T: So, still using your good sense, what are you really accomplishing by picking up bits of wood?

C: I'm taking and replacing them in different locations. That's all that's happening. Nothing changes in the life of my children.

CASE 5

This case reports successful IBT after 19 sessions in a case of asymmetry obsessions.

Freda (60 years), married, suffered from compulsive accumulation. Freda also suffered from symmetry obsessions involving aspects of personal appearance such as clothes and hair. She obsessed about wearing her clothes in the right way and would frequently change and re-arrange her clothes. The two subtypes seemed linked by the same vulnerable self-theme, 'I could be abandoned if I don't do my best at all times'. 'The best of all times' included not wasting and not replacing objects correctly. She also requested frequent embraces from her husband as reassurance of his love. Again, blending between asymmetry and abandonment proved a key factors that performing well and placing objects symmetrically guaranteed acceptance and person who left objects asymmetric deserved to be abandonned. Once Freda realized that the fear of abandon was not present in the here and now and that it was completely irrelevant to judging tasks in the here and now, the symmetry and accumulation disappeared. The following are extracts from Freda's OCD stories and her alternative reality-based stories.

OCD story: 'I could lose myself in losing my photos'

I could lose my photos and myself. It is important for me to not miss or lose anything, especially affection. I don't want to lose anything or experience regrets. I always lacked affection and when I look at the photographs, I have a feeling of warmth and tenderness and it's like the people are here with me, giving me a kiss. I can relive beautiful moments and the closer I am to the photos, the more my emotions amplify and the environment doesn't exist. It's like the here and now evaporates. I also feel if my memory fails, I'll have my photos to reassure me. The photos give me a sense of identity and belonging. If I lost them, I wouldn't know who I am.

Alternative story: 'photos are a small part of my life':

Photos are representations of people, not real people. I don't need photos to feel close and loved by people. In fact, the photos are a substitute for relations and are keeping me away from enjoying relations to the full. I have an identity and real self apart from photos. Photos are small part of my life; they are not my life.

OCD story: 'perhaps my objects are not arranged properly'

Perhaps objects are not arranged properly. It is important that objects and furniture are placed after my fashion symmetrically. This gives me great satisfaction since I have the impression of doing my job well. If I don't place them well, I would be abandoning them. Since I've lived abandoned, I wouldn't inflict this on my house and the things close to me. If the objects are not in their proper place, it means I've abandoned them and don't care for them as if I'm leaving them alone to fend for themselves. Objects in their place cannot be lost, so a house in order is not neglected.

Alternative story: 'objects cannot be abandoned or neglected'

Furniture and objects cannot feel abandoned. It's only people who feel abandoned. Objects which are moved are still the same objects; they are not lost or abandoned but simply moved about. When objects and chairs are moved and displaced, it means there is life in the house. It is not boring or cold. A place where nothing moves is like a mortuary. Things in nature (such as flowers and trees) are not symmetric. I'm energetic and dynamic. People and children like spontaneity. No one wants to appear like a statue, always in the same place.

Below is a dialogue describing Freda's blending and the deblending between 'being good' and 'exactness' at post therapy

C: I don't know why I restarted replacing and checking objects. All the objects were arranged well. All the compulsions that I got rid of have stayed OK but now I have new ones which upset me.

T: What do you do now which you didn't do previously?

C: For example, I need to tie and untie the cord in my dressing gown several times until I feel it is correct. It makes no sense. Sometimes I need to redo it 20 times before being satisfied.

T: How do you know when the belt is correct and you can stop?

C: Well, until it feels right.

T: Can you be more precise about what you mean by 'feels right'?

C: Well, I need to feel OK . . . satisfied . . . that I've done my best possible . . . that is that. I've really pushed myself.

T: What happens when you feel you have not done your best possible?

C: I experience a kind of grief. I feel sad. It's completely crazy to feel sad when a knot has not been well tied, but it's like that I feel.

T: Is there anything else which comes to mind?

C: Not really . . . except I remember when I was a child. When I found out I was adopted, I said to myself that I should always do my best possible to show my appreciation to my adoptive family. They saved me and I needed to give a lot back in return. I remember feeling if I didn't try the best I could, they would take me back to the orphanage. So I just forced myself to do all I could, to push myself as far as possible, but it was completely mad. I never succeeded. I have the impression now that I'm still that little girl trying to be perfect so as not to disappoint my parents. However, I see that it was all for nothing. They wouldn't care about my bathrobe belt or creases in my sheets'.

CASE 6

This next case also describes the important role of blending in the justification for OCD. In this case blending negligence with uncleanliness. Therapy was successfully completds in 15 sessions.

Helen (44 years), divorced and living alone, but in a relationship. Her obsessions and compulsions related almost exclusively to order and symmetry. Helen placed objects (cutlery, plates, pencils papers, Kleenex tissues, remote controls and ornaments) very precisely, and she verified constantly that the objects were well placed, often placing and replacing them. Helen was also very compulsive over what she termed 'signs of life' in the house. She literally followed a visitor around the house cleaning the toilet, sweeping the carpet and brushing furniture. Helen's clinical scales showed her initially very invested in the obsessions and compulsions. Although she completed the preliminary exercises and understood the obsessional nature of the doubt, Helen remained convinced her rituals were necessary. However, at the ninth session she worked on her vulnerable-self theme, and progressed quickly with therapy terminating successfully after the 15 sessions. Helen realized she perceived herself as a possible negligent person and that all her efforts were directed against becoming negligent. In effect she discovered she was blending the concept of negligence with the idea that objects had to be well placed and that she needed to clean up after people. This realization allowed Helen to tolerate objects out of place or not aligned 'properly' since these aspects were now separated from negligence. The following dialogue covers Helen's recognition of inferential confusion in her obsessional reasoning.

T: Let's take the following doubt: 'Perhaps the carpet in the hallway entrance is dirty'. In what context does this doubt enter your mind?

C: As soon as someone walks on it. So, in general, when someone enters the house.

T: So entering the house and walking on the carpet trigger the doubt that the carpet could be dirty?

C: Yes. It's automatic.

T: Now let's find an example of a normal doubt that you've experienced recently which comes to mind.

C: Well yesterday I needed to visit my mother who lives 50 km away and I thought I might need petrol on the way.

T: What made you think that?

C: The little light which indicates that the tank is nearly empty lit up after 5–6 km. I said to myself, it's fine because previously I had driven 50 km with the light still on. But this time I was caught for half an hour in a traffic jam, so I wasn't certain to be able to visit my mother without filling up.

T: Do you doubt if you will need fuel each time you take your car out?

C: No, only in this type of situation.

T: Yes and that's exactly what characterizes normal doubts. They arise when the context justifies doubt. The possibility of needing fuel came into your head because your senses communicated direct information to this effect. Your eyes saw the little light and your good sense told you that the amount of fuel remaining wasn't sufficient for the distance which you had yet to travel. If you didn't possess this information, would you have worried about fuel?

C: No, I would have been certain that all was OK.

T: Now does obsessional doubt also have evidence supporting it?

C: Well... I see the carpet, I know I walk on it, my senses tell me.

T: Yes, you see the carpet but your doubt concerns the possibility that it is dirty. Do you see the dirt?

C: Mostly... no.... But really there must be dirt there. I walk on pavements in the street. The pollution in the air covers the ground, and I walk over it with my shoes. It's obvious that my shoes are dirty and so the carpet is dirty since I walk on it with my shoes.

T: So in looking at the carpet you see nothing, yet you doubt whether it is dirty. Do you see a difference here with normal doubt?

C: If I don't see the little light lit up, I don't doubt if I have enough fuel. But even when I see nothing on my carpet, I still doubt.

T: Exactly. For the gas, you trust your senses and common sense. They seem sufficient and you don't need to consider anything else. For the carpet, your senses are not sufficient and you distrust them. If the obsessional doubt is not backed by reality, but you still consider it to be true. How could this be so?

C: It's based on what could be.

T: Yes... which could arrive... imagined possibilities which come entirely from you and your imagination.

C: It's as if I'm saying even if the warning light was not on, I could still lack fuel, perhaps it is deficient.

T: There you go... it could be. We can imagine thousands of possibilities, but most of the time we consider one possibility. The one our senses say is most likely from information in the here and now which seems to us relevant. Otherwise we don't consider it.

C: Unless the OCD sticks its nose in.

In the next dialogue we see how de-blending negligence and uncleanliness is aided by recognition of Helen's authentic self.

T: We've worked on the vulnerable-self theme at the last session. Can you describe how the OCD has made you think of yourself in a situation you experienced this last week?

C: Yes, well yesterday I dropped a pencil on the floor while studying at my work desk. In leaning down to retrieve it. I detected a little dirt on the living room carpet. It comes into my head that I'm negligent and that I should have made sure to clean up.

T: So according to the OCD you were negligent to not pick up the dirt before. In general, how does the OCD define negligence?

C: Well, according to the OCD, negligence is shown when you don't have everything in place, when you've left visible human traces of someone in the house. For example, leaving a crease in a cushion after someone has sat on it is negligent. Everything must be replaced back to its initial state; otherwise it's negligence.

T: In reality, do you feel this is OK? Does your common sense concur with this definition?

C: No. It's more nuanced than that. It's like the OCD exaggerates and considers behaviours as negligent which are not at all the case.

T: So the OCD confounds and mixes everything up for you.

C: Yes, absolutely, because in the end I don't listen to my common sense; I know the OCD definition is not real negligence.

T: What is negligence according to your senses?

C: Well, for sure it's not simply to not clean or tidy up. It would be more serious, letting objects that could hurt people lie around or cause danger. Or letting food go to waste and attract insects, or to not intervene in a situation where others were threatened.

T: And are you in this type of situation when the OCD tries to make you believe you are negligent?

C: No, not at all. So OCD is wrong. My good sense is clearly to tell me the right criteria for recognizing negligence, and it's never OCD situations.

CASE 7

The next case illustrates rapid progress towards resolution after 13 sessions, following understanding of the deceptive nature of the OCD reasoning devices.

Josée (40 years), is a teacher, with obsessions about contamination, chemical products, bacteria, intoxication, food poisoning and medication. Josie quickly seized the IBT principles and saw herself the imaginary part of her problem. But she experienced some difficulty generalizing this abstract knowledge to specific situations. It was necessary to analyse each OCD situation concretely. For example, at the grocer shop, she refused to place food on the counter if a previous customer had placed a chemical product by the cash checkout. Once the OCD reasoning devices had been exposed, Josie began to understand quickly the impossibility of the doubt.

At one point she began to laugh at the thought that liquid in a bottle could get into her food, or that a person taking some medicine could spill the medicine into her food. Josie termed these insights 'how the OCD fooled me'. It was still necessary to deal with each compulsive ritual at a time, but effectively not all rituals and obsessions were eliminated post treatment after 13 sessions.

Josie's OCD self-theme was that 'I'm a person easily distracted and dreamy so I'm at risk to be contaminated inadvertently'. Her authentic reality based self-theme was that 'I'm a person attentive and capable of detecting sources of contamination as well as the next person'. The following are extracts from Josie's OCD and alternative stories.

OCD story: 'I could be at risk of contamination by food'

I've heard some imported foods can be handled by dirty people who don't have the same standards as we do. Even if the food comes from local sources, it could be badly stored and have worms in it. I once bought stale tartlets with worms so it could happen to other foods. You can't always know the age of a product. An item could be older than it looks. Certain shops are filthy, and insects could crawl under wrappers.

Alternative story: 'I can trust myself to detect contaminated food'

Well-wrapped food will not come into contact with bacteria. I can tell whether food is good or not by using my senses and looking and smelling it in a normal way. I can also trust my sound of hearing when I open a lid to see if it's been tampered with or if it's dented or bruised. I have all the information available to me on the state of the food. A food being recalled has nothing to do with the way it is wrapped properly.

In the following dialogue Josie talks of her experience of resolving her key obsessional doubt "Maybe this container is damaged"

T: Last week we discussed the logic behind your doubt and found that your OCD doubt was strong because it was supported by multiple arguments that appeared logical to you. Did you take time this week to examine what arguments your OCD used to make you doubt about the state of containers?

C: Yes, and I found that taking a bit of time just to stop and reflect on these arguments that went through my mind about containers was pretty helpful.

T: Oh, interesting... Can you tell me how that was helpful to you?

C: Well, I was at the grocery store and I decided to slow down and reflect and I just realized that the reasons why I checked the containers were sometimes ridiculous (laugh)...I am a bit embarrassed to tell you that but I was thinking that maybe if there was a little hole in a can, for instance, then there would be bacteria that would get into the can and would then contaminate the product inside (laugh)...I mean, it is absurd because really, I would put back a can on the shelf because the paper around it was slightly scratched...no holes, just a scratch. I think I thought that a scratch was a hint that the can could have been really bumped and that even if it was not visible, there could have been a puncture somewhere but an invisible one (laugh) . . . but I realized it did not make sense because if it would have been really damaged, it would be obvious . . . not a slight scratch anyways!

T: So you don't mind anymore if there is a scratch on a can?

C: (laugh) no. . .because a scratch is not a hole…if there was a whole, the can would leak (laugh). . .I even drank a small carton of milk this week at work that was a bit bent on the corner and it was fine!

T: You felt it was safe to drink the milk inside that carton even if it was bent?

C: I had no problem at all. . .I just told myself, come on, it's just bent that's all! The milk inside is fine, it's not leaking right? So the milk inside is ok.

T: Do you think you will still check all the containers at the grocery store?

C: Honestly, I think I will take a quick look, yes. . .but if I see a scratch or a bump on a box, I will still buy it and eat the food inside!

T: How do you explain such a difference between how you proceeded before and how you do now?

C: Well first I look properly when I notice something wrong on a box instead of concluding that there is a hole in the box. . .so I take a look, I use my eyes to look. . .before putting it back on the shelf or throwing it away when I'm at home. Secondly, I stop going into these scenarios about what could be contaminating the food like I used to do, it was incredible! It made me feel extremely anxious because I would really imagine the contaminated food and what would happen if I would eat it (laugh). . .No, now I just stay with what I see and it's all I need to know really.

CASE 8

Finally the following is a case which did not benefit substantially from IBT. The client showed a high score on narcissistic personnality traits.

Jim divorced (46 years) lived alone, and was employed part-time in manual work. Jim's principal fear concerned the possibility of contaminating himself which led to excessive washing and showering. His showering typically took 3 hours, and he needed to divide each part of the body into sections and focus on washing each section in a strict sequence. At the same time Jim would repeat the sequence verbally to ensure he didn't miss out a step. Jim was particularly proud of his method which, according to him, guaranteed cleanliness, and he couldn't foresee any other way. Jim he did accept parts of the IBT, for example that his compulsive rituals reinforced his doubt, and that with OCD he crossed over into the imaginary. But he was more concerned throughout therapy to abide by and improve his own criteria of how to wash properly rather than using IBT. For example, when encouraging Jim to slow down his actions to be better able to catch the sequence, he noted that slowing down enabled him to be even more sure he had performed his ritual. Also he retained the notion that for any job to be well done, it required visible effort. So for Jim 'normal' washing entailed extra effort to ensure it was well done.

Identification of Jim's vulnerable-self theme: 'I could be someone who could be rejected' had a marginal impact and helped him realize the source of his daily concerns. In fact, some minor rituals (the possibility of embarrassing himself at work) did decrease, and in general the strength of his obsessions did decrease. But Jim maintained his conviction in the utility of his method. Below are some key components of Jim's OCD and alternative stories.

OCD story: 'I could forget to wash parts of my hands'

Perhaps I could forget to wash a part of my hands. Dirt and contamination can lodge everywhere in the creases of your hands and you wouldn't know. In washing your hands in a general way, you risk missing the small corner with a residue of dirt. For example, in washing the hands together, palm to palm, you risk forgetting bits. In effect, the fingers all have different lengths and are at different angles to the palm so you need to have a technique which separate out the parts of the hand one by one in sequence. The best way to keep a sequence is to say it out loud from beginning to end.

Alternative story: 'I can trust my washing without following special rules'

When I wash my hands, I rinse and soap them. I can see the mousse and feel it covering all my hands. Even if I don't separate out the washing bit by bit, I can be sure that I've washed everywhere. I see the mousse everywhere. In rubbing my hands together, I cover all possible surfaces. Nowhere do any public health guides say to follow my sequence. I don't eat food in an ordered sequence or counting my bites. The same with my hands. If I wash my hands trusting my senses and my senses say all is well, then I can be sure my hands are clean.

At the end of treatment, Jim had only shown marginal improvement due largely to his investment in his own way of washing. Jim was unwilling to accept any alternative model to his own approach. He continued to consider his technique was superior, and the belief was coupled with a fixed belief in the necessity to always apply extra OCD driven effort through the development of his method. The following dialogue illustrates this tenacity.

The following dialogue illustrates the tenacity of Jim's adherence to his own compulsive method of cleaning his hands.

T: It's difficult for you to believe that your senses are sufficient to know if your hands are clean.

C: Absolutely, it is only by using my method that I can be truly certain to have washed my hands. Appearances can be deceptive. My method is much more reliable. I've spent hours perfecting this method. I review in my head all the parts of my hand which could be dirty. I then think of the optimal method of cleaning all parts, and I order each of the operations. It's obvious that such a systematic method is more efficient.

T: But you could elaborate such a method for a multitude of things, like washing your car or shaving. Why don't you feel the need here? Perhaps you trust your senses because there is no competing OCD story.

C: No it's different. My senses have always been trustworthy in those other tasks, they've not let me down. But when it comes to the hands, the senses have failed the test. That's why I had to find an alternative.

T: Do you consider your method a compulsion?

C: Well, according to you 'yes', but for me 'no'. It's the only way to be sure of clean hands, since my senses can't be trusted here.

T: Are you completely sure your method is the most useful?

C: Well, not always. It's true I still have the impression that my hands could be dirty.

T: Well if it's a compulsion then performing it will maintain doubt not resolve it.

C: I don't agree. I'm rather of the opinion I must continue to work on improving my method. I need to reassure my subconscious as well as my conscious mind. So I'll need to redouble my efforts to perfect my method.

Case Illustrations: Clinical Data

The clinical data presented here corresponds to the case numbers 1–8 in the IBT 'Case illustrations'.

The clinical data provided by the therapists includes, in cases 2–8 measures using the clinical scales and the graphs show data from the daily diary described in the appendices 2 & 5.

Graphs shown here are restricted to the prinicpal emotion and obsessional doubts recorded over therapy sessions.

The diaries generally begin after 2–3 preliminary meetings with the therapist and following training in the diary keeping. So inital diary scores may not always correspond exactly to pre-therapy scores on the IBT clinical scales.

The diaries chart the idiosyncratic sometimes up and down course of change, and provide visual feedback to the therapist and clients on progress.

Although some clients show a progressive linear change over sessions for other clients the curve is choppy and change in the emotions does not always synchronize immediately with change in the doubts.

Please see 'Case illustrations' for more detail (including duration of therapy) regarding each of the cases.

The Yale Brown Obsessive Compulsive Scale was completed by independent evaluation in cases 2–8. Other self report questionnaire assessments (when available) included: the Obsessive Beliefs Questionnaire (OBQ-44), the Inferential Confusion Questionnaire (ICQ-EV), the Beck Depressive Inventory (BDI-II) and the Beck Anxiety Inventory (BAI).

In most cases mood and anxiety improve following IBT, as do other cognitive belief domains even though these domains were not specifically addressed during IBT.

Clinician's Handbook for Obsessive-Compulsive Disorder: Inference-Based Therapy, First Edition.
K. O'Connor and F. Aardema.
© 2012 John Wiley & Sons, Ltd. Published 2012 by John Wiley & Sons, Ltd.

Case 1 Clinical and Questionnaire scores

	Pre	Post
Yale Brown Obsessive Compulsive total Scale	23	4
Obsessional Beliefs Questionnaire	152	69
Beck Depression Inventory	20	4
Inferential Confusion Questionnaire	115	58

Case 2

Personal efficacy scale

On a scale from 0 to 100, please estimate your ability to resist the following compulsions:

	Pre	Mid	Post
1. Replay mentally past scenes to check if I did anything incorrected.	70	100	100
2. Return to places to see signs of agression.	95	100	100
3. Change thoughts of aggression by distraction.	5	90	85

Primary doubt scale

On a scale from 0 to 100, please estimate how much the following doubts are probable:

	Pre	Mid	Post
1. Perhaps I did something wrong inadvertently.	70	0	25
2. Perhaps I really hurt someone.	95	90	10
3. Perhaps I could be aggressive.	95	90	30

Secondary consequence scale

On a scale from 0 to 100, please estimate how much the following consequences are realistic if you do not accomplish your compulsions:

	Pre	Mid	Post
1. I'll be arrested and put in prison.	100	100	50
2. A catastrophe could occur.	80	70	20
3. No one would love me anymore.	90	100	40

Conviction level scale

On a scale from 0 to 100, please estimate how much you are convinced it is necessary to accomplish the following compulsions:

	Pre	Mid	Post	
1. Verify history of sites visited on the internet.	80	80	30	In context
	50	10	10	Out of context
2. Replay mentally past scenes to check if I did anything improper.	80	0	10	In context
	60	0	0	Out of context
3. Return to places to see signs of agression.	40	0	5	In context
	10	0	0	Out of context
4. Change thoughts of aggression by distraction.	100	10	35	In context
	100	0	10	Out of context

Diary

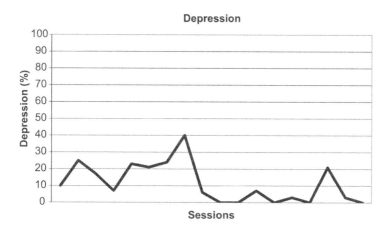

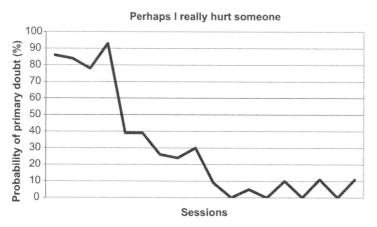

Clinical and Questionnaire Scores

	Pre	Post
Yale Brown Obsessive Compulsive Scale	22	8
Obsessive Beliefs Questionnaire	211	77
Beck Anxiety Inventory	18	3
Beck Depression Inventory	16	10
Padua Inventory	109	41
Inferential Confusion Questionnaire	94	30

Case 3

Personal efficacy scale

On a scale from 0 to 100, please estimate your ability to resist the following compulsions:

	Pre	Post
1. Asking his friends for reassurance	0	90
2. Checking the stove	20	100
3. Drawing four lines	30	99

Primary doubt scale

On a scale from 0 to 100, please estimate how much the following doubt are probable:

	Pre	Post
1. Maybe I could experience intolerable emotions.	100	4
2. Perhaps I do not have the right information.	100	12
3. Maybe the stove is not turned off.	50	0

Secondary consequences scale

On a scale from 0 to 100, please estimate how much the following consequences are realistic if you do not accomplish your compulsions:

	Pre	Post
1. There will be a fire.	50	0
2. I would look foolish or inadequate.	100	0
3. I could explode or break down if I didn't trace lines.	100	0

Conviction level scale

On a scale from 0 to 100, please estimate how much you are convinced it is necessary to accomplish the following compulsions:

	Pre	**Post**	
1. Checking the stove.	100	0	In context
	70	0	Out of context
2. Asking his friends for reassurance.	100	9	In context
	40	0	Out of context
3. Drawing lines.	100	0	In context
	0	0	Out of context

Diary

Anxiety

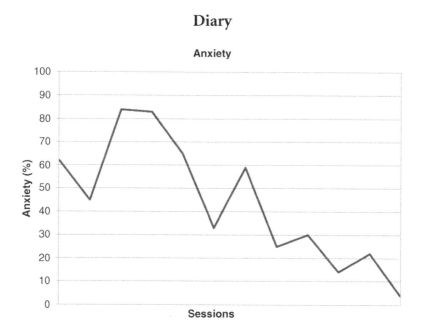

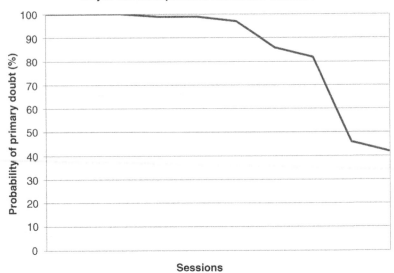

Maybe I could experience intolerable emotions

Clinical and Questionnaire Scores

	Pre	Post
Yale Brown Obsessive Compulsive Scale	29	7
Obsessive Beliefs Questionnaire	218	51
Beck Anxiety Inventory	15	10
Beck Depression Inventory	13	8
Padua Inventory	72	39
Inferential Confusion Questionnaire	136	69

Case 4

Personal efficacy scale

On a scale from 0 to 100, please estimate your ability to resist the following compulsions:

	Pre	Mid	Post
1. Remove things (posters, publicity) stuck on posters.	0	10	100
2. Remove any strange unfamiliar object.	0	15	100
3. Restrict my field of vision.	20	30	100
4. Get rid of things I've already seen once.	0	25	100

Primary doubt scale

On a scale from 0 to 100, please estimate how much the following doubts are probable:

	Pre	**Mid**	**Post**
1. Perhaps if I don't carry out these actions, a bad event will happen to my children.	100	30	0

Secondary consequence scale

On a scale from 0 to 100, please estimate how much the following consequences are realistic if you do not accomplish your compulsions:

	Pre	**Mid**	**Post**
1. Otherwise something bad will happen to my children.	100	85	0

Conviction level scale

On a scale from 0 to 100, please estimate how much you are convinced it is necessary to accomplish the following compulsions:

	Pre	**Mid**	**Post**	
1. Remove thing (posters, publicity) stuck on poster.	100	80	0	In context
	0	0	0	Out of context
2. Remove any strange unfamiliar object.	100	80	0	In context
	0	0	0	Out of context
3. Restrict my field of vision.	100	60	0	In context
	0	0	0	Out of context
4. Get rid of things I've already seen once.	100	60	0	In context
	0	0	0	Out of context

Diary

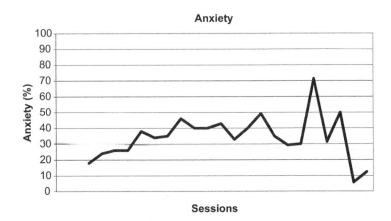

Diary

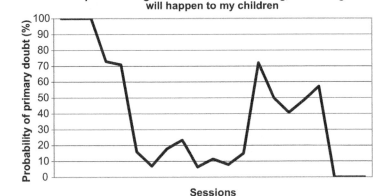

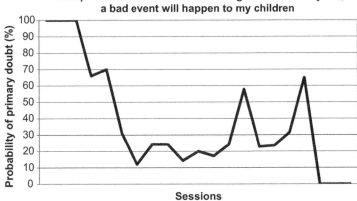

Clinical and Questionnaire Scores

	Pre	Post
Yale Brown Obsessive Compulsive Scale	28	0
Obsessive Beliefs Questionnaire	197	61
Beck Anxiety Inventory	1	1
Beck Depression Inventory	1	0
Padua Inventory	10	0
Inferential Cognitive Questionnaire	66	28

Case 5

Personal efficacy scale

On a scale from 0 to 100, please estimate your ability to resist the following compulsions:

	Pre	Mid	Post
1. Choose the right clothes to wear.	50	100	90
2. Make sure my hair is symmetrically placed.	0	0	100
3. Accumulating photos.	0	100	100
4. Give embraces to my husband repeatedly.	0	100	100

Primary doubt scale

On a scale from 0 to 100, please estimate how much the following doubts are probable:

	Pre	Mid	Post
1. Perhaps what I wear is not perfect for this day.	99	0	0
2. Perhaps my hair isn't right.	75	0	0
3. Perhaps there are faults in photos.	99	0	0
4. Perhaps I didn't kiss my husband goodnight.	85	0	0

Secondary consequence scale

On a scale from 0 to 100, please estimate how much the following consequences are realistic if you do not accomplish your compulsions:

	Pre	Mid	Post
1. I wouldn't look good.	100	100	100
2. I wouldn't feel on top of myself.	100	100	100
3. I wouldn't be able to play my part.	100	0	0
4. I would regret missing out on kiss if my husband died during his sleep.	100	100	100

Conviction level scale

On a scale from 0 to 100, please estimate how much you are convinced it is necessary to accomplish the following compulsions:

	Pre	Mid	Post	
1. Choose the right clothes to wear.	100		0	In context
	100		0	Out of context
2. Make sure my hair is symmetrically placed.	100		100	In context
	100		100	Out of context
3. Accumulating photos.	50		0	In context
	0		0	Out of context
4. Give embraces repeatedly.	100		0	In context
	100		0	Out of context

Diary

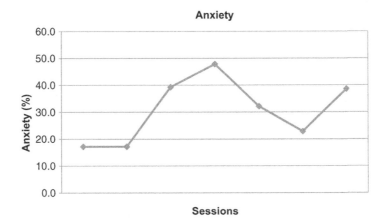

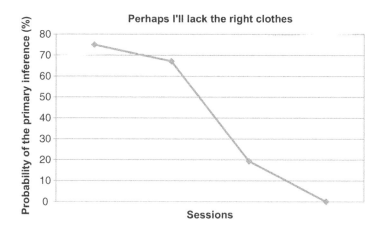

Diary

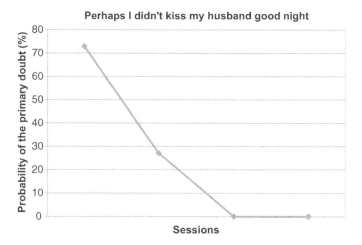

Clinical and Questionnaire Scores

	Pre	Post	6 months follow-up
Yale Brown Obsessive Compulsive Scale	27	19	0
Obsessive Beliefs Questionnaire	143	155	99
Beck Anxiety Inventory	2	4	0
Beck Depression Inventory	7	13	3
Padua Inventory	43	66	12
Inferential Confusion Questionnaire	82	58	39

Case 6

Personal efficacy scale

On a scale from 0 to 100, please estimate your ability to resist the following compulsions:

	Pre	Mid	Post
1. Think about placing objects optimally.	35	60	80
2. Placing objects at a precise angle.	15	70	80
3. Verifying by touch and by sight that objects are well placed.	25	70	85
4. Clean up everywhere after a visitor.	5	73	80

Primary doubt scale

On a scale from 0 to 100, please estimate how much the following doubts are probable:

	Pre	Mid	Post
1. Perhaps the object is not in the best place.	95	40	20
2. Perhaps the object is not facing the right angle.	90	35	20
3. Perhaps the object is not facing the right angle.	85	13	20
4. Perhaps someone has left their traces in my house.	95	35	20

Secondary consequence scale

On a scale from 0 to 100, please estimate how much the following consequences are realistic if you do not accomplish your compulsions:

	Pre	Mid	Post
1. It will not look good or efficient, but upsetting.	90	35	20
2. It won't look good, it'll be less functional and I'll seem negligent.	90	35	5
3. I'll be negligent to not place things properly.	40	25	10
4. I'll be negligent to not put back things in their initial state.	95	25	5

Conviction level scale

On a scale from 0 to 100, please estimate how much you are convinced it is necessary to accomplish the following compulsions:

	Pre	Mid	Post	
1. Think about placing objects optimally.	95	85	20	In context
	35	85	20	Out of context
2. Placing objects at a precise angle.	95	40	20	In context
	35	20	20	Out of context
3. Verifying by touch and by sight that objects are well placed.	90	35	15	In context
	45	20	15	Out of context
4. Clean up everywhere after a visitor.	95	40	20	In context
	35	20	20	Out of context

Diary

Anxiety

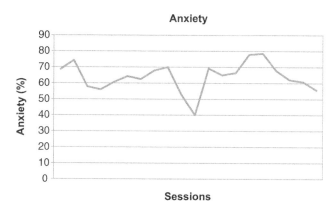

Diary

Perhaps the object is not facing the right angle

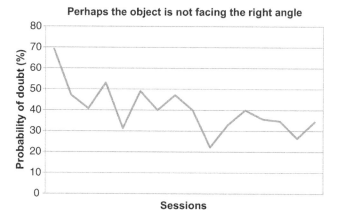

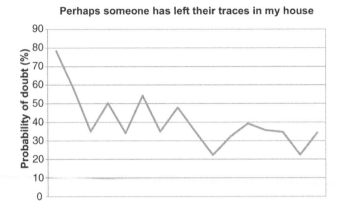

Perhaps someone has left their traces in my house

Clinical and Questionnaire Scores

	Pre	Post
Yale Brown Obsessive Compulsive Scale	36	17
Obsessive Beliefs Questionnaire	211	165
Beck Anxiety Inventory	11	5
Beck Depression Inventory	9	0
Padua Inventory	99	32
Inferential Confusion Questionnaire	90	93

Case 7

Personal efficacy scale

On a scale from 0 to 100, please estimate your ability to resist the following compulsions:

	Pre	Mid	Post
1. Empty and refill repeatedly cup of water.	75	90	100
2. Check food packages.	75	80	100
3. Check fruits and vegetables.	75	80	100
4. Wash hands.	35	80	75
5. Avoid touching chemical products' containers.	70	100	100
6. Keep mouth closed when in presence of someone who is taking medication.	100	100	100

Primary doubt scale

On a scale from 0 to 100, please estimate how much the following doubts are probable:

	Pre	Mid	Post
1. Perhaps something came into contact with the water.	20	0	0
2. Perhaps the food is contaminated inside the package.	60	10	0
3. Perhaps they are too dirty to consume.	30	10	0
4. They could be traces of chemical products on my hands.	80	10	20
5. Perhaps this product could contaminate me.	80	5	0
6. Perhaps I could absorb this medication.	10	0	0

Secondary consequence scale

On a scale from 0 to 100, please estimate how much the following consequences are realistic if you do not accomplish your compulsions:

	Pre	Mid	Post
1. I could get ill and die.	0	0	0
2. I could be poisoned.	80	5	0
3. I could be contaminated or poisoned.	10	1	0
4. I could be contaminated or poisoned.	40	5	15
5. I could be contaminated or poisoned.	20	5	0
6. I could be contaminated or poisoned.	10	0	0

Conviction level scale

On a scale from 0 to 100, please estimate how much you are convinced it is necessary to accomplish the following compulsions:

	Pre	Mid	Post	
1. Empty and refill repeatedly cup of water.	0	2	0	In context
	0	0	0	Out of context
2. Check food packages.	70	10	0	In context
	10	0	0	Out of context
3. Check fruits and vegetables.	30	10	0	In context
	10	0	0	Out of context
4. Wash hands.	80	10	15	In context
	10	0	0	Out of context

5. Avoid touching chemical products' containers.	90	10	0	In context
	70	0	0	Out of context
6. Keep mouth closed when in presence of someone who is taking medication.	0	0	0	In context
	0	0	0	Out of context

Diary

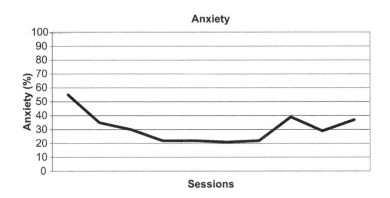

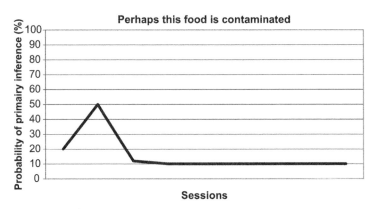

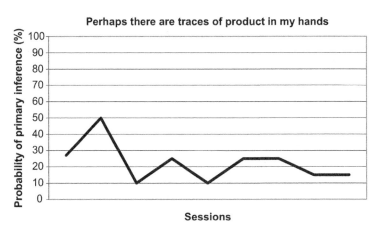

Clinical and Questionnaire Scores

	Pre	Post
Yale Brown Obsessive Compulsive Scale	20	2
Beck Anxiety Inventory	3	7
Beck Depression Inventory	0	0
Padua Inventory	51	16

Case 8

Personal efficacy scale

On a scale from 0 to 100, please estimate your ability to resist the following compulsions:

	Pre	Mid	Post
1. Wash my hands in a precise orderly sequence.	5	0	10
2. Wash my body in a precise sequence.	0	50	50
3. Count the number of steps in an action.	5	0	10
4. Plan very precisely any new actions.	92	92	100
5. Limit my contact with surroundings.	0	10	50
6. Replay an act I've done in my head.	40	30	90

Primary doubt scale

On a scale from 0 to 100, please estimate how much the following doubts are probable:

	Pre	Mid	Post
1. Perhaps my hands are contaminated.	100	100	50
2. Perhaps my body isn't washed properly.	100	50	50
3. Perhaps I could forget part of an action.	100	80	90
4. Perhaps I won't perform as I should do.	12	20	0
5. Perhaps the objects are contaminated or dirty.	90	90	60
6. Perhaps I'll forget to include all aspects.	50	40	0

Secondary consequence scale

On a scale from 0 to 100, please estimate how much the following consequences are realistic if you do not accomplish your compulsions:

	Pre	Mid	Post
1. Dirt and odour won't be eliminated and others will notice.	50	25	60
2. Others will notice and judge me negatively.	50	30	30
3. I'll have an air of dirtiness; others will keep their distance.	25	40	0
4. I'll forget to do something and others will notice.	25	20	20
5. I'll contaminate myself and others, and they won't forgive me.	75	80	35
6. I'll embarrass myself at work, and others will take note.	50	50	25

Conviction level scale

On a scale from 0 to 100, please estimate how much you are convinced it is necessary to accomplish the following compulsions:

	Pre	Mid	Post	
1. Wash my hands in a precise orderly sequence.	100	100	50	In context
	0	0	50	Out of context
2. Wash my body in a precise sequence.	100	100	50	In context
	50	0	50	Out of context
3. Count the number of steps in an action.	100	60	30	In context
	100	0	30	Out of context
4. Plan very precisely any new actions.	100	75	0	In context
	0	0	0	Out of context
5. Limit my contact with surroundings.	50	95	60	In context
	50	50	40	Out of context
6. Replay an act I've done in my head.	90	10	60	In context
	0	0	0	Out of context

Diary

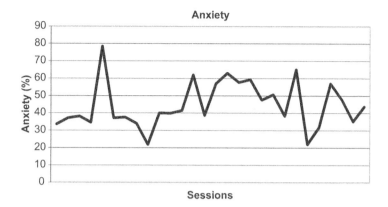

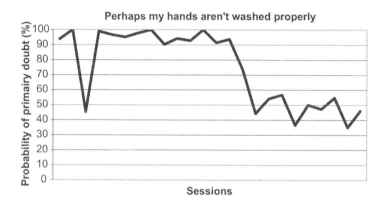

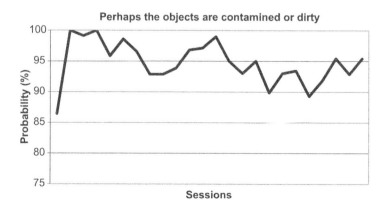

Case 8: Clinical and Questionnaire Scores

	Pre	Post	6 months follow-up
Yale Brown Obsessive Compulsive Scale	24	20	24
Obsessive Beliefs Questionnaire	109	100	128
Beck Anxiety Inventory	12	3	15
Beck Depression Inventory	13	1	12
Padua Inventory	37	9	49
Inferential Confusion Questionnaire	94	62	97

Answers to Common Queries from Clients

In this chapter we cover common queries from clients with suggested responses.

1. What is meant exactly by direct information or evidence for the doubt?

There usually are all kinds of triggers outside of you that may provoke an obsessional doubt. So obviously, there is information around you when you doubt. For example, you may just leave the house, see the door, and then doubt whether the door has been locked properly. However, what is meant with no direct information or evidence for the doubt is that there is no information in reality around you that supports your doubt. For example, while locking the door, you may sense or feel something out of the ordinary, like not being able to turn the key as far as usual. In that case, there is specific direct information or evidence for a doubt such as 'The door may not have been locked properly'. Obviously, this information is not conclusive, but it is sufficient to call the doubt a normal doubt. Obsessional doubts, however, occur without this type of information or evidence, and this is an important aspect of being able to tell the difference between obsessional and normal doubt.

2. I never really have certainty before the doubt occurs. I doubt all the time. So where is this certainty before the doubt?

There is some variation among people with OCD as to how generalized their doubt is. Some people only doubt in particular situations they encounter during the day,

Clinician's Handbook for Obsessive-Compulsive Disorder: Inference-Based Therapy, First Edition.
K. O'Connor and F. Aardema.
© 2012 John Wiley & Sons, Ltd. Published 2012 by John Wiley & Sons, Ltd.

and in calmer moments wonder why they were so upset or started to doubt anything at all. Others have doubts that continue to persist all day, and continue to experience the doubt as a valid concern no matter what situation they are in. In those cases, the certainty may not be apparent, even though there is certainty 'before' the doubt, which exists in what your senses tell you. Your senses have already told you all you need to know.

3. I do not doubt. I am certain that my doubts are real

Sometimes people with OCD are convinced that their particular obsessional concerns are the only possibility that exists. Then it seems as if there is no doubt. For example, you may be utterly convinced that there are dangerous germs on your hands, or that you do have a serious illness. However, in general, if we are really sure, we don't need to check or repeat actions. Do you need to constantly check to see if the walls in the room are still there? If you are repeating an action, you can't be completely certain. There is doubt.

4. My doubts are more like a feeling. There is no particular thought going through my mind

OCD can become very automatic, which makes it seem there are no thoughts related to your compulsions or discomfort. However, behind this feeling there always is a doubt. You can ask yourself a series of questions to uncover the doubt. First, ask yourself, 'What would happen if I would not carry out the ritual?' That usually uncovers the first layer of thoughts that have to do with your primary doubt. However, continue to trace these thoughts back to the primary doubt. For example, with washing compulsions the immediate concern might be that you will be contaminated, or for checking compulsions you may have thoughts like 'The house will burn down if I don't check'. Ask yourself 'When will I be contaminated?' or 'When will the house burn down?' The answer might be something like 'The doorknob might be dirty' or 'I might have left the oven on'. These are so-called primary doubts that give rise to everything else. Without them, you would feel no need to check or wash. Remember, your therapist can help you with identifying your primary doubts.

5. My doubts seem to come out of the blue. I don't think about anything in particular, and they suddenly appear. So are my doubts different from those of other people with OCD?

It's not uncommon that there are no immediate thoughts associated with the doubt. For example, think about driving. As you learnt how to drive, every action required a particular thought. Look in the mirror, change the gear, accelerate, brake and the like. As you became more practised, these actions no longer required any conscious thought. OCD is no different, your rituals and even doubts no longer seem to require any justification anymore, since they have become largely automatic. However, that does not mean that there was no justification initially. More importantly, you can still trace back the justification behind these doubts with some creativity. Act as if the doubts you recognise are someone else's. Then, try to imagine the justification this 'other person' could have for such doubts.

6. My doubts are totally senseless. I can't think of any justification for them

Obsessional doubts often appear 'unreasonable' even to the person experiencing them. However, do you feel the same way when you are in the OCD trigger situation where you doubt? Most people with OCD find their doubts absurd yet feel differently in the trigger situation where the obsessional doubt occurs. Then, suddenly, there are all kinds of thoughts that seem to support the doubt. So try to go back to the last time that you acted on an obsessional doubt, and see how you justified it back then.

7. Isn't my doubt possible even if the chances of it being true are very small?

A lot of things are possible, but in no way does that account for your OCD. Let's say, for example, that you would doubt whether or not there is a dog sitting behind you right now. It is easy to come up with all sorts of ideas and facts that could support the doubt ('Dogs exist', 'I heard of dogs entering neighbours houses', 'It is always possible' etc.). However, you do not doubt the fact that there is no dog behind you. The doubt doesn't even enter your mind, and even though you may consider it to be possible you very quickly dismiss this doubt as a very arbitrary and irrelevant doubt. So we are not arguing that the doubt is impossible, but what we argue is that the doubt is *irrelevant* to reality in the here and now.

If you would truly believe that the obsessional doubt is not relevant, then the doubt would not even occur. And the fact of the matter is that obsessional doubts are not really different from the above dog example. OCD has a great number of tricks up its sleeve to make it seem as if obsessional doubts are different, and that they actually do have something to do with the reality around you. However, if you look closely, you will always find that obsessional doubt occurs without direct evidence in the here and now. There is nothing in reality around you to support the doubt. Since there is nothing in reality, the doubt is not even 0.0001% possible. The doubt can only be 100% imaginary.

8. So my doubts are simply imaginary? It's all in my imagination?

The word 'imagination' is sometimes used in this kind of dismissive way: "Oh don't be silly It's just in your imagination', 'You're imagining things' or 'You're making up things'. However, imagination is much more than that, and in no way do we use the word 'imagination' in a dismissive kind of way. In fact, it is a faculty similar to other faculties like perception. We all rely on our imagination to make sense of the world around us, and it helps us to function where perception is ambiguous. The imagination can play an important part in normal life, and plays a role in how we arrive at conclusions. The difference for people with OCD is that there is a confusion, which makes it seem as if the imagined doubt has something to do with reality or perception, while in fact the obsessional doubt is in no way related to the world around you. Imagination trumps the senses whereas normally there is little or no overlap between perception and imagination, and the two faculties operate independently of each other. This idea about imagination is quite different to simply saying, 'It's all in your imagination, its silly'.

9. How can my doubt be 100% imaginary if I can justify it with all kinds of facts that come from reality?

The OCD story can contain elements that originate from reality, but as we said earlier, it has come about on a purely imaginary basis in that there is nothing in the here and now to support the obsessional doubt. Of course, there may be all kinds of facts 'wheeled' into the story that make the doubt seem more plausible and probable. The facts you wheel in to support the OCD story are generally of an abstract remote nature, e.g 'people can get infected', 'bird flu exists'. However, you will need to ask yourself the question whether these facts serve reality or whether they serve your imagination. If the doubt was not provoked by reality around you and no real evidence justifies the doubt, then why are these facts relevant? In other words, the facts have become part of a 100% imaginary process. Remember, no one ever got OCD from the fact that something is possible, or that it happened before to someone else. People with contamination concerns for example will frequently cite the existence of bird flu SARS as a 'fact' supporting their concern. But neither bird flu nor any real event elicited their OCD, rather such facts are produced to confirm the already existing fear. These facts or possibilities are merely rhetorical devices by which you come to feel your doubt as real. They are rhetorical, because you apply them in a situation where they are irrelevant, since they are in the service of your imagination and not the reality around you.

10. So if I trust my senses, all will fine? Are the senses never fallible?

This argument, where one might say 'Senses can be wrong', is of course quite true, but irrelevant. Firstly, as we have said before, the senses are indeed fallible but they're what connects us with reality. Indeed our senses are our only connection to reality. OCD does not help you guard against the fallibility of the senses. But it worsens your connection to reality, since in the OCD Bubble you are disconnected from reality and *less* aware of what is going on around you.

11. Why do other approaches not target doubt?

Clients may ask why other CBT therapies do not use IBT strategies. The reason lies principally in the distinction between intrusions and inferences. Some cognitive models recognize all intrusions as potential obsessions depending on how the person reacts. Intrusions can take many forms. Such intrusions may involve a questioning, but more usually they are a mix between observations, images, memories, thoughts, fantasies or insights. Everyday in everyway we have thousands of pop up thoughts, some quite senseless and sporadic, running through our minds. Here are just a few: 'That's a strange looking guy', 'Will he go drive through that space?' or 'What a loud mouth'.

However, in the IBT approach, although both people with and without OCD experience them, such 'pop up' thoughts are not the source of obsessions, rather obsessions begin with inferences. In particular, they begin with doubting inferences arrived at on the basis of a false reasoning narrative. Such inferences are not spontaneous intrusions. They are the gateway leading the client further into obsessional behaviour.

Therapist Queries

In this section we cover some common therapist queries about the IBT programme in question (Q) and answer (A) format.

The IBT Programme : Strategies and Principles

1. Q: The client initially complains that the exercises are not behavioural enough.
    A: Exploration of the model is delicate and essential for clients to understand the primacy of the doubt. The good news is that most click with IBT once they've grasped the key elements.
2. Q: Do I always need to follow the sequence of the programme?
    A: No. The outlined sequence is optimal and it is essential to cover all steps of IBT. But the therapist can be flexible. For example, in the case of a self-obsession, the self-theme can be addressed immediately.
3. Q: Is it necessary to address appraisals in IBT?
    A: This question needs to be answered in two parts. For the client, the first part involves understanding the sequence. Doubts precede consequences and appraisals and so constitute the primary target. But yes, of course, appraisals are clinically important, cause distress and may even need to be addressed first of all if the appraisals are impeding therapeutic alliance. For example, if someone is so ashamed of their problem they do not wish to face it, clearly the appraisal of shame may need to be overcome to embark on any therapy. It is also possible, as others have noted, that repeated failure to deal with obsessions leads to its own pessimistic mind-set. From the IBT perspective, it is clinically important that appraisals are not understood to

Clinician's Handbook for Obsessive-Compulsive Disorder: Inference-Based Therapy, First Edition.
K. O'Connor and F. Aardema.
© 2012 John Wiley & Sons, Ltd. Published 2012 by John Wiley & Sons, Ltd.

be the source of obsession but follow on from it. Evidence suggests that appraisals are not change anyway as a consequence of IBT.

The second part relates more to combining IBT with more traditional cognitive approaches. This is possible; however, in our experience, if IBT is successful, it is unnecessary to use other techniques to deal with obsessional anxiety or consequences since diminution follows naturally from resolution of obsessional doubt within the IBT process. However, as noted previously, other cognitive behavioural techniques may be useful in cases where avoidance and/or safety behaviours are inadvertently maintained.

4. Q: But isn't IBT a bit limited? You're just dealing with the cognitive element with no attempt to improve other psychosocial aspects, emotions, or the person's life skills.

A: It's true: IBT is a specialized cognitive therapy for OCD and related belief disorders. It may be incorrect to jump to conclusions that a client's problem relates to low self-esteem or to a social skills dysfunction since these are often consequences of the OCD, even though they may be the client's focus. A major tenet of IBT is that mostly the clients possess all the talents they require to overcome OCD, but OCD makes them doubt it. Hence the IBT approach is to strip away the OCD and then when the real client has repositioned themselves in the real world, review the case and consider any further remediatl action. In any case, the client will be much more likely to consider improving real-life skills as needed when free of OCD. Usually mood improves too following IBT.

5. Q: What's the relationship between IBT and acceptance-based therapies?

A: Essentially, both have a similar endpoint that the client does not react to previous obsessional thoughts in an obsessional way. In IBT, the endpoint is successful resolution of obsessional doubt, not its acceptance.

Clinical Issues

6. Q: The client is constantly in distress at each session.

A: Emotion can easily overtake the person, especially if they are absorbed into the secondary imaginary consequences. It may be necessary to address metacognitions. The client may be judging themselves or the problem badly or even punitively. The client may have developed the idea that they can never be free of OCD and foresee a dismal future which upsets them.

7. Q: What if the client has multiple obsessions?

A: Multiple obsessions will usually connect to one self-theme. This may make it essential in such cases to identify and reposition the person with respect to their self-theme. Usually if this is done, the IBT strstegies will generalize more easliy from one obsession to the other.

8. Q: When should I consider the client is not progressing?

A: There are always clients who do not respond to treatment. There are a variety of ways of defining treatment and recidivism. One accepted way is to consider all increase less than 30% as clinically insignificant. One of our important research findings is that clinical improvement at midtreatment (10–12 sessions) predicts successful outcome at the end of treatment. So if there is no clinical improvement after 10–12 sessions, the lack of progress needs to be clarified with the client. In our studies of IBT, we have found that only 15% do not respond favourably. Obviously decisions to continue or not should be based on actual evidence of improvement, not a clinician's illusion that progress is just around the corner.

9. Q: What should I do if the client has not improved at midtreatment?

A: Generally speaking, improvement at midtreatment after about 10–12 weeks is a robust predictor of outcome. Identify the component of IBT to which the client does not respond, and try to find out the obstacle which might be that (1) the client doesn't understand IBT properly, (2) the client considers that even prior to therapy IBT won't work.

In the case 1, it's a good idea to break down the information into short steps. Make sure the client masters each component by asking for repetition and checking the responses to the quizzes and worksheets.

In case 2, this problem may relate to a pre-existing expectation of therapy or a feeling that the client is a special case where the principles of the programme do not apply. Assuming the client has been able to comply with the exercises and quizzes and understands and accepts the model, then the problem may be outside stress or unreported problems. A narcissistic element might be in play here.

IBT has been shown to succeed in all subtypes, so if it doesn't succeed, there are two obvious reasons: (1) the person does not have OCD (e.g. they have complex cognitive tics); and (2) IBT is not delivered or complied with properly. Both of these issues should be readily detected by the experienced therapist. It is always possible that the client does not wish to follow the programme or applies themselves intermittently, giving the clinician the illusion that they will improve.

10. Q: What should I do with incorrect quiz answers?

A: Please go over the answers with the client. The quiz is a way of assuring that the practical implications of each step are understood. If an answer is incorrect, it is necessary to do some revision with the client.

11. Q: How important are nonspecific factors in IBT?

A: Obviously, the therapeutic alliance is important in any therapy. Although different psychotherapy schools have their own approaches to defining ingredients, clearly the basics are that the client needs to feel at ease to express themselves and be listened to, understood, protected, guided and confident in the progress of the therapy. But alliance is dynamic, and in our experience interacts with integration of the therapy content. The alliance and the therapy strategies are not static or independent. For example, once clients understand that IBT works for them, the working alliance can improve.

12.   Q: The client has difficulty creating an alternative story.

      A: Typically in this case, clients will either think they must create a huge story or think they need to be convinced immediately. It is worth experimenting with building up a story organically.

13.   Q: At the end of treatment, the client still believes the doubt is possible.

      A: Go back to the basic doubt exercises in the early steps of therapy. It is important to always check the basics and that the client has understood the basic IBT principles.

14.   Q: Neither I nor the client seem able to find the right doubt.

      A: This can be problematic due to the secondary nature of some doubts. So it is important to backtrack to the base doubt. The base doubt is the first doubt which takes the person away from reality.

15.   Q: The obsessional story is so bizarre, it could be psychotic.

      A: Don't be distracted by the bizarre nature of the story. It is likely to be treatable identically to a nonbizarre one, even though it is drawn from a more idiosyncratic source and justification. We once saw a client convinced that other people could get inside her if she didn't wash properly. In fact, her story was driven by a vulnerable theme about being used and exploited, and the story taken from a highly imaginative sequence in a film where a character she identified with experiencing her body being possessed by others. All the same OCD reasoning errors applied in this case as in nonbizarre cases.

16.   Q: What if the doubt keeps changing?

      A: This probably means you have located a secondary doubt or offshoot doubt, the same as with consequences since they are a secondary product of the main doubting inferences. These secondary doubts are less stable and may change more according to context or situation. For example, a client may initially say, 'I think others might be looking at me', and think, 'Maybe I don't walk straight'. Maybe the next time the client may say, 'No, it's not that, it's more that they are looking at the way I move my bum'. All this could be traceable to the base doubt 'When I'm with others, I think maybe others think I'm not normal'.

17.   Q: Are there other strategies to help the client become aware of reasoning problems?

      A: One supplementary technique is to ask the client to relisten to or reread their own dialogue between sessions. This exercise can stimulate reflection.

18.   Q: What if the person expresses no doubts, only certainties?

      A: In some delusional-like OCD, it may appear there is a firm conviction about the reality of the obsessional doubt. It may be that the client believes the maybe is a certain 'maybe', but in reality there is a doubt, as illustrated in the following dialogue.

C: My hands are surely dirty, I know it.

T: But how are you 100% sure?

C: Because of my intelligence.

T: But what do your senses say is there?

C: Well, I don't trust my senses. They could miss out.

T: So you're unsure of your senses here?

C: Yes.

T: You doubt them?

C: Yes, I doubt they're right.

19. Q: How can I contest facts which seem to support OCD behaviour?

A: Clients may initially contest IBT by tenaciously producing facts about infections or other dangers to support the OCD. The therapist can here highlight the selectivity and incoherence in the citing of such abstract facts. One example here is 'microbes'. Microbes, of course, do exist – but why is the client citing this fact in some situations, but not in others? Usually a client afraid to touch an object due to microbes is not afraid of breathing in microbes in the air. When comparing the obsessional doubt to other situations where the client uses the senses normally, the response might be 'Well, it's not the same. My doubt is important and different.' Usually, however, other non-OCD situations (e.g., crossing the road) are equally as dangerous as the OCD consequences. The aim here is to let the client understand that the facts do not cause the fear; the fear precedes the facts, and the facts are there just to confirm the imaginary story generating the fear. A vulnerable self-theme underlies the obsessional conviction. When the client grasps how doubts are connected through the vulnerable OCD self-theme, they will also recognize how only threats to the idiosyncratic self-theme trigger the doubts. This awareness of the central role of the feared OCD self-identity can help the client identify potential OCD trigger risk situations. If a threat is only a threat because it touches the self-theme, then it is part of the obsessional response pattern.

Quiz Answers Sheet

Quiz 1: When OCD Begins

1b, 2b, 3b, 4d, 5c, 6f

Quiz 2: The Logic Behind OCD

1b, 2a, 3d, 4d, 5b, 6d

Quiz 3: The Obsessional Story

1b, 2a, 3b, 4d, 5c

Quiz 4: The Vulnerable Self-Theme

1d, 2b, 3b, 4a, 5d, 6b

Quiz 5: OCD is 100% Imaginary

1b, 2d, 3d, 4c, 5c, 6c

Clinician's Handbook for Obsessive-Compulsive Disorder: Inference-Based Therapy, First Edition.
K. O'Connor and F. Aardema.
© 2012 John Wiley & Sons, Ltd. Published 2012 by John Wiley & Sons, Ltd.

Quiz 6: OCD Doubts are 100% Irrelevant

1b, 2d, 3b, 4d, 5d, 6d

Quiz 7: The OCD Bubble

1d, 2a, 3d, 4d, 5b

Quiz 8: Reality Sensing

1c, 2d, 3d, 4c, 5a

Quiz 9: A Different Story

1b, 2b, 3a, 4a, 5d, 6a

Quiz 10: Tricks and Cheats of the OCD Con Artist

1ab 2d, 3d, 4b, 5a, 6b

Quiz 11: The Real Self

1b, 2a, 3a, 4d, 5b, 6b

Quiz 12: Knowing and Doing: Moving On and Preventing Relapse

1c, 2b, 3a, 4a, 5b, 6d

Appendix 1

Inferential Confusion Questionnaire (ICQ-EV)

Please rate your agreement or disagreement with the following statements using this scale:

Scale:

1	2	3	4	5	6
strongly disagree	disagree	somewhat disagree	somewhat agree	agree	strongly agree

	Answer 1 to 6
I am sometimes more convinced about what might be there than by what I actually see.	
I sometimes invent stories about certain problems that might be there without paying attention to what I actually see.	
Sometimes certain far-fetched ideas feel so real they could just as well be happening.	
Often my mind starts to race and I come up with all kinds of far-fetched ideas.	
I can get very easily absorbed in remote possibilities that feel as if they are real.	
I often confuse different events as if they were the same.	
I often connect ideas or events in my mind that would seem far-fetched to others or even to me.	

Clinician's Handbook for Obsessive-Compulsive Disorder: Inference-Based Therapy, First Edition.
K. O'Connor and F. Aardema.
© 2012 John Wiley & Sons, Ltd. Published 2012 by John Wiley & Sons, Ltd.

Certain disturbing thoughts of mine sometimes cast a shadow onto everything I see around me.	
I sometime forget who or where I am when I get absorbed into certain ideas or stories.	
My imagination is sometimes so strong that I feel stuck and unable to see things differently.	
I invent arbitrary rules, which I then feel I have to live by.	
I often cannot tell whether something is safe, because things are not what they appear to be.	
Sometimes every far-fetched possibility my mind comes up with feels real to me.	
I sometimes get so absorbed in certain ideas that I am completely unable to see things differently even if I try.	
In order to tell whether there is a problem or not I tend to look more for that which is hidden than what I can actually see.	
Even if I don't have any actual proof of a certain problem, my imagination can convince me otherwise.	
Just the thought that there could be a problem or something wrong is proof enough for me that there is.	
I can get so caught up in certain ideas of mine that I totally forget about everything around me.	
Often when I feel certain about something, a small detail comes to mind that puts everything into doubt.	
I sometimes come up with far-fetched reasons why there is a problem or something wrong, which then suddenly starts to feel real to me.	
I often cannot get rid of certain ideas, because I keep coming up with possibilities that confirm my ideas.	
My imagination can make me lose confidence in what I actually perceive.	
A mere possibility often has as much impact on me as reality itself.	
Even if I have all sorts of visible evidence against the existence of a certain problem, I still feel it will occur.	
Even the smallest possibility can make me lose confidence in what I know.	
I can imagine something and end up living it.	
I am more often concerned with something that I cannot see rather than something I can see.	
I sometimes come up with bizarre possibilities that feel real to me.	
I often react to a scenario that might happen as if it is actually happening.	
I sometimes cannot tell whether all the possibilities that enter my mind are real or not.	

Appendix 2

IBT Clinical Scales

Perceived Personal Efficacy in Resisting Compulsive and Other Neutralizing Behaviour

Personal Efficacy Scale

On a scale from 0 to 100, please estimate your ability to resist the following compulsive behaviours and neutralizations:

	Pre	Mid	Post
1. _____	_____	_____	_____
2. _____	_____	_____	_____
3. _____	_____	_____	_____
4. _____	_____	_____	_____
5. _____	_____	_____	_____
6. _____	_____	_____	_____
7. _____	_____	_____	_____
8. _____	_____	_____	_____

Clinician's Handbook for Obsessive-Compulsive Disorder: Inference-Based Therapy, First Edition.
K. O'Connor and F. Aardema.
© 2012 John Wiley & Sons, Ltd. Published 2012 by John Wiley & Sons, Ltd.

9. _____ _____ _____ _____

10. _____ _____ _____ _____

Primary Doubt Scale

On a scale from 0 to 100, please estimate how much the following inferences are probable:

	Pre	Mid	Post

1. _____ _____ _____ _____

2. _____ _____ _____ _____

3. _____ _____ _____ _____

4. _____ _____ _____ _____

5. _____ _____ _____ _____

6. _____ _____ _____ _____

7. _____ _____ _____ _____

8. _____ _____ _____ _____

9. _____ _____ _____ _____

10. _____ _____ _____ _____

Anticipated (Secondary) Consequences Scale

On a scale from 0 to 100, please estimate how much the following inferences are realistic if you do not accomplish your compulsions:

	Pre	Mid	Post

1. _____ _____ _____ _____

2. _____ _____ _____ _____

3. _____ _____ _____ _____

4. _____ _____ _____ _____

5. _____ _____ _____ _____

6. _____ _____ _____ _____

7. _____ _____ _____ _____

8. _____ _____ _____ _____

9. _____ _____ _____ _____

10. _____ _____ _____ _____

Conviction Level Scale

On a scale from 0 to 100, please estimate how much you are convinced it is necessary to accomplish the following compulsions:

	Pre	Mid	Post	
1. _____	_____	_____	_____	(in context)
				(out of context)
2. _____	_____	_____	_____	(in context)
				(out of context)
3. _____	_____	_____	_____	(in context)
				(out of context)
4. _____	_____	_____	_____	(in context)
				(out of context)
5. _____	_____	_____	_____	(in context)
				(out of context)
6. _____	_____	_____	_____	(in context)
				(out of context)
7. _____	_____	_____	_____	(in context)
				(out of context)
8. _____	_____	_____	_____	(in context)
				(out of context)
9. _____	_____	_____	_____	(in context)
				(out of context)
10. _____	_____	_____	_____	(in context)
				(out of context)

How to use clinical scales addressing OCD doubts, anticipated consequences and conviction levels

The probability of obsessional doubt and the realism or likelihood of anticipated consequences are assessed transversally using clinical rating scales that ranging from 0 (not at all) to 100 (extremely). Since the anticipated consequences follow on from the obsessional doubt, a convenient format to separate obsessional doubts (i.e. primary or initial inferences) and anticipated consequences (i.e. secondary inferences) is to use a logical template of the form 'If . . ., then . . .' The following example involving fear of contamination will now be used to describe this logical template: 'If the hands are dirty, then I will contaminate others'. Here, in logic, the first clause after 'If' is the primary inference (or premise); the clause after 'Then' is the secondary inference (or corollary). If the primary inference is not clear, it is possible to work back from the consequences and ask, 'And that will happen if what state of affairs (is true), or (happens)?' So, in the following example, the client (C) spontaneously volunteers a consequence to the therapist (T).

C: If I don't wash my hands, I will contaminate others.
T: And others will be contaminated if that state of affairs is true?
C: Well, if my hands are dirty.

After having properly identified the obsessional doubt (e.g. if my hands are dirty) by differentiating it from the anticipated consequence (e.g. others will be contaminated), the therapist may now use the clinical scales to assess the IBT relevant components related the this fear of contamination:

The Perceived Ability to Resist Scale assesses how participants perceived their resistance to rituals according to the following question: to what extent do you believe that you are capable of resisting your washing ritual?

The Probability of Obsessional Doubt Scale evaluates degree of belief in obsessional doubt as a real probability, that is likely to be true, according to the following question: to what extent is it probable that. . .(example: your hands may be dirty)?

The Realism of Anticipated Consequences Scale assesses degree of belief in the realism in anticipated consequences according to the following question: if your hands are, in fact, dirty, to what extent is it realistic to think that you could . . . (example: contaminate others by not washing them)?

Self-monitoring diary

The probability of obsessional doubt and the realism of anticipated consequences can also be assessed longitudinally throughout therapy using a daily self-monitoring diary as described in Appendix 5.

The Degree of Conviction (DCP) Scale evaluates degree of convictionin the need to perform rituals to prevent anticipated consequences according to the following question: to what extent are you convinced that you must perform your washing ritual to avoid contaminating others?

Appendix 3

Therapy Evaluation Form and Scale[1]

Therapy Evaluation Form
(Adapted from Devilly & Borkovic, 2000)

Please use this scale to answer the following questions:

0	1	2	3	4	5
Not at all	Not much	A little	Moderately	A lot	Enormously

1. At this point, how much has therapy helped you?
2.
   (a) At this point, how much do the following elements contribute to help you?
   ___ be able to *talk* about my obsessions and compulsions
   ___ better understanding of how my obsessions and compulsions are maintained
   ___ receive advice and suggestions from my therapist
   ___ homework
   ___ information I receive
   (b) If there are any other elements that help you, please mention them below and write down how much they have helped you:
   _____
   _____

[1]Adapted with permission from Devilly & Borkovic, (2000) by Laverdure, Pelissier and O'Connor (2002).

_____

_____

_____

_____

(c) Amongst all the elements named above, what are the three most important ones for you? Please write them down *from the most important to the least.*

1st _____

2nd _____

3rd _____

3. _____ At this point, how satisfied are you with therapy?

Please indicate how much you believe, *right now*, that the therapy you are receiving will help to reduce your problems. Belief usually has two aspects: (1) what one *thinks* will happen and (2) what one *feels* will happen. Sometimes both aspects are similar; sometimes they are different. Please answer the questions of Part I in terms of what you *think* and those of Part II in terms of what you really and truly feel.

Part I

1. At this point, how logical does the therapy you are receiving seem?

1	2	3	4	5	6	7	8	9
Not logical at all				Somewhat logical				Very logical

2. At this point, how useful do you think this treatment will be in reducing your symptoms?

1	2	3	4	5	6	7	8	9
Not useful at all				Somewhat useful				Very useful

3. How confident would you be in recommending this treatment to a friend who experiences similar problems?

1	2	3	4	5	6	7	8	9
Not confident at all				Somewhat confident				Very confident

4. By the end of therapy, how much improvement in your symptoms do you think there will be?

0%   10%   20%   30%   40%   50%   60%   70%   80%   90%   100%

Part II

For this set, please close your eyes a moment and try to identify what you really *feel* about the therapy and its possible success. Then, answer the following questions.

1. At this point, how much do you really feel that therapy will help you reduce your symptoms?

1	2	3	4	5	6	7	8	9
Not at all				Somewhat				Very much

2. By the end of the therapy period, how much improvement in your symptoms do you really *feel* will occur?

0%   10%   20%   30%   40%   50%   60%   70%   80%   90%   100%

3. During the last week, how much time a day, approximately, were the obsessions present?

1	2	3	4	5	6	7	8	9
0 to 5 min.	6 to 15 min.	16 to 30 min.	31 to 60 min.	1 to 2 hr	2 to 3 hr	3 to 5 hr	5 to 8 hr	more than 8 hr

4. During the last week, how much time a day, approximately, were the compulsions present?

1	2	3	4	5	6	7	8	9
0 to 5 min.	6 to 15 min.	16 to 30 min.	31 to 60 min.	1 to 2 hr	2 to 3 hr	3 to 5 hr	5 to 8 hr	more than 8 hr

5. In 3 months, how much time a day do you think the obsessions will be present?

1	2	3	4	5	6	7	8	9
0 to 5 min.	6 to 15 min.	16 to 30 min.	31 to 60 min.	1 to 2 hr	2 to 3 hr	3 to 5 hr	5 to 8 hr	more than 8 hr

6. In 3 months, how much time a day do you think the compulsions will be present?

1	2	3	4	5	6	7	8	9
0 to 5 min.	6 to 15 min.	16 to 30 min.	31 to 60 min.	1 to 2 hr	2 to 3 hr	3 to 5 hr	5 to 8 hr	more than 8 hr

7. At this point, what have you least liked in this therapy?

_____

_____

_____

_____

8.   At this point, what have you liked the most in this therapy?

_____

_____

_____

_____

Therapist Evaluation Scale

By using the following scale, evaluate your degree of agreement for each statement. For each statement, write the number that best reflects your attitude toward your therapist. Your answers are confidential.

1	2	3	4	5	6	7
Strongly agree	Generally agree	A little agree	Neutral	A little disagree	Generally disagree	Strongly disagree

	Write a number	
1.	–	My therapist could certainly confront me more.
2.	–	My therapist appears as a confident and sure person.
3.	–	What my therapist says does not contradict what she seems to think or to feel.
4.	–	My therapist seems to have difficulty to tolerate my fears and my apprehensions.
5.	–	My therapist is free to reveal his/her own thoughts or feelings when I ask her (him).
6.	–	My therapist is a kind person.
7.	–	I always understand exactly what my therapist says when he/she talks to me.
8.	–	My therapist encourages me to continue my efforts.
9.	–	When I succeed a stage toward recovery, my therapist presents new things to work on.
10.	–	My therapist seems comfortable with herself/himself.
11.	–	My therapist tries to avoid my questions when I attempt to know her/him more.
12.	–	Sometimes my therapist leaves me confused about what he/she tries to say to me.

13.	–	Sometimes, my therapist shows positive and friendly reactions toward me than he/she does at other moment.
14.	–	In general, I feel that my therapist respects me as an individual.
15.	–	My therapist is clear when he/she expresses himself/herself to me.
16.	–	My therapist seems to be a cold person.
17.	–	My therapist tries to see things like I see them.
18.	–	My therapist is uncomfortable when I ask for information concerning himself/herself.
19.	–	My therapist seems frequently unfit and gauche.
20.	–	I can be very critical or very grateful toward my therapist without provoking any changes concerning his/her feelings for me.
21.	–	My therapist seems very interested in my case.
22.	–	My therapist always presents me with new challenges to help me increase my progress.
23.	–	My therapist likes me more when I behave in a certain way rather than in the other ways.
24.	–	My therapist seems afraid and uncertain of himself/herself.
25.	–	If I wish so, my therapist is ready to use our time so I can better know him/her.

Notes for therapy sessions[2]

| Date: _____ | Session: _____ | Therapist: _____ |
| Session: _____ | | |

A) Appointment
☐ The client was late more than 5 minutes.
☐ The client is not present (without warning).
☐ The client changed appointments less than 24 hr before.
☐ The client changed appointments more than 24 hr before.

B) Self-monitoring
☐ Not completed
☐ Partially completed
☐ Not brought to interview
☐ Completed

Others (questionnaires, etc.):

	☐ Not do	☐ Incomplete	☐ Complete
	☐ Not do	☐ Incomplete	☐ Complete
	☐ Not do	☐ Incomplete	☐ Complete

File notes

(A) *Review of the week/intervention goals*

_____

_____

_____

_____

_____

_____

_____

_____

_____

_____

_____

_____

Date of the next meeting: _____

(B) *Intervention and model comprehension*

0	1	2	3	4	5	6	7	8
Absent		Minimal		Acceptable		Very good		Surpass expectations

(C) *Therapeutic alliance*

0	1	2	3	4	5	6	7	8
Absent		Minimal		Acceptable		Very good		Surpass expectations

(D) *Awareness of changes*

0	1	2	3	4	5	6	7	8
Absent		Minimal		Acceptable		Very good		Surpass expectations

Homeworks

Previous homework

☐ The therapist did not give homework.
☐ The therapist did not revise the homework.
☐ The therapist revised the homework.
☐ The therapist revised the homework in detail and integrated it during the session.

Difficulty in use of homework

☐ The homework is not well explained.
☐ Did not give written instructions or did not verify the understanding of the client (make repeat).
☐ Did not give relevant homework.

Actual homework

The therapist

☐ did give homework
☐ did not give homework

Homework

		Frequency/Quantity
Task 1		
Task 2		
Task 3		

Review of previous homework (to fill before the next appointment)

	Not attempted	Attempted but abandon	Different homework but relevant	Degree of success (%)	Success greater than required	Frequency/ amount (of homework)
Task 1				%		
Comments:						

Task 2				%		
Comments:						
Task 3				%		
Comments:						

Impact

☐ The homework had an impact on the knowledge of the client.
☐ The homework had an impact on the emotional state of the client.
☐ The homework had an impact on the behaviour of the client.

(E) *Global evaluation of the degree of cooperation from the client in the carrying out the homework*

0	1	2	3	4	5	6	7	8
Absent		Minimal		Acceptable		Very good		exceed expectations

(F) *Global evaluation for the quality of homework*

0	1	2	3	4	5	6	7	8
Absent		Minimal		Acceptable		Very good		exceed expectations

_____

Signature
Licence # _____
_____

[2]Adapted by O'Connor, 2005.

Appendix 4

Avoidance and Situational Profile Scale

Avoidance

People who have OCD tend to avoid objects, places or situations which are, or at least perceived to be, associated with obsessional thoughts. Avoidance can serve to (1) prevent the occurrence of obsessional thoughts, (2) minimize the possible consequences should the obsessions occur and (3) prevent anxiety or the feeling of guilt which can be caused by the occurrence of obsessions. Please name the things which you avoid because of your obsessional thoughts.

Places (e.g. hospitals, the subway, the dentist, etc.)

People (e.g. people with illnesses, people with injuries, etc.)

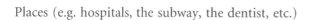

Situations (e.g. being alone with an injured person, being too close to someone of the opposite sex, children, etc.)

Information (e.g. movies, television, newspapers, radio, books, conversations, etc.)
Objects (e.g. knives, syringes, etc.)

Activities (e.g. driving, walking in the forest, etc.)

Other

Please place in order of difficulty.

Easiest to confront   0
                                       10
                                       20
                                       30
                                       40
                                       50
                                       60
                                       70
                                       80
                                       90
Most difficult to confront   100

Situational Profile: Part #1

What are the situations, the states, the activities or the events during which your obsessions or your compulsions are more likely to occur or to increase?

For example, some people find that their compulsions are more likely to occur when they are stressed, tired or sad; others when they have nothing to do or a boring task to accomplish, or when they are alone.

Here are some examples...

Examples of situations and activities:

> Conflictual situation
> Social situation
> Situation at work
> Repetitive activities or tasks
> Difficult tasks
> When you are on vacation
> When you have nothing to do

Examples of events:

> If you receive good/bad news
> If you have an accident
> If you get sick
> Illness or death of a close other
> Love or friendship breakup

Examples of states:

Tired	Sad
Bored	Stressed
Excited	Disappointed
Frustrated	Isolated

Please list all the situations, states, activities or events that may trigger or increase your obsessions and your compulsions.

Situations/States/Activities/Events	Probability of OCD increase (from 0% to 100%)

Situational Profile: Part #2

What are the situations, states, activities or events during which your obsessions or your compulsions are at their lowest or have a tendency to decrease?

Situations/States/Activities/Events	Probability of OCD decrease (from 0% to 100%)

Appendix 5

Diary

Instruction Guide for the Therapist

Introduction

Self-monitoring is a very important tool for understanding the process of change during therapy. Experiments show that the majority of clients with OCD are able to do it well. However, the therapist and his/her attitudes are essential for success. If the task is well structured, if the client understands well and if the client is well motivated and reinforced by the therapist, quality results are obtained.

Basic daily self-monitoring is conducted using a little individualised notebook and is composed of four kinds of variables:

Symptoms (duration, distress)
Emotional state
Primary doubt and anticipated secondary consequences

Self-monitoring is introduced gradually. The first week, the clients evaluate the symptoms. Starting in the second week, clients evaluate the symptoms and emotional state. Starting in the third week they evaluate all variables. During the first few weeks a standardised notebook is used in which idiosyncratic items are written.

Kieron O'Connor, PhD, 2002 (Adapted from: Mark H. Freeston, PhD & Kieron P. O'Connor, PhD, Nov. 1997). Fernand-Seguin Research Center Montreal, Quebec

Later, an individualised booklet is made which contains all of the items. In this way, we ensure the fidelity of the items over the course of treatment and we show, in a very behavioural way, the importance that we attribute to self-monitoring.

The client brings the notebook back to each session. If they forget the notebook, they bring it back the next session.

How to Explain Self-Monitoring, Establish Its Importance, Motivate the Client and Prevent Obstacles

The following points are important to point out to clients:

Explain and establish importance of self-monitoring

Self-monitoring (which means writing each day certain behaviours, thoughts or emotions) allows the therapist to understand what is happening between sessions.

It is difficult to change something if we don't pay any particular attention to it; self-monitoring allows people to learn about their difficulties. Being conscious of difficulties is the first step of the process of change.

An important part of the therapy is to carefully examine your difficulties. Writing them down each day helps you establish exactly what is happening each day. When we live with a problem, we get used to our reactions and we don't notice all of the different variations which can be related to different factors.

Self-monitoring is a tool which enables us to see if the therapy is going well, to see if there is an obstacle in the process, to understand the obstacle more, and to find solutions.

The gathered information allows us to adjust the treatment for each person and to plan strategies that enable gains to be maintained long term.

Motivate the client and prevent difficulties

It is important to fill in the booklet at the same time each day, to establish a routine. Therefore it is necessary to find a moment which occurs each day: coffee after supper, before brushing your teeth at night, after having fed the cat, etc. The more self-monitoring fits into a routine, the more the data is accurate and less of an arduous task. (The therapist helps the client identify the best moment.)

It is normal to find self-monitoring 'annoying' and hard the first few weeks, but people get used to it and become used to doing it. Once the person is used to it, it doesn't take more than 5 minutes per day.

Self-monitoring is written in little notebooks which are discreet. This way, the person can carry them in their pocket, or purse or their bathroom kit. This way there is no reason for not doing it when the normal routine is disturbed, for example when you are travelling.

Possibly paying attention to the symptoms will worsen them and may be their trouble or degree of preoccupation will increase. It is rare that this occurs, and in these rare cases, it is generally temporary. For some people, it is even the opposite which happens – they find that their behaviours take place less often than they thought. In any case, self-monitoring is a way for starting to see your difficulties in a different way.

Some people are afraid to put 'the wrong rating' down. The ratings are relative and we look for each person's experience, as such there is no right rating in the absolute sense. Filling out the notebooks daily diminishes the stakes. Even if mistake ourselves a little today, we can take it up again tomorrow.

If ever you have difficulties in filling out this notebook, it is important that the therapist knows. That way both of you find a solution to the problem together. Self-monitoring is important in helping us understand what is going on and is not to embarrass you.

General Behaviours and 'Troubleshooting'

The following points explain the role of the therapist and the behaviours to adopt in confronting various situations which may arise in completing diaries.

Check the client's understanding by asking them to repeat the instructions. It is often very useful to give written instructions or to ask the client to take notes.

Go back to the self-monitoring during each session. Even if there is nothing special, *always* make a comment: 'I see that Wednesday was a good/bad day', or 'It is interesting to see just to what point the duration is relatively stable, but the degree of disturbance varies'. This behaviour on the part of the therapist reinforces self-monitoring more than any other strategy. It also allows the therapist to closely follow clients. This way the client becomes more motivated and the therapeutic relationship is consolidated by a displayed active interest. As well, by closely following clients, the therapist can even be surprised to find important phenomena.

In the first few weeks, return to the routine aspect of the task:

'When did you fill out the notebook? Did you have difficulty remembering to do it? What can you do to make the task even easier?'

1. The client should always have at least one or two extra notebooks in case the appointment be postponed. Giving too many notebooks (for example, for the entire therapy) at the beginning is not a good idea, because this takes away the ability to talk about self-monitoring at the end of session.
2. Periodically verify that the people use the same reference point as at the start. (See the section on operationalising the variables.) 'Just to be sure that we are talking about the same thing, 100 means. . .'
3. If the ratings do not seem to reflect other changes brought forward by the client, it is important to investigate, without making a demand for change. The two main reasons are the fear that the therapy will be terminated and the superstitious fears related to saying that things are going well.

'It sometimes arises that people are afraid to diminish their ratings. Sometimes they are afraid that if they say that things are going better that there will be consequences. These consequences could be, for example, that the therapy will be ended immediately. Or, the fact that saying that things are going well may be bad luck and things will start to go wrong. Is it possible that something similar is happening here?'

4. If you suspect that the client is filling out the notebook just before each session (the handwriting does not vary, pen is always the same colour, etc.), it is important to raise this question delicately.

'We know that some people have a harder time at being regular in their habits, despite their good intentions. How do you find the task of having to fill out the notebook daily?'

5. It often occurs that some people arrive with an empty notebook or with just the first few days filled out. This could be due to the fact that the person may believe that if they miss a few days, that the whole week is ruined. In this case, it is important to discuss the occasional missing data, and to stress that if the person returns to it the next day, almost nothing is lost: it is better to miss one day or two than an entire week.

6. If you suspect that the 'forgotten' or 'lost' notebook(s) is (are) not being filled out, it is important to raise the possibility by using the 'problem solving' approach. 'It seems to me that this the xth time that the same thing has happened. I am asking myself what we can do to facilitate the task?'

Anchoring Ratings

General instructions

The principal variables (except duration) are evaluated on a scale of 0 to 100, which is located on the cover of the notebook. For some variables, the fact that there is a scale in words ('none' to 'extreme') and a scale of 0–100 allows people to generally locate themselves with the words before prescribing numbers. This allows people to translate, in a more standardized way, the experience as being 'a little' or 'average' within the numbered scale.

Because OCD is a chronic disorder with an evolution which often fluctuates in intensity, it is important to solidify the scale in a realistic way. If this is not done, it is easy to have floor effects for certain variables. Therefore, for many variables, the last month(s) serve(s) as a reference point. The maximum on the scale is 'the worst attained in the last month' and not 'the worst I have ever had in my life'. If the last month is the worst month in the last year, refer to something a little bit more typical. If the present severity surpasses the reference point, the person can write 100 and the therapist can understand that, in reality, it is more than 100.

Symptoms Two basic items measure the symptoms, notably the duration and the degree of distress caused by the obsessional and/or compulsive symptoms.

Item 1: Duration. The duration refers to the number of hours and minutes in the day that the symptom is present. It is important to see, with the person, *their* definition of 'present': a continual fashion (without end) versus a repetitive fashion within a period, paying complete attention versus in the back of the mind, wanting to do the compulsion versus doing it, etc. What is important is that the definition 'present' makes sense to the client.

Item 2: Distress. The person will evaluate to what extent the OCD symptom(s) disturbed them during the day. This is a measure of intensity (see the note above on how to operationalize the maximum point).

Emotional state

Item 3: Emotional state. The emotional state refers to the client's general emotional state during the day and not just the emotional responses to OC symptoms. We observe three or four dimensions. The first three are depression, anxiety and irritability. For each, you identify a word or expression that the person uses spontaneously to represent that dimension for them.

> Depression: down, discouraged, sad, demoralised, etc.
> Anxiety: anguished, panicked, stressed, worried, etc.
> Irritable: aggressive, frustrated, pissed off, etc.

A fourth dimension can be added for an emotion or a state which is important to the individual but cannot be classified by the other three, for example, uncomfortable, guilty, uneasy, etc. Once the individualised word or expression has been chosen, it will be written in the booklet and the dimension becomes defined by this word for the client.

Doubting inferences Primary doubting inferences refer to the expectations that the people may have about the probability of an event or state occurring. The anticipated secondary inferences about consequences refer to the extent to which the people may consider this consequence to be realistic or not. Clients will evaluate two primary doubting inferences and two secondary consequences during treatment. These inferences will be related to two distinct compulsive (or neutralizing) behaviours. One behaviour will be chosen according to whether personal efficacy in resisting is reasonably elevated (and therefore should change early in treatment) and one for which the personal efficacy is very low (and is therefore the ultimate test). These OCD behaviours will be identified according to the scale administered by the therapist before treatment (see OCD Study Protocol for precise instructions).

To identify the inferences:

1. Put in order of importance the compulsions according to the personal efficacy scale ratings.
2. For the first item, choose a behaviour which is between 30% and 40% of the highest personal effectiveness (therefore, starting from the behaviour the easiest to resist).

    For example, if 10 items, choose the fourth.
    For example, if 7 items, choose the third.
    For example, if 4 items, choose the second.

3. For the second item, choose the behaviour with the weakest personal efficacy (therefore, the behaviour which is hardest to resist).

Items 4 and 5: Primary doubting inferences: Identify the two statements on the primary inference evaluation scale which correspond to the behaviours identified in steps 2 and 3.

Items 6 and 7: Anticipated secondary inferences: Identify the two statements on the secondary inference evaluation scale which correspond to the behaviours identified in steps 2 and 3.

If the therapist has access to the available software, visual graphs can be cmputed at different stages of IBT therapy as personal maps of progress. Generally, clients respond favourably to such feedback. It also refreshes the client's memory of their starting point, and can form a basis for discussion of expectations of future progress.

Week from _____to_____   Week from _____to_____
Code:_____   Code:_____

Extremely	81–100	Maximum
Very much	61–80	
Moderately	41–60	
A little	21–40	
Not much	1–20	
Not at all	0	Minimum

Extremely	81–100	Maximum
Very much	61–80	
Moderately	41–60	
A little	21–40	
Not much	1–20	
Not at all	0	Minimum

Week from _____ to _____
Code: _____

Extremely	81–100	Maximum
Very much	61–80	
Moderately	41–60	
A little	21–40	
Not much	1–20	
Not at all	0	Minimum

1. Please note the amount of time spent on obsessions and compulsions today.

Date						
Day						
Amount of time						

2. How much did your obsessions and compulsions disturb you today?

Date						
Day						
Rating						

1. Please note the amount of time spent on obsessions and compulsions today.

Date						
Day						
Amount of time						

2. How much did your obsessions and compulsions disturb you today?

Date						
Day						
Rating						

Week from _____ to _____
Code: _____

Extremely	81–100	Maximum
Very much	61–80	
Moderately	41–60	
A little	21–40	
Not much	1–20	
Not at all	0	Minimum

1. Please note the amount of time spent on obsessions and compulsions today.

Date						
Day						
Amount of time						

2. How much did your obsessions and compulsions disturb you today?

Date						
Day						
Rating						

1. Please note the amount of time spent on obsessions and compulsions today.

Date						
Day						
Amount of time						

2. How much did your obsessions and compulsions disturb you today?

Date						
Day						
Rating						

3. Please assess your emotions for the day.   3. Please assess your emotions for the day.

Date							
Day							

Date							
Day							

3. Please assess your emotions for the day.   3. Please assess your emotions for the day.

Date							
Day							

Date							
Day							

4. Please assess how probable is the following: 4. Please assess how probable is the following:

_____   _____

_____   _____

_____   _____

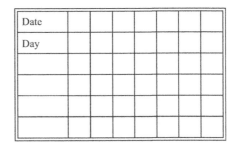

Date							
Day							
Rating							

Date							
Day							
Rating							

5. Please assess how probable is the following: 5. Please assess how probable is the following:

_____   _____

_____   _____

_____   _____

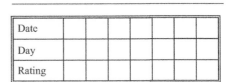

Rating								

Rating								

4. Please assess how probable is the following: 4. Please assess how probable is the following:

_____   _____

_____   _____

_____   _____

Date							
Day							
Rating							

Date							
Day							
Rating							

5. Please assess how probable is the following:

Rating							

6. Please assess how realistic it is for you:

Date							
Day							
Rating							

7. Please assess how realistic it is for you:

Rating							

6. Please assess how realistic it is for you:

Date							
Day							
Rating							

7. Please assess how realistic it is for you:

Rating							

5. Please assess how probable is the following:

Rating							

6. Please assess how realistic it is for you:

Date							
Day							
Rating							

7. Please assess how realistic it is for you:

Rating							

6. Please assess how realistic it is for you:

Date							
Day							
Rating							

7. Please assess how realistic it is for you:

Rating							

Bibliography: Key IBA Publications and Other References

Aardema F, O'Connor KP. Seeing white bears that are not there: Inference processes in obsession. *Journal of Cognitive Psychotherapy* 17, 23–37, 2003.

Aardema F, Emmelkamp PMG, O'Connor KP. Inferential confusion, cognitive change and treatment outcome in obsessive-compulsive disorder. *Clinical Psychology and Psychotherapy* 12(5): 337–345, 2005.

Aardema F, O'Connor K, Emmelkamp P, Marchand A, Todorov C. Inferential confusion in obsessive-compulsive disorder: Inferential Confusion Questionnaire. *Behaviour Research and Therapy* 43(3): 293–308, 2005.

Aardema F, Kleijer TMR, Trihey M, O'Connor KP, Emmelkamp PMG. Processes of inference, thinking, and obsessive-compulsive behaviour in a normal sample. *Psychological Reports* 99: 213–220, 2006.

Aardema F, O'Connor K, Emmelkamp PMG. Inferential confusion and obsessive beliefs in obsessive-compulsive disorder. *Cognitive Behaviour Therapy* 35(3): 138–147, 2006.

Aardema F, O'Connor K. The menace within: Obsessions and the self. *Journal of Cognitive Psychotherapy* 21: 182–197, 2007.

Aardema F, Radomsky AS, O'Connor K, Julien D. Inferential confusion, obsessive beliefs and obsessive-compulsive symptoms: A multidimensional investigation of cognitive domains. *Clinical Psychology and Psychotherapy* 15(4): 227–238, 2008.

Aardema F, O'Connor K, Pélissier M-C, Lavoie M. The quantification of doubt in obsessive-compulsive disorder. *International Journal of Cognitive Therapy* 2(2): 188–205, 2009.

Aardema F, O'Connor K, Côté S, Taillon A. Virtual reality induces dissociation and lowers sense of presence in objective reality. *CyberPsychology, Behavior, and Social Networking* (online version ahead of print – February 16, 2010).

Clinician's Handbook for Obsessive-Compulsive Disorder: Inference-Based Therapy, First Edition.
K. O'Connor and F. Aardema.
© 2012 John Wiley & Sons, Ltd. Published 2012 by John Wiley & Sons, Ltd.

Aardema F, Wu K, Careau Y, O'Connor K, Julien D, Dennie S. The expanded version of the Inferential Confusion Questionnaire: Further development and validation in clinical and non-clinical samples. *Journal of Psychopathology & Behavioral Assessment* 32: 448–462, 2010.

Aardema F, Wu K. Imaginative, dissociative and schizotypal processes in obsessive compulsive symptoms. *Journal of Clinical Psychology* 67: 74–81, 2011.

Abramowitz JS, McKay D, Taylor S (Eds). *Obsessive-Compulsive Disorder. Subtypes and Spectrum Conditions.* USA: Elsevier, 2008.

Calvocoressi L, Mazure CM, Kasl SV, Skolnick J, Fisk D, Vegso SJ, Van Noppen BL, Price LH. Family accommodation of obsessive-compulsive symptoms: Instrument development and assessment of family behavior. *Journal of Mental Disease* 187(10): 636–642, 1999.

Clark DA. *Cognitive-Behavioural Therapy for OCD.* New York: Guilford Press, 2004.

Devilly GJ, Borkovec T. Psychometric properties of the credibility/expectancy questionnaire. *Journal of Behavior Therapy and Experimental Psychiatry* 31: 73–86, 2000.

Fauconnier G, Turner M. The way we think: *Conceptual blending and the mind's hyidden complexities.* New York: Basic Books,k 2002.

Ferrier, S., & Brewin, C. R. (2005). Feared identity and obsessive-compulsive disorder. *Behaviour Research and Therapy,* 43, 1363–1374.

Frost RO, Steketee G (Eds). *Cognitive Approaches to Obsessions and Compulsions: Theory, Assessment and Treatment.* Oxford: Elsevier Science, 2002.

Grenier S, O'Connor K, Bélanger L. Le trouble obsessionnel-compulsif et l'insight: une revue critique de la littérature. *Canadian Psychology/Psychologie Canadienne* 47(2): 96–109, 2006.

Grenier S, O'Connor KP, Bélanger C. Surinvestissement des doutes obsessionnels et de leurs conséquences anticipées chez les patients qui souffrent d'un trouble obsessionnel-compulsif (TOC): un portrait sociodémographique et clinique. *Revue Francophone de Clinique Comportementale et Cognitive* 11(4): 17–25, 2006.

Grenier S, O'Connor KP, Bélanger C. Obsessional beliefs, compulsive behaviours and symptoms severity: Their evolution and interrelation over stages of treatment. *Clinical Psychology & Psychotherapy* 15: 15–27, 2008.

Grenier S, O'Connor KP, Bélanger C. Belief in the obsessional doubt as a real probability and its relation to other obsessive-compulsive beliefs and to the severity of symptomatology. *British Journal of Clinical Psychology* 49(1): 67–85, 2010.

Guay S, O'Connor KP, Gareau D, Todorov C. Single belief as a maintaining factor in a case of obsessive-compulsive disorder. *Journal of Cognitive Psychotherapy: An International Quarterly* 19(4): 369–378, 2005.

Julien D, O'Connor KP, Aardema F, Todorov C. The specificity of belief domains in obsessive-compulsive symptom subtypes. *Personality and Individual Differences* 41(7): 1205–1216, 2006.

Julien D, O'Connor KP, Aardema F. Intrusive thoughts, obsessions, and appraisals in obsessive-compulsive disorders: A critical review. *Clinical Psychology Review* 27(3): 366–383, 2007.

Julien D, O'Connor KP, Aardema F. Intrusions related to obsessive-compulsive disorder: A question of content or context? *Journal of Clinical Psychology* 65(7): 709–722, 2009.

O'Connor KP, Robillard S. Clinical observations on inference processes in obsessive-compulsive disorders. *Behavior Research & Therapy* 33: 887–896, 1995.

O'Connor KP, Robillard S. Interventions cognitives pour les troubles obsessionnels-compulsif. *Numéro spécial, Revue Québécoise de Psychologie sur les Comportements Compulsifs* 17: 165–195, 1996.

O'Connor KP, Robillard S. A cognitive approach to modifying primary inferences in obsessive-compulsive disorder. *Journal of Cognitive Psychotherapy* 13(4): 1–17, 1999.

O'Connor KP. Intrusion and inference in obsessive-compulsive disorder. *Clinical Psychology and Psychotherapy* 9: 38–46, 2002.

O'Connor KP, Aardema F. Fusion or confusion in obsessive-compulsive disorder. *Psychological Reports* 93: 227–232, 2003.

O'Connor KP, Aardema F. The imagination: Cognitive-precognitive, and meta-cognitive aspects. *Consciousness and Cognition* 14: 233–256, 2005.

O'Connor KP, Aardema F, Bouthillier D, Fournier S, Guay S, Robillard S, Pélissier M-C, Landry P, Todorov C, Tremblay M, Pitre D. Evaluation of an inference based approach to treating obsessive-compulsive disorder. *Cognitive Behavior Therapy* 34(3): 148–163, 2005.

O'Connor K, Aardema F, Pélissier M-C. *Beyond Reasonable Doubt. Reasoning Processes in Obsessive-Compulsive Disorder and Related Disorders.* Sussex UK: John Wiley & Sons, Ltd., 2005.

O'Connor KP, Aardema F. Editorial: Self-themes in obsessive-compulsive disorder. *Journal of Cognitive Psychotherapy* 21: 179–181, 2007.

O'Connor K, Koszegi N, Aardema F, van Niekerk J, Taillon A. An inference-based approach to treating obsessive-compulsive disorders. *Cognitive and Behavioral Practice* 16(4): 420–429, 2009.

O'Connor K, Aardema F. Living in a bubble: Dissociation, relational consciousness and obsessive compulsive disorder. *Journal of Consciousness Studies* (in press).

O'Connor KP, Pélissier M-C. Reasoning in anxiety, OCD and related disorders: Can formal reasoning theories inform us about psychopathology? In: S. Selek (Ed), *Different Views of Anxiety Disorders.* In Tech: Open Acces (in press).

Pélissier M-C, O'Connor KP. Deductive and inductive inference in obsessive compulsive disorder. *British Journal of Clinical Psychology* 41: 15–27, 2002.

Pélissier M-C, O'Connor KP, Dupuis G. When doubting begins: Exploring inductive reasoning in obsessive-compulsive disorder. *Journal of Behavior Therapy and Experimental Psychiatry* 40(1): 39–49, 2009.

Prochaska JO, DiClemente CC. *The Transtheoretical Approach: Crossing Traditional Boundaries of Therapy.* Homewood, IL: Dow Jones–Irwin, 1984.

Rachman, S. (1994). Pollution of the mind. *Behaviour Research and Therapy*, 32, 311–314.

St-Pierre-Delorme M, Purcell-Lalonde M, Perreault V., Koszegi N, O'Connor K. Inference-based therapy for compulsive hoarding: A clinical case study. *Clinical Case Studies* 10(3): 1–13, 2011.

Taillon A, O'Connor K, Dupuis G, Lavoie M: Inference-based therapy for body dysmorphic disorder. *Clinical Psychology and Psychotherapy*, 2011 (published online)

Wells A. *Emotional Disorders and Metacognition: Innovative Cognitive Therapy.* Chichester, UK: Wiley, 2000.

Wu K, Aardema F, O'Connor K. Inferential confusion, obsessive beliefs and obsessive-compulsive symptoms: A replication and extension. *Journal of Anxiety Disorders* 23(6): 746–752, 2009.

Yorulmaz, O, Dirik G, Karaali O, Uvez E. The psychometric properties of the inferential confusion scale based in Turkish patients with obsessive-compulsive disorder. *Turkish Journal of Psychiatry* 21(2): 135–142, 2010.

Index

a different story step   4, 159–73
  bridging   160–3
  client exercise sheet   168–70
  client training card   171
  client worksheet   166–7
  counter-stories   62, 160
  decision chart   164
  do's and don'ts of narratives   163
  live-in stories   60
  reality sensing   60, 163, 169–70
  rehearsals   163–164
  storytelling   65, 66, 159
absorption into imaginary sequences   177
abstract facts   50–4
accommodation   11, 18, 29
adjusting the focus   24
alternative narratives *see* counter-stories
anticipation   18, 206
anxiety
  IBT evaluation   11, 14, 15, 19
  knowing and doing: relapse prevention
    step   206
  logic behind OCD step   49, 55
  OCD bubble step   136
  reality sensing step   152–3

  when OCD begins step   23, 32–4, 36–7
apparently comparable events   177
appraisal therapy   221
arbitrary stopping rules   97
attention   11, 213
authentic self   2, 4
automatisation   46–47
aversion of client to doubt   47
avoidance   18, 19
awareness of precursors   43–4, 46–9
Axis II personality disorders   11

bacterial contamination   29, 133, 165
BDD *see* body dysmorphic disorder
beliefs   226–7
believe-in stories   61
blending
  de-blending   102
  metaphor and literal meanings   101–2
  negligence   101
  OCD doubt is 100% imaginary
    step   99–102
  perfectionism   99, 100–1
  tricks and cheats of the OCD con artist
    step   187

Clinician's Handbook for Obsessive-Compulsive Disorder: Inference-Based Therapy, First Edition.
K. O'Connor and F. Aardema.
© 2012 John Wiley & Sons, Ltd. Published 2012 by John Wiley & Sons, Ltd.

blood contamination 9–11, 31, 148
body dysmorphic disorder (BDD) 11
body focused repetitive behaviour 11
bridging 161–2

category errors 49, 176–7
CBT *see* cognitive-behavioural therapy
certainty 150–3, 163
challenging beliefs and values 226–7
chemical contamination 132–3, 164–5
cognitive avoidance *see* avoidance
cognitive-behavioural therapy (CBT) 10, 226
cognitive ritualizing 221
common sense
  knowing and doing: relapse prevention
    step 225
  OCD doubt is 100% imaginary step 107, 112
  reality sensing step 144
comorbid disorders 11, 221
competing therapy models 226
competing messages from external
    authorities 226
compliments 191, 202
compulsions
  knowing and doing: relapse prevention
    step 213
  logic behind OCD step 55
  OCD bubble step 136–7, 140
  real self step 191–2
  reality sensing step 146, 155
  when OCD begins step 23, 32, 34, 36–7
confidence, lack of 24
confused self 77
consolidation 2, 4–5, 157–229
  a different story step 4, 159–73
  knowing and doing: relapse prevention
    step 4–5, 205–20
  real self step 4, 189–203
  tricks and cheats of the OCD con artist
    step 4, 175–87
  troubleshooting and problem solving 5, 221–29
content of obsessional thought 13–14
contraindications 227
conviction in and out of OCD situation 16

coping skills 207–8
counter-stories
  a different story step 159–64, 169–73
  obsessional story step 63
  reality sensing step 145–6
  vulnerable self-theme step 82–4
counting 97, 108
credibility
  a different step 162, 171–3
  doubt and possibility step 123
  knowing and doing: relapse prevention
    step 215
  OCD bubble step 135
  tricks and cheats of the OCD con artist
    step 179
cross-over points
  OCD bubble step 129, 130–1, 138–41
  reality sensing step 143, 153

de-blending 102
death 27–8
deconstructing OCD 150
decontextualization 47–8
delusional disorders 17
depressive disorders 11
derealisation 129
desires 195, 196–7
detachment 129
detail
  a different story step 170
  obsessional story step 60
  reality sensing step 146
detecting obsessional elements 75–6
diagnostic instruments 11
direct evidence
  a different story step 169
  OCD doubt is 100% imaginary step 93, 110, 113
dirt contamination
  IBT evaluation 14
  logic behind OCD step 46
  obsessional story step 58
  reality sensing step 145
  tricks and cheats of the OCD con artist
    step 177–8
  when OCD begins step 26–7
discussing doubts 182–3

dissociating with OCD   129–30, 141
doorknobs   26–7
double jeopardy   182
doubt
    a different story step   159–61, 168–70
    anatomy of obsessional doubt   117–18
    aversion of client to   47
    categories of doubt   50–4
    client perceptions   28–9
    distrust   147
    doubt and possibility step   115–27
    IBT evaluation   10, 14–17, 19
    imaginary   93–6, 105–7, 146
    implications   116
    impossibility of obsessional
        doubt   116–17, 127
    integration of IBT model   7
    intellectualizing   29–30
    irrelevance   93, 115–17, 121–3, 125–7,
        143–4
    knowing and doing: relapse prevention
        step   205–10, 215
    letting go   205
    logic behind OCD step   43–5, 47–8
    multiple   30, 77–9, 82
    normality   31
    obsessional story step   58, 61, 66
    OCD bubble step   133–9
    OCD doubt is 100% imaginary
        step   91–6, 97, 103–10, 112–13
    phobic doubts   31
    primary doubts   24, 25–9, 31–3, 227–8
    reality sensing step   143–4, 146–7, 148,
        150–6
    resolution   62, 119, 178, 216, 218
    selectivity   121
    selfless   74–5
    shameful   30
    sources   29
    step by step approach   2–4
    subjectivity   91
    tricks and cheats of the OCD con artist
        step   175–87
    troubleshooting and problem
        solving   221, 227
    trusting the senses   148
    uncertainty and lack of confidence   24

vulnerable self-theme step   73–7, 80–4
when OCD begins step   23–41
doubt and possibility step   3, 115–27
    anatomy of obsessional doubt   18
    applying the principle   122
    client exercise sheet   123–5
    client quiz   127
    client training card   126
    client worksheet   120–2
    creating OCD from neutral
        situations   123–5
    credibility   123
    decision chart   119
    implications of doubt   116
    impossibility of obsessional
        doubt   116–17, 127
    irrelevance of doubt   115–17, 121–3,
        125–7
    probability   120
    resolution of doubt   119
    selectivity of doubt   121
doubting stories   159–60

education and foundation   2–3, 21–87
    logic behind OCD step   2, 43–56
    obsessional story step   2–3, 57–71
    vulnerable self-theme step   3, 4, 16–17,
        73–87
    when OCD begins step   2, 23–41
ego-dystonic obsessions   97
ego syntonicity   28
emotional processes
    IBT evaluation   10
    knowing and doing: relapse prevention
        step   206–7, 213, 215
    when OCD begins step   23, 27
epidemics   93
ERP *see* exposure and response
    prevention
evaluation of IBT   9–20
excitement   213
explaining the bubble   130
exposure   206, 222–4
exposure and response prevention (ERP)
    therapy   222–24
exposure-based therapy   10
extra effort   149

falsehood of obsessions   144, 150–1, 155–6
fatigue   213
feared OCD self   194, 197
feelings   195, 196–7
fly in the head models   208
focus   24, 213

general rules   50–4
generalization across obsessions   178,
    224–5
goals   198, 203, 206, 216
going against reality   143–2, 150–52, 156
going beyond the senses   134, 138–41, 144
guilt   75, 97

habituation   207, 223
hearsay   50–4
hierarchy of efficacy in resisting
    compulsions   13
hoarding   100
holidays   213

identity   74–5, 85–7
imaginary doubt   93–6, 105–6, 146
imaginative processes
    a different story step   166–7, 170
    knowing and doing: relapse prevention
        step   207, 209, 213
    logic behind OCD step   47
    OCD bubble step   129–30, 134–5, 138–41
    OCD doubt is 100% imaginary
        step   91–7, 99, 105–6, 113
    real self step   192
    reality sensing step   143–4, 146–7, 150,
        153–6
    tricks and cheats of the OCD con artist
        step   175, 176–7, 181
    troubleshooting and problem
        solving   223
implications of doubt   115–16
impossibility of obsessional doubt   116–17
impulsion phobias   18–19
inadvertent slippage   214
inductive reasoning   98–9
inferential confusion   12–13
    contributing factors   98–9
    doubt and possibility step   116

explanatory value   97
OCD doubt is 100% imaginary step   95,
    96–9
    process   96–7
real self step   192
reality sensing step   143–144
    therapist effects   228
    thought-thought fusion   98
tricks and cheats of the OCD con artist
    step   176–7
    troubleshooting and problem
        solving   223, 227
vulnerable self-theme step   80
when OCD begins step   26–7
infestations   109–10
initial doubt *see* primary doubt
inner senses   151
integration of IBT model   6–7
intellectualizing doubt   29–30
intervention   2, 3–4, 89–156
    doubt and possibility step   3, 115–27
    OCD bubble step   3, 129–40
    OCD doubt is 100% imaginary step   3,
        91–113
    reality sensing step   4, 143–56
intolerance of uncertainty   24
inverse inference   175–6, 177
irrelevance of doubt
    doubt and possibility step   115–16, 117,
        120–1, 125–7
    OCD doubt is 100% imaginary step   93,
        105
    reality sensing step   143–4
irrelevant associations   175–6

jumping ahead too fast   225
justification
    a different story step   161, 168–9
    doubt and possibility step   120, 127
    logic behind OCD step   43, 45, 50–4, 56
    OCD doubt is 100% imaginary step   91,
        103, 110
    vulnerable self-theme step   77, 79

keeping thoughts in mind   208–10
knowing and doing: relapse prevention
    step   4–5, 16, 205–18

client exercise sheet   215
client practice card   218
client quiz   217
client worksheet   213–14
coping skills   207–8
decision chart   212
exposure   206
inadvertent slippage   214
keeping thoughts in mind   208–10
last stages of therapy   210
letting go   205
mastery   206
reinforcement   210
relapse prevention measures   4–5, 18,
   210, 217
repositioning the self   208

lack of confidence   24
law of habituation   207, 222
led astrays   59
letting go   205
life roles   200–201, 215
literal meanings   101–2
live-in stories   60, 160–1
living the fear   181, 184, 187
locked doors
   a different story step   162, 168–70
   obsessional story step   63
   OCD doubt is 100% imaginary step   104,
      108
   tricks and cheats of the OCD con artist
      step   180, 181
   vulnerable self-theme step
      77–9, 82
   when OCD begins step   32–4
logic behind OCD step   2, 43–56
   automatisation   46–7
   aversion of client to doubt   47
   awareness of precursors   43–4, 46–9
   client exercise sheet   52–4
   client quiz   56
   client training card   55
   client worksheet   50–1
   decision chart   48
   decontextualization   47–8
   imaginative processes   47
   prompting the reasons   45–6

reasoning behind the doubt   43–4, 46–8,
   50–4, 56
logical template   25–8

magic pen exercise   61–2
maintaining thoughts   208–10
mastery   206
memory   24
mental rituals   98, 140, 153, 221
metaphors   1–2
   blending   101–2
   real self step   189
   troubleshooting and problem
      solving   227
mismatching   180, 184, 187
misplacing the self   74, 78–9, 81, 83–5
money contamination   14
multiple doubts   30, 77–9, 82

narrative units   3, 57–9, 66
narratives
   a different story step   159–73
   do's and don'ts   163
   knowing and doing: relapse prevention
      step   209–11
   OCD bubble step   129, 132
   OCD doubt is 100% imaginary step   98–9
   reality sensing step   143, 146–7, 150,
      151–2
   tricks and cheats of the OCD con artist
      step   176, 180–1, 184, 186
   troubleshooting and problem
      solving   221
   vulnerable self-theme step   75–6,
      77, 83
negligence   74, 101
neutralization
   IBT evaluation   10, 13, 17, 19
   obsessional story step   64
   OCD bubble step   131
   OCD doubt is 100% imaginary step   97,
      103
   real self step   192
   troubleshooting and problem
      solving   221
non-self   189–90, 195, 202
normality of doubts   31

obsessional doubt
  doubt and possibility step   115–19, 123–4, 127
  impossibility   116–17, 127
  knowing and doing: relapse prevention step   207, 209–10
  logic behind OCD step   43, 45, 47–8, 52–5
  obsessional story step   58, 66
  OCD bubble step   134–9
  OCD doubt is 100% imaginary step   91, 92, 94–6, 104–11, 112–13
  reality sensing step   143–4, 153–4, 155–6
  resolution   118–19
  tricks and cheats of the OCD con artist step   175–8, 185–6
  troubleshooting and problem solving   221
  vulnerable self-theme step   75–7, 80–4
  when OCD begins step   24–5, 28, 30–4, 35–7
obsessional preoccupations   14, 23
obsessional sequence   35–7
obsessional story step   2–3, 57–71
  believe-in stories   61
  client exercise sheet   67–9
  client quiz   71
  client training card   70
  client worksheet   65–6
  counter-stories   62
  creative exercises   61–2, 68–9
  decision chart   63
  detail   60
  doubt creating stories   61
  led astrays   59
  live-in stories   60
  narrative units   57–9, 66
  outing the story   59–60, 67
  personalization   61, 65, 67–8
  power of narratives   60–1
  recording narratives   59
  rhetoric and reason   57–60, 63–4, 66
  smooth transport   60
  storytelling   58–9, 65–6
OCD bubble step   3, 129–40
  client exercise sheet   138–9
  client quiz   141
  client training card   140

client worksheet   134–7
client's perception   130
cross-over points   130, 131, 138–41
decision chart   132
disadvantages   130
dissociating with OCD   129–30, 140
explaining the bubble   130
going beyond the senses   134, 138–41
reality sensing   143, 147, 155–6
reasoning   131
security   136
stress   136–7
tricks and cheats of the OCD con artist step   179
OCD controlling the therapy   225–6
OCD doubt is 100% imaginary step   3, 91–113
  blending   99–102
  client exercise sheet   107–11
  client quiz   113
  client training card   112
  client worksheet   104–6
  de-blending   102
  decision chart   103
  direct evidence   93, 110, 113
  imaginary doubt   93–6, 104–6
  imaginative processes   91–7, 99, 104–6, 113
  inferential confusion   95, 96–9
  irrelevance of doubt   93, 102
  neutralization   97, 102
  perceptual processes   94–7, 112
  possibility versus reality   92, 104
  reasoning   98–9, 105, 113
  subjectivity of doubt   91
  testing behaviour   102
  thought-thought fusion   98
one-dimensionality   194
out-of-context facts   178, 180, 184
outing the story   59–60, 67
over-reliance on possibility   177
overuse of the senses   147, 155, 156

partial understanding   225
perceptions of others
  real self step   192, 196–201, 202–3
  when OCD begins step   25

perceptual processes
  OCD bubble step   134–5, 138–9
  OCD doubt is 100% imaginary
    step   94–7, 112
  reality sensing step   147, 149, 153–6
  when OCD begins step   24
perfectionism   99, 100–1
personal experiences   50–4
personal hygiene
  a different story step   162
  logic behind OCD step   48
  OCD bubble step   131–2
  OCD doubt is 100% imaginary step   93
  reality sensing step   145
  vulnerable self-theme step   74, 77–9
  when OCD begins step   25–6
personalization
  a different story step   170
  obsessional story step   61, 65, 67–8
  vulnerable self-theme step   76–7
phobias   91
phobic doubts   31
planning ahead   218
poison   63–4, 180
positive self-attributes   189–91, 194–196,
    202, 206, 208
power of narratives   60
pre-emptive neutralization   18
primary doubt   25–30, 31–2, 227–8
principles   1989, 206, 222
probability   120, 143–4
Prochaska–DiClemente's model   6–7
programme overview   1–7
prompting the reasons   45–6

questioning   23–4
questionnaires   11, 12–13, 19
quick looking   154

radioactive contamination   15, 53, 104
real self step   4, 189–203
  client exercise sheet   196–201
  client practice card   202
  client quiz   203
  client worksheet   194–5
  decision chart   193
  desires and feelings   193, 195

differentiating OCD nonself   190–1, 194,
    202
feared OCD self   194, 197
inferential confusion   192
one-dimensionality   194–5
perceptions of others   190, 194
positive self-attributes   189–90, 196–201
self-components   191–2
values and goals   198, 203
varied life roles   200–201
reality sensing step   4, 143–56
  alternative narratives   145–6
  basic steps   155
  client exercise sheet   155
  client training card   155
  client worksheet   153–4
  cross-over points   143, 151
  decision chart   149
  deconstructing OCD   150
  detail   146
  doubt distrust   146
  extra effort   149
  falsehood of obsessions   144, 151–2,
    155–6
  going against reality   144, 151–52, 155
  overuse of the senses   147, 155, 156
  reality-based information   145, 153–6
  self-sabotage   136–7
  trusting the senses   146, 148, 152–3,
    155–6
reality values   18
reality-based information
  a different story step   163–4, 169–70
  reality sensing step   145–6, 153–6
reasoning
  a different story step   159, 161–3
  doubt and possibility step   127
  inductive   98–9
  logic behind OCD step   43–4, 47–9, 50–4,
    56
  obsessional story step   57–60, 63–4, 66
  OCD bubble step   130–1
  OCD doubt is 100% imaginary
    step   98–9, 107, 113
  tricks and cheats of the OCD con artist
    step   175, 176–7, 181
  vulnerable self-theme step   76, 77, 80, 83

recording narratives   59
rehearsals   163–4
reinforcement
  knowing and doing: relapse prevention
    step   213
  OCD bubble step   136–7
  tricks and cheats of the OCD con artist
    step   175, 178
relapse prevention *see knowing and doing:*
  relapse prevention step
religious devotion   99, 100
repetitive behaviour   11, 97
repositioning the self   190, 208, 218
resistance *see* treatment resistance
resolution of doubt   118–19, 159–60, 178,
  216, 218
response prevention (RP)   222–23
reverse reasoning   181
rhetoric
  a different story step   163
  obsessional story step   57, 59–60
  tricks and cheats of the OCD con artist
    step   175
role playing exercises   45
RP *see* response prevention
rules   50–4
ruminative disorders   17, 18–19, 211

SARS *see* severe acute respiratory syndrome
scare stories   226
secondary consequences   15–16, 23
security   136, 137
see-sawing comprehension   221
selectivity of doubt   121
self-absorption   130
self-components   191
self-fulfilling prophecies   18
self-perception   190–94
self-sabotage   131, 136–7
self-themes *see vulnerable self-theme* step
selfless doubt   74–5
sense gaps   63
severe acute respiratory syndrome
  (SARS)   226
sexual disturbances
  IBT evaluation   19
  knowing and doing: relapse prevention
    step   218

logic behind OCD step   45–6, 49
obsessional story step   59
OCD is 100% imaginary step   99, 104–5
tricks and cheats of the OCD con artist
  step   181
when OCD begins step   27
shameful doubts   30
situational triggers
  IBT evaluation   19
  OCD is 100% imaginary step   94
  when OCD begins step   32–4, 35
smooth transport   60, 170
sources of doubt   29
spider phobias   91
staring   147, 153, 156
step by step approach   1–5
stopping rules   97
storytelling
  a different story step   159, 166–7, 170
  obsessional story step   58–9, 65–6
stoves, leaving on   32, 68
stress   136–7, 213–14
subjective disequilibrium   15
subjectivity of doubt   91
symbolic nature of OCD   228–9

targets of exposure   223–24
testing behaviour
  IBT evaluation   17–20
  OCD doubt is 100% imaginary step   102
  tricks and cheats of the OCD con artist
    step   182
  troubleshooting and problem
    solving   223
thought-thought fusion   98, 223
three-step logical template   25–8
tic disorders   11
transtheoretical behavioural model of
  change   6–7
treatment resistance   7
tricks and cheats of the OCD con artist
  step   4, 175–87
  client exercise sheet   184–5
  client training card   186
  client worksheet   179–83
  deeper reality   179, 181, 187
  discussing doubts   182
  double jeopardy   182

implication of reasoning devices   175–7
inverse inference   175–6, 177
last stages of therapy   178
living the fear   181, 184, 187
mismatching   180, 184, 187
out-of-context facts   177, 180, 184
reinforcement   175, 178
reverse reasoning   181
testing behaviour   182
trusting the senses   177, 181–2
triggers *see* situational triggers
troubleshooting and problem solving   5,
     221–29
   appraisal therapy   222
   challenging beliefs and values   226–7
   cognitive ritualizing   221
   competing therapy models   226
   competing messages from external
      authorities   226
   contraindications   227
   exposure and response prevention
      therapy   222–4
   general clinical points   221–29
   generalization across obsessions   224–5
   inferential confusion   223, 228
   jumping ahead too fast   225
   metaphors   226
   OCD controlling the therapy   225
   primary doubt   227–8
   see-sawing comprehension   212-22
   symbolic nature of OCD   228–9
   targets of exposure   222–3
trusting the senses
   knowing and doing: relapse prevention
      step   207
   real self step   191–2
   reality sensing step   147, 149,
      152-2, 156
   tricks and cheats of the OCD con artist
      step   177, 181–2

uncertainty   24
upside-down reasoning   181

values   198, 203, 226–7
varied life roles   200–201, 215
verification subtypes   14–15
vivid imagery   27–8
vulnerable self-theme step   3, 4, 16–17,
      73–87
   client quiz   87
   client training card   85–6
   client worksheet   80–1
   confused self   75
   counter-stories   82–4
   detecting obsessional elements   75–76
   identity   74–5, 85–7
   misplacing the self   74, 75, 78–9, 81, 83–5
   narratives   75–6, 83
   personalization   76–7
   selfless doubt   74–5

washing rituals *see* personal hygiene
when OCD begins step   2, 23–41
   adjusting the focus   24
   client exercise sheet   35–7
   client quiz   41
   client training card   40
   client worksheet   32–4
   creative exercise   38–9
   decision chart   31
   doubt, uncertainty and lack of
      confidence   23–4
   intellectualizing doubt   29–30
   logical template   24–8
   multiple doubts   30
   normality of doubts   31
   phobic doubts   31
   primary doubt   24, 25–9, 31
   shameful doubts   30
   sources of doubt   29